'We Ain't Got No Drink, Pa'

A Little Girl's Struggle to Survive in the Slums of 1920s South East London

HILDA KEMP WITH CATHRYN KEMP

Copyright © Hilda Kemp and Cathryn Kemp 2015
Photographs © Albert Kemp

The right of Hilda Kemp and Cathryn Kemp to be identified as
the authors of this work has been asserted in accordance with the
Copyright, Designs and Patents Act 1988.

This edition first published in Great Britain in 2015 by
Orion
an imprint of the Orion Publishing Group Ltd
Orion House, 5 Upper St Martin's Lane,
London WC2H 9EA

An Hachette UK Company

1 3 5 7 9 10 8 6 4 2

A CIP catalogue record for this book
is available from the British Library.

ISBN 978 1 4091 5840 0

Typeset at The Spartan Press Ltd,
Lymington, Hants

Printed and bound by CPI Group (UK) Ltd, Croydon, CR0 4YY

The Orion Publishing Group's policy is to use papers that
are natural, renewable and recyclable and made from wood
grown in sustainable forests. The logging and manufacturing
processes are expected to conform to the environmental
regulations of the country of origin.

Every effort has been made to fulfil requirements with regard
to reproducing copyright material. The author and publisher
will be glad to rectify any omissions at the earliest opportunity.

www.orionbooks.co.uk

Hilda Kemp
29th July 1921 – 18th February 2003

Dearest Nan,

How are you? That's probably a stupid question to ask you as you've been dead for almost 12 years now. But that's just it. You don't feel 'deceased' to me. You feel as alive as you were as a young girl, skipping and laughing your way through the slums of Bermondsey.

Since I started writing this tribute to your life, it's been just like the old days. You holding court (in my head), telling me story after story, reliving even the darkest moments of your extra-ordinarily brutal upbringing, sharing with me the love you had for your mother and siblings, showing me that in even the most difficult circumstances there is always room for laughter and love.

You have been resident in my head and heart. But then it's not like you ever really left. Can I make that point clear, Nan? Just in case you decide to haunt me in other ways. No, you never left.

I've shared many a conversation with you since you died, and I swear I've been able to hear you cackle your responses with that great capacity for joy (you were always doubled up with laughter), and your equal tendency for sorrow. I've had the slightly disturbing pleasure of hearing your voice again as I've written the words on these pages. Once or twice, I swear you've even scolded me for saying something the wrong way.

You came alive for me during the days and weeks I pieced together the story of your life. I heard you whispering in my ear, joking in my head. I even felt you arch an eyebrow at me, as you sometimes used to do when I'd overstepped the mark as a youngster. I was instantly corrected, showing you still have the power to make me feel like a small child.

I can't take the credit for what is contained within these pages.

These are your words, your stories, your life. I felt like I was the channel, guiding the words out from you, crafting them into something that resembled your memoir, and all the while hoping I did you justice.

You were the matriarch of my family. You were the maternal head and the overflowing heart. You loved us all with fierce loyalty and passion. Yet you suffered terribly at the hands of your father. You suffered extremes of poverty and deprivation, living in filthy, desperate dockside rooms. But you never lost your infectious laugh or your dream that you could build a better life than the one you'd been brought into.

Remarkably, you succeeded. You met the love of your life, your Bert, and you took your future into your hands. You never lost the twinkle in your eye or your innate sense of theatre. You lived life with gusto, just how it should be lived, and this book, your book, is my offering to you.

Even though it has been a strange pleasure reigniting our conversations so that I could write you the book I'd always promised you, I would like my head back now, please. Hearing any voice, apart from my own, should not be encouraged. I told you I'd write your memoirs and so, finally, I've come good on that promise. Sorry it took me so long, Nan, you know how it is. Life sometimes gets in the way of a good story.

Your loving granddaughter,
Cathryn
September 2014

CHAPTER I

Bermondsey Slum

1928

The first we knew he was back was when we heard his key scratch on the door. It scratched again, then again, as my pa kept missing the lock. He was attempting to open the door to our dark, dingy rooms on the ground floor of a tenement in Bevington Street, Bermondsey, south-east London. The more he fumbled, the more drunk we realised he was, and so we huddled together for protection, listening to the expletives as they slurred out of Pa's mouth.

When I say 'we' I mean my younger brother, Les, and baby sister, Joanie, and me, of course. I was the eldest child at seven years old, and it was me the young 'uns turned to for protection, not that I could do much in the face of what was coming.

The three of us moved instinctively together behind the wooden table in the centre of the tiny room that served as a front room and kitchen. We had a small scullery out back where we had our weekly Friday night scrub down in the old tin bath that hung on a nail in the yard, and one bedroom with the big iron bed we all shared. So there was nowhere to hide from Pa, but God knows we tried, every time we heard our father's drunken temper as it built up outside our door.

I put my arms around little Joanie, who snuggled into my arms, her thumb in her mouth and her dark hair nestled against my shoulder. She already knew not to cry out in case she attracted Pa's wrath, even though she was just a baby. Instead of wailing, she started to cry softly. She was only just two years old, a toddler, but already she knew the fear of his fury. Les was almost four years old; a cheeky, fun-loving little boy, except, of course, when he was faced with his father's drunken rage. Then he cowered with the rest of us, his stick-thin legs curled up against him and his big dark eyes wide with fear as we huddled together for safety.

There was no one else there to protect us. My ma was asleep in the bed. Her latest illness had taken her hard. I was worried about her but right now I was more frightened for our safety.

We never knew how it would go with Pa when he got like this. Sometimes he returned home, covered in coal dust and grime from his heavy work down at the docks, and fell straight into bed, snoring minutes later in a drunken stupor. More often he would swear and rage, and then turn round to look for someone to blame for the black parts of his soul. It was always Ma and me who bore the brunt of his foul moods and raging tempers, trapped by these tiny dank rooms in this tall dark building. I felt the building tower over me, much like his temper, the danger of it frightening me to the core.

It was late. None of us had dared go to bed because Pa, or 'That Man' as I called him, often came home and he'd wake us with a swift kick, or grab one of us by the ear and drag us from the bed. He'd pull his victim into the kitchen to feed him or pour him a drink of whatever he had kicking around. It wasn't safe to sleep, we were vulnerable on nights like this.

So we stayed awake, sitting cross-legged on the kitchen floor, pretending to play games while yawning and rubbing our eyes, shivering a little from the cold as we wrapped the thin, scratchy blanket we shared around us. All the while, my heart would be thumping, knowing what might come.

We all felt the tension, waiting for That Man to come home and never knowing what state he'd be in. My stomach would feel tight, my senses on high alert, waiting for the sound of his heavy dockers' boots to announce his arrival.

Last orders would've been called nearly an hour ago. None of us would dare ask where he'd been or what he'd done. He'd probably been out earning his next evening's drink money by bare-knuckle fighting down by the docks or on the Old Kent Road or at The Ring in Blackfriars. These were the places where all the fighters would go to punch the living daylights out of each other for pennies. That money, which we sorely needed to buy medicine for Ma or for food for the littl'uns, would be thrown down his throat and there was nothing in the world we could do about it.

His key scraped against the lock. It fumbled, then scratched again. Les looked at me, his face pale. Our eyes locked for a moment, registering our terror. We heard the key turn. Then the door slammed open, kicked wide by those boots. We jumped. Joanie let out a wail and I shushed her, cuddling her close with trembling hands.

The first thing we saw were those terrible big boots. Then we saw Pa's dark frame silhouetted against the blackness of the hallway outside. For a second nobody moved. Then Pa walked in, swaying as he entered. He wiped his chin and stood surveying the room, his face a picture of mean, sodden rage. His cap had slipped to one side, making him look almost comical.

Pa was 27 years old but already he looked like a man who was disappointed with his lot in life. Despite having a wife and three healthy children, he wore the surly sneer of someone who thought he deserved more. Perhaps that was why he made such a show of fighting. It was a way of proving himself and raising himself above the men of his class and status.

I looked up at him. He was a small, stocky man, but he seemed to tower above me. I noticed that his jacket, made out of sacking cloth and tied with string round the middle, was ripped on one arm. Evidence of his fighting, if we needed it. His lip was starting to swell up and he had a trickle of blood running from the corner of his mouth, which he wiped away like swatting a fly. *More work for Ma*, I thought to myself. She would need to stitch his only jacket to hide the tear while he strutted about Bermondsey. There was only enough time to think these small, insignificant thoughts before That Man lurched into a chair, grabbing the back of it for support in his drunken swagger.

He looked around, searching for someone to take him on. He wasn't done, I could see from his gait that he wanted more violence, more confrontation, like an itch he had to scratch. I knew it had to be me. Who else was there to take his rampaging temper? As I was the eldest, I felt it was my job to protect the others, even though I was not much more than a baby myself.

I couldn't expect Ma to stand between her husband and her children as she was already poorly with a heart complaint. Her heart was always too big for her, we would say, as if knowing that made our worries about her recede. They didn't of course, and there was never enough money to pay for a doctor. The idea of calling a doctor and being whisked into hospital with medicine and clean, crisp white sheets was a fairy tale fantasy, a scenario as far from our lives as it was possible to be. So I looked after Ma the best I could and she called me her 'littl' nurse' and we pretended everything was okay, because what else could we do?

The light from the hearth cast shadows around the room.

The peeling wallpaper that had once been jolly, with faded pink roses on pale green winding stems, made awkward shapes against the gloom. Pa looked black against the shadow – prowling, dangerous. He saw us then, huddled together near the hearth, and he growled at us, 'Fuckin' move, you lazy bastards, I need to warm me feet. Go on, get out of here, you ungrateful cunts.'

The other two moved against the far wall, as if by crouching there they could stay undetected, out of harm's way. I stayed where I was. I watched Pa warily as he gripped the chair and pulled his backside down onto it. His body moved out of rhythm with itself, he stank of beer and fag smoke and there was now a line of bloody dribble running down the dark stubble of his chin.

'What are you fuckin' starin' at? Get me a drink, girl,' he snarled, running his large, dirty hands through his oily hair.

'We ain't got nuffink,' I said, cowering a little under his gaze.

His eyes were bloodshot; small pins of red in his flat face. I hated him; no, I despised him with every ounce of flesh on my skinny body. Every part of me loathed this monster. He made our lives a living hell, when they were already tough enough with the hardship of poverty.

'Well get me a fuckin' sandwich then, I shouldn't 'ave to fuckin' ask ya, 'ilda. I've been workin' down them docks all day, the least a man should expect is 'is dinner when 'e gets 'ome.' With that, he looked up at me, sniffing the air, like an animal scenting its prey. 'An' where's that lazy cow of a mother?'

'She's upstairs, Pa. Restin', like. She ain't well, Pa, 'er 'eart's givin' 'er gyp.' I trembled as I spoke, my eyes averted. There was no point giving him the means to start a fight, yet.

With that he rubbed his chin with his right hand, then

crashed it down onto the table. I jumped out of my skin with the suddenness of it. 'I don't want to know what that lazy bitch is doin', she should be 'ere, feedin' 'er 'usband. Now go an' get me a fuckin' drink NOW.' He slammed his fist down again, to make sure I understood, and by God I did.

'This bloody family. I ain't done nuffink to deserve the likes of you lot. Work me fingers to the bone I do, and what for, I ask you? To be cheeked by me own flesh an' blood.'

I looked, puzzled, at his fingers. There was no bone show-ing there. Instead they were thick digits, like sausages, the red veins lying under the grime of the dockyard. His fingernails were filthy and stained yellow with the tar from his baccy. I also knew he hadn't been at work today. He'd been refused work at the dockside, or so his mate Billy's wife told Ma this morning. His foul mouth and quick temper had got him into trouble with the foreman at the dock gates again, so how can he have worked his fingers to the bone?

Confused, I watched him as he launched the fury that froze me to the spot. My feet refused to move from under me, even though my mind was yelling to my legs to run away, run as fast as I could and get out and away from That Man. No good would come of tonight. The violence was coming, I could see him building up to it. I could only brace myself for the onslaught.

'We ain't got no drink, Pa.' I shook as I spoke and then somewhere inside me I found the anger, the courage to answer him back. I now knew he was going for me, so I reckoned I might as well go down fighting after all. 'We ain't got no grog cos you drank it all.'

My voice sounded shrill, sharp in the black fog of the room. I could instinctively feel the others shrink into the wall, hoping they might disappear. I wished they could. This way, he'd forget about them and focus just on me. They, at least, would be safe tonight.

'What did you say, girl? I've never 'eard such fuckin' cheek, an' comin' from a daughter of mine wiv a mouth on 'er. I'll bloody teach you for that. You don't ever disrespect your old man. What the 'ell did that bitch of a mother teach you?'

And with that he launched. I had just enough time to brace myself, then the first blow landed.

My pa was a fighter, a proper fighter. He knew how to hit so the bruises didn't show. He knew how to hurt me and I knew I would regret my cheek.

He landed the first blow as a cuff to my face. I felt the skin on my face move in shock then the saliva followed; I spat it onto the floor. I staggered sideways, almost hitting the hearth, with a surprisingly quick movement, he grabbed my hair that hung, brown, lank and dirty, and pulled as hard as he could. I tried to stop my cry, even then I didn't want to startle the babies, but I couldn't, it hurt too much.

'Let me go, Pa, I'll find you a drink, I promise,' I whimpered, only just loud enough for him to hear.

He dragged me by the hair to the door. 'Cheek me an' I'll chuck you out. I don't want you, your ma don't want you. You're no good to anyone you littl' cow.'

With that he reared his face up at me, his eyes screwed into ugly violence. His breath was as sour as the drinking holes he frequented, his skin was grey and mottled red with the booze and his latest fight.

'I'll find you a drink, Pa, I promise I will, I promise.' My voice sounded small next to the storm that was building in him. Again he yanked my hair, dragging my body after him. I felt the door swing open. My head hit the side of it and was jerked round to face the blackness of the open doorway.

I glanced back quickly with the smallest turn of my head which was in his fierce grip, tearing at my scalp.

'It's okay, I'm okay,' I mouthed to Les and Joanie. They were huddled into the grime of the wallpaper, staring at me with huge, fearful eyes. I willed them to stay there, quiet and still, so no harm would come to them.

My head burnt with the pull of That Man's thick fingers. 'I'll fuckin' throw you out, you littl' cunt. What d'you say to me, your pa? What d'you fuckin' say?'

The spittle from his reeking mouth hit my face. I tried to hide my revulsion, my pain, because I knew it excited him even more.

'I'm sorry, Pa. I shouldn't 'ave said that to you. I ain't a bad girl, I promise, Pa. I'll do whatever you say next time, won't I?'

I tried to look him in the eyes but my face was twisted round towards his body, my hands holding my head where the roots of my hair were tearing from my scalp. That must have satisfied him, because he threw me back into the room where I stumbled into the chair and grabbed the table for support. I backed off as slowly as I could, away from the babes, keeping his attention on me, wishing him to calm himself, to quieten down. For a second his eyes met mine and I almost saw something that in another man might've been regret, except it was him, that bastard old man of mine. Whatever it was, it vanished in an instant, leaving that panting, sweating, stinking brute with the remainder of his drunken anger still written on his face.

'Get me a sandwich, then,' he slurred. He looked tired now, defeated, as if the attack had drained him.

Rubbing my head, I edged towards the bread that lay under a grey-streaked piece of linen on the table top. There was half a loaf left, just enough to feed us children in the morning. It might possibly be our only meal of the day, but that wouldn't worry him. I could hardly bear to give it to him, but I knew I had no choice. As if to underline our plight, my stomach growled with hunger.

We went to bed with empty stomachs but grateful Pa's temper hadn't been worse. We climbed onto the iron bed, next to Ma's warm body. Three small children, a urine-stained mattress and a single blanket. I covered each of the littl'uns with their coats and finally settled down myself.

'No 'arm done, sleep now, it'll all be better in the mornin'.' I almost meant it.

We huddled together, not just for warmth, but for the comfort of being together, relatively unscathed by the night's events. I started telling them the same story I told them every night. It wasn't a fancy story, there were no princesses nor handsome princes to rescue them from wicked wizards.

Instead, I told a story about a family who had three children. The mother and father were always happy and loved their little ones. There was always enough to eat, and they lived in a little house that was always warm. There was no need to triumph over evil, because it simply didn't exist in that world we created in our minds. Eventually I heard small snuffles coming from the others and I knew I could finally sleep. I said my prayers. I never asked for much, just the courage to live another day under the same roof as my wicked Pa. This time though, I added a new prayer. I asked God in heaven for a proper family. One with a father who loves his children, and brings them sweets and gives them cuddles, though I knew my prayer would never, ever be granted.

CHAPTER 2

Bare Knuckle

1929

A clenched fist met solid bone. There was a crack, then a moan from the onlookers. One of the men swayed back, his face a mess of blood and gristle. Pa swung his fist back again, and launched the next blow. This time it found his opponent's chin, and he staggered back with the impact. There was a split second when nothing happened. The crowd that stood around the men in a rough circle, as though it were a boxer's ring, went instantly quiet. Then Pa moved again, his bare torso streaked with dirt and grime from the day's work lugging great sacks from the barges and into the warehouse that stood behind him. He drew back his right arm, and in one elegant move he landed another punch to his opponent's cheek. This time the bare-knuckle fighter fell backwards with a spray of sweat and hit the hard dockyard stone. With a victorious yell, Pa dropped his body on top of his victim with heavy finality.

There was a cry from the crowd then several men rushed to pull Pa up from the motionless body of the loser. Ted Johnson held his hands aloft, knowing he was the dockside champion. The crowd that gathered round him erupted, braying for more. Angry faces, men who'd lost their money betting on That Man's vanquished rival, spat out insults, then turned to pull their man from the floor. Pa's opponent, another docker most likely, was out cold and suffering the indignity of being dragged off to the nearest pub by his mates. Men were shouting and waving scraps of paper after having spent their day's wages on illegal betting. They surged towards Pa with excitement, the day's back-breaking work now forgotten.

I swayed as I stood with my back to the warehouse, keeping in the shadows in case I was spotted. This was no place for a young girl. I was eight years old and had never before witnessed a boxing match. Ma had sent me out to find Pa and ask him to go and forage for firewood, or steal some tar blocks from the roads as they made the best fires. I'd run around the dockyards until I found him. It was only 7 p.m., early enough for a girl to be out, but the sight of Pa bellowing his victory made me wish it was later so I would never have seen his triumph.

Despite that, I couldn't find it inside me to leave. Part of me was fascinated by his stories of the fights he won and lost, and I felt like I was seeing a different side to my old man even though it was just as brutal. Somehow I'd never thought of him as a champion, but seeing the adulation of the crowd of dock workers, it struck me as a sordid kind of fame.

Men were starting to move off now the fight was over. They'd collected their winnings and were leaching away from the dockside. I hoped they were going home to their wives and children, but knew it was more likely they were heading to the local pubs. Pa bent down to pick up his shirt, wool coat and cap. I could hear his voice above the sounds of the men talking and laughing. He was regaling his pals with the match, revelling in the spectacle and the blood lust. It was time for me to leave. No one had noticed the young girl in the dirty grey dress standing at the back of the crowd, so focused were they on the heat of the two men's battle. I could be spotted at any minute, though, and so, inching along the warehouse precincts, I edged away from the scene of Pa's victory, wishing I'd turned and run away when I had the chance because I couldn't bear seeing his blood-thirsty glory any longer.

Back at home, I ran in and launched myself into Ma's arms. 'What's all this, 'ilda?' was all she said. I buried my face in her apron, feeling the bump of the new life growing inside her underneath the worn cotton, wishing the images of the fight would drain away from my mind, like the blood from the face of the pale fighter who came off worse in the fight. I didn't reply. Ma stroked my hair with her hand. I'd cut off my long tresses after Pa had dragged me by them, crying a little when my wavy brown locks had fallen to the floor.

Later that night, we waited again for That Man to crawl out of the pub with his winnings spent on booze and his bruises the only things left to show for his triumph. Les and Joanie were curled up in bed. I'd checked on them just after 11 p.m. and they were both breathing softly, their faces almost luminescent in the moonlight and damp with night sweat.

I heard Pa's return before I saw him. His rough London voice rose above the sound of two other men as they careered their way home. They were drunk, and loud, and shouting obscenities at each other in a play of mock fighting.

Pa lurched through the door, still hollering after his mates. I felt a lump in my throat of pure tension. I tried to swallow but my mouth was suddenly dry. I had to go into the kitchen. I couldn't leave Ma in there, alone, even though I was only a young girl.

'What d'ya fuckin' mean, there ain't no dinner left?' he growled. He was tanked up on cheap ale, and full of his own pride at his fighting prowess.

'Wife, all I ask for is my fuckin' dinner on the table when I get in from a day workin' like a slave. Is that too much to fuckin' ask?' His voice was raised to shouting pitch. Les and Joanie wouldn't be asleep for long, I just hoped they'd be sensible and stay where they were. No sense in getting involved.

At that moment I appeared in the doorway.

That Man's head swivelled towards me, and I knew in an instant I should've stayed hidden. The sight of me seemed to rile him even more.

He turned back to Ma and stalked over to where she was sitting, her hands clutching her knitting in her lap, her mouth set in a line, of fear or determination, I didn't know which.

'Ted, there ain't no dinner left because I gave it to the kids. They were hungry tonight and there wasn't much in the pot,' said Ma, adding, 'you've been out all evening, Ted. How was I to know you'd 'ad nothing for yer dinner?'

Her voice trembled. Her hands smoothed over her belly as she spoke.

'You've got another fuckin' baby in there that needs feedin' and who's goin' to go out and work? Who's the one who 'as to work all the hours God sends to keep you all?' Pa snarled.

His face was level with Ma's. His breath must've stunk of stale beer but Ma didn't move an inch. She looked back at him, silent and dignified. This seemed to inflame him even more. He shouted again, this time he spat into the corner of the room I was cowering in.

Pa stumbled slightly, then took a step back. He looked like he was thinking about what to do next.

His large, brutal hand moved quickly. Before I'd had time to draw breath, he slapped Ma across the face. She put a hand up to shield herself but he grabbed it, pulling her up to her feet to face him. I watched as her knitting rolled its way down her skirt and onto the wooden floor. One of the knitting needles came loose from the row of stitches, leaving the empty loops stranded.

I gasped as That Man held Ma's arm, bringing her right up to his face so her swollen tummy rested against his torso. It looked like a lovers' embrace, except for the pain in Ma's face.

'Stop it, Ted, you're 'urtin' me,' she begged.

He laughed at that, clearly enjoying her distress. He shook off her arm, leaving behind a red ring round her wrist that would bruise by tomorrow.

As he released her, he swung his right fist round and this time hit her hard on the side of her belly. He was careful not to hit her bump. He knew just where to hurt without causing too much damage. Ma groaned, and staggered sideways, falling into the side of the table.

I started crying. I felt so helpless watching my mother being beaten.

'Ted, stop it, you'll hurt the baby!' Ma cried, clutching her stomach and feeling for the chair behind her.

He didn't stop, though. He slapped her again, then again, then raised his fist and brought it up to her face. She was crouched on the floor awkwardly, trying to lift herself back up.

'This is your warning, Em. If I don't get my dinner on the table when I get in, you'll get it bad, d'ya understand?' His voice was harsh and slurred, his gait awkward.

Ma nodded in response. She said nothing. I expect, like me, she was just praying for him to stop.

Pa turned round and pulled out a chair. Sitting down, he sat heavily, expectant, as Ma pulled herself back up. She didn't look at him as she limped slowly round to the range. Even though it was past midnight, even though Ma was pregnant and weary, even though Ma had been beaten by him and was clearly in pain, she knew she had no choice but to prepare him his dinner.

The injustice stung me to babyish tears. There was nothing I could do to make this better, except help Ma peel a couple of potatoes and set the pot to boil.

We worked in silence. That Man stared at us as we cooked, his small, mean eyes glittering in the dim light.

Pa had learnt his craft during his brief stint in the Army, after returning from the Boer War. He'd honed his fighting technique, the speed of his right hook, the left coming in to finish what the right fist had started. Now he boasted he'd fight anyone 'fer a penny'. He was agile on his feet, surprisingly so in light of his stocky frame and his love for the drink. He had a violent temper, a need to win and an ego that demanded the attention that small-time pugilism gave to men in the East End. It was a way of being 'somebody' and Ted Johnson loved the feeling he was 'someone' special. I sound hard on him, and I expect I am, but I saw him stagger through that door more times than I could count, boasting of having spent his winnings on beer and his 'pals'. We never got to see that money, but by God we saw his rages.

I knew even at such a young age that I couldn't change my father, but that night I think I finally knew it for sure. He was made to fight; his life was a battle for survival every single day. As a child he'd been beaten by his father and had boiling water poured on him by his stepmother. His life had been one of violence and very little love. I guess that's what made him who he was. Ted Johnson would never put down his fists and settle his quarrels in any other way, he didn't know how to, and I saw that so clearly I wish I'd been blind to it still.

*

'Give me your faces, Joanie and Leslie Johnson. I ain't never seen such a lot of filthy faces in all me life, I swear I ain't,' I joked, as my sister and brother tumbled out of the bed.

It was a cold morning, the type that made me want to stay under my thin blanket and coat for as long as possible to avoid the chill of the floorboards and the soft plumes of mist as my breath hit the cool air. Both of them yawned and shivered in the chill grey light of the morning, rubbing their eyes to adjust to the dim light coming from the open doorway, and greeting them with the harsh reality of life in the slum we called home. It was already past seven o'clock.

Ma was still in the bed we all shared, her belly swollen with her fourth child, my latest sibling and an extra mouth we would have to feed. Her pregnancy was hitting her hard this time and so she was spending more and more of her days propped up, breathing shallow breaths and grimacing in pain when she thought I wasn't looking.

None of us knew what the trouble with her was and at three shillings and sixpence a visit, a doctor was a luxury far beyond our meagre pockets. Ma always said she thought it was her heart that hurt, giving her giddy spells and leaving her short of breath and permanently sallow-looking. Ma, or Emily, to give her her real name, had been a good-looking woman until the relentless poverty, and worries caused by That Man her husband, had robbed her of her beauty. Her brown hair had been glossy, and she always said she could turn heads in the borough in her day. Now the slim figure had disappeared as a result of the serial pregnancies; one baby following another by a few years, until this latest one, which seemed more than she could bear.

Despite that, I still thought she was beautiful, even in her patched and faded flowery apron and with her hair tied back off her face. It was the kindness that shone from her for us kids that made her pretty in my eyes. She always had a smile on her face for us, and her touch was always gentle, always caring. So different from That Man.

It was hard to see how they had got together in the first place. But they had, and now this woman, who everyone in the streets around us turned to for advice or help with their problems, was becoming a shadow of her former self. She no longer sang as she scrubbed clothes at the end of each day. Now, I did most of the washing as best I could because Ma was so tired, and had bags under her eyes to prove it. I was just a child but already I was my ma's right-hand woman and had been since the age of six when I was old enough to dress myself and my siblings and help out at home with the chores that had to be done each and every day. I scrubbed the floor and I washed the clothes, even though I was barely tall enough to reach into the tin bath we used. I helped Ma wherever I could as life for a housewife in east London was one of hard, relentless graft. I hung the clothes on the line in the yard out the back and I ripped up bits of newspaper to hang on the nail in the lavvy.

But, still, Ma was becoming weaker by the day. There was little we could do except hope and pray that by some miracle she'd get better soon. Everything Ma had ever taught us, about being honest, upright and caring, was done despite That Man. She kept us clean, she made sure we all looked 'spick an' span'. She had the sunniest smile for miles around, and yet she faced that monstrous man every night without losing her gentle nature or her love of a good joke. She really was a woman of importance to us, she worked hard for all of us and asked for nothing in return.

She was one of 21 siblings, born in Merrick Place, to her mother, also Emily, and her father, Joseph Scoggins, who was a leather dresser journeyman, which meant that he worked in a tannery, converting the hide into leather by means of the stinking alchemical processes. Her brother Billy later became the famous Bermondsey Billy Wells, a welterweight boxer. He was a local celebrity. Everyone knew Bermondsey Billy, and he was greeted with drinks and slaps on the back in the pubs that he and Ted frequented. Billy was Ma's family's hero. He had escaped the drudgery of his station in life. Ma was younger than him, but spoke about him with pride, saying ''e'd made something of 'imself'. Every few months, we'd be taken, scrubbed and clean, to Ma's parents' home in The Grange, just a few streets away, and sometimes Billy would be there, with his shiny silver cups as proof of the prize fights he had won.

We'd troop up the rickety wooden stairs to the first floor tenement, which comprised two bedrooms, a kitchen and scullery. How her parents had brought up 21 children in the cramped, filthy rooms was anybody's guess. Ma had always said the first time she slept in a bed rather than on the floor was when she married Pa and they finally got a few rooms of their own. It must've felt like she'd gone up in the world!

Ma and Pa lived with her parents at The Grange for the first year of their marriage. Ma gave birth to me in the smaller of those dark, dirty rooms. But they were forced to leave after Pa stole two of Billy's cups and pawned them for beer money. I always thought that was a stupid thing to do to a prize boxer! Billy went mad with rage when he found out, throwing us all out of the flat, and giving Pa a beating in the process. Pa might have been tough but he couldn't compete with Billy's expert fists. Billy rarely lost a fight. That was why we only saw Ma's family rarely, even though they lived so close to us.

The last time we'd gone was on Grandpa's birthday. Ma had washed our clothes with extra vigour the night before to make sure we were smart, but That Man had started a fight with her and had smashed her face against the kitchen table by way of ending their argument.

I'll never forget us arriving at her parents' house, us children all smart looking but pale after the night's events, Ma casting her eyes to the floor with the shame of her purple bruised eye and cut forehead which brushing her hair to one side could not hide. Pa strutted in with us, as usual, and no one said a word. We ate cake and drank tea, or milk for us kids, and left earlier than usual. I can still recall trying to swallow that cake, but finding my throat was tight with tension.

I used to ask myself why neither Billy nor Joseph ever intervened. And why didn't Ma ever ask them for help and protection against that womanising thug, her husband? I suppose they thought she'd made her bed, now she had to lie in it. I'd pondered this many times over the years, and in my childish way I'd felt heartbroken that Ma seemed so alone against That Man.

I had no time for the worrying thoughts this morning, though. It was easier to dismiss my fears when there was work to do, and naughty children to get clean and dressed for school.

I yawned slightly as I walked into the scullery, goosebumps crept up my arms and I rubbed them down to try and generate a little heat. It wasn't yet cold enough to have frost inside the window panes but I knew it wasn't far off. This cold was more a damp kind of chill, the type that settles in your bones and won't let go. Even so, I was grateful for winter as it was the only time of the year the smogs eased a little, freeing the borough from the stench of the factories and fug of the city. As winter breezes whipped up the Thames, we shivered in our woollen coats and too-small boots as we scurried between home and school, but at least we could breathe for a while, till the spring melt started the slow sinking back into the stews of summer.

We were always underdressed. There was never any money for new clothes. We each of us had one set of clothes and nothing for Sunday best. Pa was the only one who owned a set of best clothes: a dapper brown wool suit and a white shirt and tie. The suit regularly saw the inside of the local pawnshop when there was not enough left in Ma's purse to buy food at the start of some weeks. 'What Pa don't know, don't hurt 'im,' she always said with a crafty wink, but even though she made light of it, it must've been a worry coming up with the extra pennies to pawn it back in time for Sunday morning. Pa never said anything, or maybe he didn't notice. He was always too busy drinking and betting with his cronies down at the Dog and Gun to worry about what was going on at home in his absence.

But this wasn't the time to dwell on Pa, or pawnshops. The children had to get washed and dressed before I could even start on getting breakfast together.

'Will you stand still. This ain't the time to fidget. You're goin' to make us late, you rascal,' I said, with a grin, as I held Les's angelic little face in my hands and scrubbed him clean. He gave me a smile, and with his brown locks and dark eyes, he stole my heart away. How could I possibly scold him? 'Right, that's your face done, now give me your 'ands. I bet them 'ands are just as dirty. I don't know what you get up to, I really don't!' I exclaimed.

I couldn't help but laugh at Les's sweet smile, which hid his cheeky personality and love of mischief and jokes. He grinned back at me, and showed me his palms. Just as I thought, they were ingrained with dirt from his larks playing up at the docks or down at Southwark Park. I scrubbed his hands, making the water go black, and when he was clean I rubbed them dry with another cloth before handing him his clothes from the chair by the hearth.

I'd boiled the shirts and blouses in the copper the previous evening. It was set in brickwork over the fireplace and I was always very careful not to scald myself because I'd seen Ma do it when she wasn't paying attention. Once the water, which had to be poured in jug by jug-full, was simmering nicely I added the Reckitt's Blue, a tablet of carbolic soap wrapped in a small piece of muslin and tied up with string. If I was careful I could make it last several washes. Then once the water had turned its distinctive blue colour, which made the shirts go white, I squeezed them out as best I could and put them through the mangle we had in the yard. Then I put Les's and Pa's shirts out in front of the hearth. My own blouse went on the end of the iron bedstead and was rarely dry by the next day. That night had been cold though, so we were all going to have to go to school and work with the clammy feel of damp material against our skin.

'Go an' get yerself dressed, you 'orror,' I shouted to Les with mock anger, and he scampered off into the bedroom. I could hear him singing as he took off his only pair of long johns by himself. He was only four years old but he was older than his years. We all had to be in order to survive, and he managed to dress himself with his collar sticking up to show the effort it had cost him. I undressed as quickly as I could so that I wouldn't lose the residual heat from my nightgown in that chill room.

That's how it was for us. We were cold all winter, and then we were hot all summer. We wore damp clothes because we couldn't afford to buy a second set. Yet we barely noticed because that's how it was for everyone in the borough. Our neighbours were no different. The old lady Mrs Mackintosh who lived on the floor above us wore the same clothes every day and there was no sign she'd ever washed them. A widow, she'd struggled to cope without her husband, and it was only looking after her grown-up son that seemed to keep her going through the drudgery and poverty of her daily life.

Ma, being the soft touch she was, took them up some dinner once or twice a week. Pa always grumbled about her 'puttin' food into other people's mouths' but she replied that it was good, Christian kindness, and when he stopped putting our food money into the pockets of the local publicans she would stop helping others. She often got a belt for saying that.

'Now then, Les, are you goin' to be difficult or can I wipe that saucy smile off your face?' I winked at Les as he walked over to me. He was growing taller by the day, turning into a real beanpole, and I was worried about how we'd afford a new pair of breeches for him.

'Alright 'ilda, I'm 'ere,' he said in his little voice. 'No need to get your knickers in a twist.'

'I won't 'ave that language from the likes of you,' I frowned. I knew where he picked up these phrases, but there was nothing I could do about Pa's filthy mouth. 'Say that again an' I'll wash your mouth out wiv the Reckitt's Blue.'

He looked completely unconcerned, and scampered off once I'd brushed down his hair and wiped his face.

'Goodness, I can't stand 'ere chattin', I've got to get the kettle on, and make Ma 'er tea,' I cried, looking up at the clock and seeing it was already 7.30 a.m. The kettle clattered as I tiptoed to reach the range and placed it awkwardly on top. I'd lit it upon waking, with a piece of rolled up newspaper. There was a steady heat emanating from it and I almost stopped there a second to appreciate it. From the shelf above the mantelpiece I pulled down three plates and four cups. Ma never ate first thing, she said she didn't like having breakfast. I'd ask if she was perhaps saving the bread for us kids, but she'd always denied it with a wave of her hand.

Beyond the chimneys and the yards, the other women's washing and the weaving streets, were the docks where Pa made his precarious living. They were the robust and noisy source of our livelihood. Even from here, if you squinted hard enough, you could make out the masts of the ships that drew in and out of the wharves daily, bringing their strange cargoes to the docks where an army of men worked like ants to unload the timber from Scandinavia, the spices from India and Africa, the gums and glues which had such a sweet-sour heavy aroma and the fruit and veg which came from goodness knows where. We never saw any of it, that was a fact. What we didn't have, we didn't miss, though, and those murky warehouses that lined the waterfront could as well have contained gold bars for all the good they did us.

Pa's working days were spent among the bustle and noise, with the great juddering masts of the ships that lined the wharves, teetering over the cold stores at the end of our road. There were always the shouts from men lining the barges, throwing ropes to the smaller boats that were pulling in the steamers. The caws of seagulls joined the melee, mixing with the lively shouts and barked orders issued by men on the dock side, and the sound of the Thames, brown and churning as she discharged her vessels laden with goods. These sights and sounds were the backdrop of our lives, and we were bound to the sea beyond our briny horizon in a myriad of ways. Pa's livelihood was centred on it, and with him our fortunes lay, as did our grumbling bellies and our clothes with layers of darning.

I didn't ask questions. What went on with the money was between Ma and Pa, though I prayed for the day I could earn a wage and see the look on Ma's worn face when I handed my pay packet over to her. I grabbed the remnants of yesterday's loaf of bread, which was wrapped in a cloth, and started carving thin slices from it. There was a pot of jam on the shelf and a tin of condensed milk.

We'll need something in our tummies for the cold today, I thought, as I opened the tin with fierce jabs, licking the sticky sweet milk off my fingers as I went. I poured the viscous liquid into the steaming tea in the four cups and hastened to give Ma hers.

Back in the kitchen, Joanie was perched up at the table, a spirited girl of three years old, and already wanting to be as independent as her big brother Les. She'd submitted to being dressed and I'd managed to brush her hair before she wriggled free of me and climbed onto one of the kitchen chairs.

I cut the bread and scraped a thin layer of jam onto it. Joanie grabbed the first slice out of my hands, and I scolded her, placing my hands on my hips just like Ma did.

She laughed at me and I couldn't help but smile. Les munched on another slice of bread, chattering away to Joanie about his school day ahead. Once they'd both eaten and showed me their rinsed hands, I grabbed Les's flat cap and shushed him out of the door. I listened to the sound of his hobnail boots as they clattered down the stone steps and out into the street.

'Blimey I'm in a right doze this mornin',' I said to myself and started to clear up the plates, rinsing them in the stone sink. I cut off another slice of bread, carefully using the knife as Ma had taught me, and spread a thin layer of jam over it. Gulping down my tea, I added an extra splash of condensed milk, licking the drips from the side of the can before looking round guiltily to see if Ma could see me. She was still abed and so I quickly mopped round the floor, placed the wooden chairs back to the table and made sure we were all spick and span, just as Ma liked.

Joanie had slunk back into bed with Ma. With a last look round the tiny kitchen, I pulled on my navy wool coat, my pride and joy, tied back my hair with a ribbon which was my only ornament, bought when Pa was in one of his rare generous moods, and skipped out of the door, catching my breath on the cold air as I met the outdoors with an inward sigh.

Almost instantly I bumped into Mrs Mackintosh. She was carrying a small basket containing half a loaf of bread and a packet of lard.

' 'Ello, darlin', 'ow are you all today?' she asked with a smile.

I was late for school but I couldn't be rude, so I stopped and we chatted for a moment. Just as I was about to leave she grabbed my hand and with the other dug around in the pockets of her black skirt, bringing out several small sweets wrapped in shiny silver paper.

'For you an' your bruvver an' sister, darlin',' she said, nodding as I started to protest. 'I always say, ain't it a pity the way fings are for you and your mother at 'ome. A pity,' she repeated, wagging her head from side to side.

She wasn't the only one of our neighbours who liked to give little treats to Les, Joanie and me. They all knew about Pa. They all knew he gave us a hard time, and most of the time they heard him do it. The walls of the tenements were paper thin, and then, of course, we had the black eyes and bruises to show for it. I accepted the sweets, a small lump appearing in my throat.

'Thanks, Mrs Mackintosh, but I've got to run,' and I clattered down the steps and onto Bevington Street.

*

Waiting for me, outside our front door, were two of my friends from down the street: Margaret and Nellie. Both stood kicking their heels on the cobbles, with white, thin legs and too-small winter coats. We all smiled when I jumped out, and linking arms we hurried off to school. All of us had chores each morning. We all helped our mothers and we were often late, but we all waited to walk into school together regardless of whether we'd get into trouble. It was the fierce loyalty of girls who live the same kinds of difficult lives. Our friendship was one of our main consolations, but we never had time to dawdle.

Round us, housewives were already sweeping and scrubbing their doorsteps and the surrounding cobbles, marking their territory even though it was barely past eight o'clock. I could hear the sounds of our district; the women starting the morning gossip with exclamations of ''E didn't, I don't believe it, 'e's got a nerve your old man ain't 'e?' and 'Well she said to me, don't you go botherin' my Joe, 'e's got enough on 'is plate.'

There was one thing you could guarantee, living here: everyone knew everyone's business. There was no such thing as privacy; as I said, the walls of the tenement buildings were thin, the lavvies out in the dingy little yards were shared by four or five families, folk slept three or four people to a room and had maybe one other room that doubled as the scullery and parlour to live, talk and play, so the streets became our home. At all hours of the day and night children were out playing, dodging the carts plastered with Peek Frean and Pears Soap adverts and the steaming piles of dung left by the horses that pulled them.

The smell of the horses and horse dung, the whiff of sugar and vanilla from the custard and biscuit factories, and the spices and medicinal herbs in the cold stores created a heady mix, but overpowering all of them was the stench of the tanneries; acrid and heavy against the surprisingly salty smell of the Thames lapping against the end of our road. Added to this was the sounds of children shouting, housewives gossiping and the clatter of horses' hooves. It was never boring, I'll say that for Bermondsey. We might have been poor as church mice but we had the most exciting, exotic playground of any London child. We considered ourselves richer than kings when we were racing around the docks, watching ships coming in to harbour and throwing stones into the Thames. It was freedom, and we loved our rowdy, exciting borough.

I walked towards the school on Bevington Street. I loved being there, away from the worries at home. At school I felt safe and I took great pride in being a 'scholar', making sure I listened attentively to my teachers.

It was always disappointing when it came to home time, and today was no different. I sloped back, my head spinning with the three 'r's – reading, 'riting and 'rithmetic – that formed the basis of our studies. It wasn't what you'd call a wide education, but it did for the likes of us. Us girls also learnt cookery and housewifery, though God knows I knew enough about that already! I always wondered why the boys never learnt those skills, but never questioned it. That wasn't the done thing and I'd have got a clip round the ear for my cheek.

Les and I walked home together, chattering about our day. We bundled into the house, throwing off our coats and calling for Ma. There was no sight of her, either in the scullery or the yard. Confused, we looked at each other, our faces registering the first feelings of alarm. There was no note, and no sign that anything was taken, so I told Les to ask around and see if he could glean where Ma was.

Ma had been seen, hunched up like an old woman, being taken off by ambulance to the 'ospital at the other end of Southwark Park. She was having the baby! At once we were excited and nervous. We munched on the remaining bread, smearing it with jam and finishing off the condensed milk, and waited for news.

Pa arrived a couple of hours later, saying we had a new baby brother and wasn't that 'sumfink speshul'. He seemed genuinely pleased, or maybe it was the fact he got to celebrate by 'wettin' the baby's 'ead' that made him so animated, as it wasn't long before he took his leave of us, putting me in charge and disappearing into the night with barely a backward glance.

For the next ten days I did all Ma's jobs, even scrubbing the steps. Every morning I got Les up and dressed for school, and every evening I fed him, Joanie and Pa (who was being surprisingly well behaved) their dinner, washed their clothes for the next day, put the wet clothes through the mangle and hung them out. I told jokes to keep Les amused and kept him smiling so he didn't worry about how Ma and the baby were doing. I stroked Joanie's hair and tucked her up every evening with the blanket and her coat covering her. Each night I fell into bed and was asleep almost as soon as I shut my eyes.

At the end of the ten days, we trooped in from yet another school day, our collars up round our ears to stave off the biting cold of that blustery March day, and there was Ma, back in the kitchen like she'd never been away. She looked tired but happy to see us and we rushed up to cuddle her, talking nineteen to the dozen.

It took a moment to remember we had another sibling, which was what all the fuss was about. Then came a cry from the bedroom. It was the distinct high-pitched yell of a new-born baby. Without thinking, we raced into the bedroom to see a bundle of blankets wrapped in the top cupboard drawer, which was open, revealing the crinkled, red face of a yelling infant. We looked at Ma and she started laughing.

'Come 'ere, you soppy 'apporths, and meet your new brother Ronald.'

We didn't need any more introductions than that! We huddled around him, cooing and touching his little fingers and tiny nails, exclaiming with delight each time he yawned or opened his eyes in between yells.

'Aw ain't 'e lovely,' I said, staring in wonder as Ronald gripped one of my fingers.

' 'E's so small!' said Les, who said he wouldn't touch him for fear of breaking him.

Ma looked at us and smiled. Even though it was another mouth to feed, another little person to wash and clothe, it was a moment of pure joy for us all. It was just another ordinary day in the slums, but we had a new brother to love, and it was that love that always got us through each twist and turn of our embattled lives.

CHAPTER 3

Gettin' a Beatin'

1931

The clock's dark face showed midnight. The soft glow of the hearth kept a bare kind of light in the scullery. Ma's outline shifted, her head nodding as she fought against sleep. I was there, as usual, keeping vigil with Ma while she waited for Pa to come home from his drinking hole, this stifling August night.

Ma eased her misshapen body out of the chair and walked awkwardly over to the small window, her hands clasping her back for support even though she was still a young woman of 30. There was nothing much to see in the small communal yard out the back, just today's washing hanging in limp, grey shapes like exhausted ghosts against the grim, dirt-streaked brick of the yard wall.

Behind the boundaries of the wall were more tenement buildings, looming over the cobbled streets with lines of black windows and chimney pots in regimented queues. Then, of course, there were the docks and the ships that lay in our harbours. By day the bustle of activity was the backdrop to our existence. By night, the waters of the Thames foamed against the dockyard walls. The catcalls and shouts of the workers were silenced. The dock gates were locked, but the dense blackness of the night contained other noises, from the seething river to the calls of the whores who worked the back alleys. We had never experienced real silence, the sort that scoops out noise leaving, what? The sound of my ticking heart and shallow breaths perhaps.

Ma tried to ease the window open a crack wider, in the hope of catching a breeze to move the hot soupy air inside our little room. As she swayed at the window the stench of the tanning factories seemed to fill the hot, stifling room even more.

On nights like this it felt like the city was smothered under a veil of soot and smog. The soot coated the dark brick walls that towered over the tiny winding streets; covering the cobbles, the stray dogs and us folk who lived, played and worked here. We breathed soot and dust, it became part of us and us part of it. Choking beneath the factory fumes, we Londoners were as much a part of the smog as the soot itself. Our aroma was that of this neighbourhood and these streets, it was unmistakable, however hard we tried to scrub it all away during our weekly bath. Tonight the smell of the bones from the glue works joined the rest, creating a cloying odour that we carried round with us wherever we went, rendering us, unmistakably, Bermondsey people.

On overheated nights like this I didn't know why Ma bothered to wait up for Pa. I vowed to myself with the fervour of the very young (I was now ten years old) that I would never wait up for any man, let alone a drunken old sod like That Man.

I could barely call him by his name, let alone by his relationship to me. I knew from the minute I was old enough to have a thought in my head that he would never be the father I wanted or needed. I always knew he was a bad man. Yet still we waited, me sat with a pair of Les's socks, darning over the places I'd already fixed with my tight little stitches. Ma, back in her chair, did nothing, her darning sliding off her knees as she sighed restlessly. Every now and again, she raised her head to look at the clock above the doorway, the hands relentlessly ticking onwards with no sign of him.

33

Then, just as I felt my head nodding onto my chest, Ma stood up abruptly and called out to Les, who was fast asleep.

'Les luvvie, I need you to go and get your pa. Come on now, get up an' make yerself useful,' she called into the darkness.

For a minute I thought she hadn't shouted loudly enough, then there was a small thud where Les's feet hit the bare floorboards and the sound of material as it was dragged from the chair and onto his body. Seconds later, my little brother appeared at the doorway, yawning and blinking into the gloom.

'All right, Ma, I'll go and find the old bugger,' he said, pushing his dark hair back across his face.

He was six years old but already he spoke like a man, and had the look of the man of the house, weighed down by responsibilities far beyond his tender years. The light caught his profile and for a second he looked almost animated. He moved towards the door and was cast back into darkness.

'Dunno why you both wait up for 'im. What's 'e ever done for you?' he said as gruffly as his boy's voice would allow. 'I'll find 'im and I'll give 'im wot for, I will, Ma. I don't like 'im treating you like this, nor you, 'ilda,' he said with his little-boy logic.

Of course Ma and I knew the answer to that. If we'd been found asleep by Pa on his return, we'd have been in trouble. He took a perverse pleasure in waking one or all of us on his return from his nights stalking the streets, looking for Lord knows what to give joy to his twisted soul.

'Now don't you go lookin' for trouble, my boy. 'E ain't all bad an' he's your father, whether you like it or not,' said Ma quietly.

My heart broke for her, as it did every time I saw the disappointment at her lot in life in her eyes, and yet her stubborn refusal to see the bad in anyone, even him. Even him, the worst father any girl ever had.

'You be safe now, Les,' I muttered under my breath. I wouldn't have sent him out into the seedy city streets this time of night for anything. It wasn't that the streets were dangerous – my God everyone knew everyone in Bermondsey. You couldn't shit without the people three streets away knowing it! But it was That Man who was the trouble that lay in store for Les. Pa wasn't going to be pleased that a search party had been sent to find him, whatever the hell he was up to.

Despite the searing summer heat, Les pulled on his heavy wool jacket, the only one he owned, and walked out of the house, tipping Ma a slight wink and touching his head where his cap usually sat as he went. His footsteps descended the short flight of steps and then receded into the distance.

We stood at the window watching his small dark frame move silently into the night, weaving past the drunks who hollered and catcalled at him before losing interest and lurching on their way. Several black lumps pissed against one of the tenement buildings, and the sound of someone shouting 'Oi, you bastards, get out of it' filled the air. The shapes staggered backwards, raised their hands in acknowledgement and teetered away into the back streets, home to an angry wife and hungry children most likely. The clock ticked, reminding us that time was passing. It was almost one o'clock now and I could feel a dribble of sweat run down my back. The waiting was the worst part, not knowing what state Pa would be in and how he'd greet the search party. Les was in for it, I reckoned, but I guessed Ma and I wouldn't get off lightly either.

Ma picked up her darning then put it down again almost

at once. I tried to make conversation to ease the growing tension.

'Bread an' dripping for breakfast tomorrow, Ma. Don't you worry, I'll get the littl'uns fed an' up for school. You just stay in bed an' 'ave a lie-in,' I said, even though I was dog-tired after my day at school. I had to help Ma, because who else could do it?

Sometimes I wondered if it was like this for everyone. Did all children in London go to bed with a knot of fear in their stomach, hoping the next day would be better? I knew we weren't the only ones who feared their father. Nellie, one of my pals, regularly came to class with bruises on her wrists where her old man had grabbed her and hurt her. She lived with her mother, Eva, and two siblings two doors down from us in Bevington Street. Eva would never speak to any of her neighbours and we all knew why. Her husband Reg was a mean old sod as well, and often beat her. She was ashamed of so public a spectacle after one time when Reg grabbed her by the hair and pulled her down the road, yelling and cursing, before punching her to the ground in front of all us children and neighbours. Despite the fact that we all saw what took place, none of us would ever dare say a word. It was an unspoken rule in our part of London that this violence was an inevitable part of our lives. No one ever stepped in if a man was beating his wife.

It was an odd sight, seeing my friend's mother being attacked, and us all watching, silently. In my heart of hearts I knew it was wrong to say nothing but I was caught in the reality of life in our impoverished part of Bermondsey. Reg worked down the docks with Pa, and often went out drinking with him. It was a guess, but I imagined the same sorts of things happened in their house as they did in ours. Eva would, most probably, complain there was no money to feed her three kids and Reg would give them all a belting for their trouble.

Strangely, Nellie and I never spoke about the violence we suffered at home, but we were close friends, looking out for each other and sharing secrets and dreams like little girls do. We never mentioned our black eyes and our bruises. We never spoke about the terror we faced nightly at home, but escaped it together when we could.

We skipped around the playground, holding hands, as close a pair of pals as you'd be likely to meet. When we could, we'd race out of school and watch the ships from Tower Bridge, or play hopscotch on the street. I'd plait Nellie's long red curls, which I, with my shoulder-length dark brown hair, secretly envied, along with Nellie's translucent skin with fine blue veins. I felt so ordinary next to her with my grubby red cheeks and cheerful smile. Sometimes we'd just sit on the edge of the cobbles and make little dolls from discarded pegs. We were happy when we were away from home, and perhaps we both knew why we clung together in friendship so completely, and how much comfort it gave us playing together in our little fantasy worlds, away from the harsh reality of our lives.

One time we were sitting outside the tenements making peg dolls and selling them to other children for ha'pennies when my pa turned up, demanding the money from us. We both turned to him with our sweetest, little girl faces and denied ever selling them, instead handing him one if he'd like to take it to sell instead. Pa was lost for words! He stuttered a bit, refused to even touch the little doll with painted black eyes and a scrap of material for a dress, and stalked off, his masculine pride affronted, leaving Nellie and me snorting with repressed giggles. It wasn't often we got one up on our fathers, but when we did we enjoyed it immensely!

I always paid for my cheek, though, and when Pa got home that night I got a beating with his thick belt. I was sore for days after that, but it was worth it to see him flounder.

Suddenly the door slammed open. Pa's heavy dockers' boots had kicked open the unlocked door in a display of power and vicious temper. His eyes were wild, his hair disordered and standing up in spikes, his clothes, which he was hastily rearranging, gaped open revealing his stocky barrel chest with straggles of black hair. He wasn't a tall man, but what he lacked in stature he more than made up for in temper. He was pulling his shirt into his trousers, which had been hastily retied. Les followed behind him, his eyes glittering black. I couldn't read his expression but I knew it was bad.

'What the fuckin' 'ell are you doin' sendin' me own boy out to spy on me?' he roared, without waiting for an answer, his face pointed in hostility towards Ma.

Emily, who was a brave woman, braver than me, stood up shakily, like she'd been bracing herself for this moment. She met his glower.

'What the 'ell are you doin', you miserable ol' bitch?' he shouted, not caring that two of his children were in the room, and that the youngest, Joanie and Ron, were probably awake by now. No, none of this mattered to That Man; our feelings and fears were nothing to him. Time and time again he proved that.

He turned to me this time, his face a picture of sneering injustice. ''Ow dare you think you can set a tail on me! Who do you think you are?' he shouted.

'Sorry, Pa,' was all I could say. My nerves had got the better of me. I felt a betraying trickle run down my left leg, hot liquid against my clammy skin. I shivered, feeling ashamed to my bones. He'd frightened me so much I'd wet myself. I'd never done that before. I side-stepped away from the damning puddle, but no one noticed. All eyes were on That Man as his sense of wounded pride gave voice to his fury.

Pa slammed his fist down hard on the wooden table, making his point as only a drunken bully can. 'You'd better give me a good reason, Em, or I'll beat you, I will.'

And with that, he shook his right fist. The one that he'd only yesterday boasted to us that he'd knocked his opponent out stone cold with. Pa had won a fight in a rough pub on the Old Kent Road last night. He'd come home full of his swagger and bravado, showing us the big veiny fists that had done the damage. He'd spent his winnings buying drinks for himself and his fair-weather friends down at his usual drinking hole the Dog and Gun, but he was in such a good mood that, for once, we didn't mind and joined in his fit of good temper, grateful for the reprieve. Well, the reprieve hadn't lasted long.

'So, what were you doin' to keep you out of your bed this late? And don't tell me no lies, Ted Johnson, I know when you're lyin' to me,' said Ma. Her voice was so calm, with only a faint tremor, that I almost believed she wasn't frightened. Before Pa could answer, Les, his voice trembling with anger, spat out the truth.

'I found 'im, Ma, and you won't like what I saw.'

We all turned to Les, in shock. If he noticed, he didn't let on. He was hell-bent on telling us what he'd seen. 'I found 'im wiv 'is trousers round 'is ankles down Surrey Docks.'

I was dreading what Les might say next. His little boy's face was screwed up as if he wanted to spit out something dirty or unclean. At this, Pa's face swivelled towards Les, but Les kept going. I loved him for his spirit in that moment, even though it would mean dire consequences for all of us.

'I saw Pa wiv three women, Ma. 'E 'ad 'is trousers down,

'e 'ad 'is back to me but I know what I saw, Ma. 'E was 'avin' it off wiv them. I saw 'is arse, Ma.'

With that, Les stopped talking. His eyes swept the room, challenging and fierce before his face finally crumbled and he became, again, what he really was, a young boy who'd witnessed something no boy of his age should have to.

'Get to your bed,' said Pa. His voice was low and he spoke slowly, which was, in a strange way, more frightening than his shouting. Les looked at Ma.

'Do as your Pa says,' Ma answered faintly, her hands now pulling at her throat in an anxious gesture. Les looked for a minute like he was going to refuse, then before he could speak, Pa grabbed his shirt collar and roughly pushed him towards the door. Les stumbled as he went.

'I won't tell you again, get to your bloody bed, you ingrate, or I'll give you worse than that,' threatened Pa, grabbing his belt buckle and making as if he was going to take it off and give him a beating. It wouldn't have been the first time.

I wondered how it was that Les escaped his belt that night. Pa's actions were never rational. He seemed to me to be hell-bent on wreaking revenge on women, either by cheating on them or by attacking his wife and daughter. We all knew Pa had been treated badly by his stepmother when he was a child, and maybe that's what made him so mean to Ma and me. Les got away saying his damning words and received only a shove. Who could say why Pa acted the way he did?

Les shook off Pa's hands and ran from the room, clearly defeated, and we all heard his sobs as he tried to muffle them with the blanket.

Pa turned slowly to Ma. She must have been desperate to comfort her child, but she didn't dare move. I couldn't read Pa's expression, as the single candle end that had been burning on the mantelpiece above the range flickered out in waxy finality. The room was quiet and dark with an air of grim expectation.

I barely saw the first punch as it landed on Ma's face, it came so fast and so sharp. She gasped, a small noise, before a more guttural moan came from her bent frame. He punched again, this time to her left side, leaving her in no doubt of his feelings.

'Stop, Pa, stop it. She ain't done nuffink wrong. Why don't you leave 'er alone?'

I heard my voice echo slightly in the kitchen. I hadn't realised I was going to say anything. My reaction was forced from me like the air in Ma's lungs on impact.

'You old bugger, leave 'er alone!'

I could hear how ineffectual my words were in the gloom. They sounded weak, tinny. I knew I was going to get it from him and I could do nothing to stop him now. Perhaps I should've let him hit her, I could've edged to the side of the room, backing away from the violence and rage of his self-pity and thwarted lust. But I couldn't, for my sins I just couldn't.

'An' what's it to you, you ungrateful littl' cow,' he snarled, his teeth bared, his hackles rising. He wasn't as drunk as I'd originally thought. Sometimes he was more dangerous when he was only half-cut, as he had enough beer inside him to fuel his rages and yet was still able to think with that small, vicious brain of his. His pride was hurt, and that was the most fearful of his moods.

My eyes darted to the door. Could I escape him? But he saw me, and quick as a flash he struck again, punching me squarely on the nose.

The shock was the first thing to hit me, even though I should've seen it coming. The pain followed later, along with the thick warm sludge of blood as it dripped onto my blouse, spoiling it. *It'll never wash out*, I thought frantically, before sinking to my knees as the impact rebounded through me. The implosion of pain took me by surprise and I covered my face with my hands as tears drawn half from the shock and half from the pain threatened to fall.

'Let that be a lesson to you,' said Pa, as he wiped his hand on his trousers, shaking it, then stretching his fingers out to realign the bones and muscles that had caused so much anguish already. 'No one disrespects me, d'you 'ear me, 'ilda, no one, not even you, and definitely not your mother. I work like a slave for 'er, an' all I get back is cheek.'

I could hear the petulant whine of self-justification in his voice and I definitely didn't want to hear that, not after everything. I slowly raised myself to my feet, gripping the back of a wooden chair. Unsteadily, I headed out of the kitchen and into the bedroom, grabbing a soiled rag from the table as I went to stem the flow of blood.

Joanie was asleep now, her chest rising and falling with warm breaths, her forehead moist with night sweat and Bermondsey grime. Ron had woken during the shouting, and his cries had added to the chaos, but my sister had picked him up and shushed him back to sleep in her arms. They were curled up together on the bed. He might only be two years old but he had already learnt there was no comfort to be had from Ma when Pa was on the rampage. Les had his back turned from the door but I could hear his breathing sharp and quick. He wouldn't sleep till he'd calmed down. There was no need for the blanket tonight so I lay down and held my nose with the rag, hoping the blood would stop flowing soon and I could escape into the relief of sleep.

I slept until the sound of the streets waking up broke my fragile dreams. I eased myself up out of the bed, feeling for my sore nose. The bleeding had stopped overnight, but I was caked in blood. Moving into the empty kitchen, I poured water from the jug into the cold basin and gently wiped away the worst of last night's injury. I looked up into the cracked mirror on the mantelpiece and saw the first bloom of a black eye. I washed my face, feeling the water washing away the soot and the brown, dry blood.

Mustn't grumble, I thought to myself. *Ma's got it 'ard enough as it is*, and I looked at myself one last time, steeling myself for the day ahead and determined I wouldn't let That Man get me down.

Pa had sloped out early, down to the dockyard gates to hustle his way to the front of the queue for work. We wouldn't see him till later that evening. There were rumours that work was becoming scarce for casual workers, and even the regular jobs with the Port Authority might be cut.

He told us it was the effect of the Great Depression that had swept through America a few years before. Pa told us he'd seen headlines predicting that it was coming our way, and he'd heard on the streets that families were found starved to death, young mothers feeding their children rather than themselves and falling prey to sickness and disease as a result. He shuddered as he spoke about the 'Great Slump'.

And now it was upon us and, despite the never-ending bustle and chaos of the dockside, Pa was finding it harder and harder to fight his way to the front of that queue for work. And God only knows what lay in store for us if Pa's work dried up.

Time to get the kids up, I said to myself, with a brusqueness I didn't feel. Our worries lay heavy on me, especially with a bruised face to show for my sins this morning. But I bustled into the bedroom, just like Ma did, and shook Les and Joanie till they woke up with yawns and protestations of tiredness.

'Up you both get, it's time for your breakfast,' I said with a determined grin on my face.

'Bloody 'ell,' exclaimed Joanie, who was too young to be swearing at the tender age of five, 'you look terrible!'

'Oh nuffink to worry your 'ead about Joanie Johnson, and less of the swearin' if you please,' I chirped back, not wanting her to see how sore I felt, in so many ways.

Les looked at me, and realised where I'd got my new face. His eyes sunk to the floor and I could see he looked ashamed that he'd left us to Pa and his fists.

'There's nuffink you could've done, Les,' I murmured, and put my arms round him, 'nuffink at all. Come on, it looks worse than it feels, I promise.'

Les looked at me, scanning my face for any hint I was lying to him, but my bright, determined smile would not betray my pain for anything and eventually he leapt up, grabbed his shirt and trousers, and said, 'What's for breakfast, 'ilda?'

'Bread an' drippin' today,' I answered. 'The pot's on the range, the tea'll be good 'n'ot an' you'll 'ave sumfink in your bellies for school,' I said, warming to my theme of keeping the home fires burning.

Within seconds Leslie and Joanie were sat, fidgeting, at the table in the kitchen. The pot on the stove released plumes of steam and I poured the water out into the chipped teapot before dividing the good, hot brew into four cracked teacups. I took a cup through to Ma who was stirring.

She looked up at me, saw my face and her lips pursed together. 'You all right, sweetheart?' she asked softly, easing herself up onto an elbow and using her free hand to stroke back my hair from my face.

I winced a little but smiled back, meeting her gaze with steady knowing. We both knew there was nothing we could do about Pa and his ways. In those days in the borough, you could only leave your husband if you had money or some-where better to go. Even then, there was no guarantee Ma would've kept her children if she'd fled her marriage. There was no money, and no way out, and we both knew it.

'We make the best of it, don't we, girl,' Ma said, more as a statement than a question.

'Course we do, Ma,' I replied, and my love for her, this woman of importance, this respite for us children from such a domineering and brutal man who spent his time drinking, betting, womanising and beating us all at his whim, felt like it would swallow me whole. I looked at her livid purple-and-yellow black eye, more evidence of last night, and said, 'We're twins now, anyway.' I pointed to my face, to my own telltale bruising.

We should've been used to it by now, but somehow we never were.

CHAPTER 4

Boot Brush Lil

1932

A loud thump on the door shattered the companionable peace Ma and I were enjoying as we sorted clothes to hang out to dry. We looked at each other, startled from our reverie. I may even have been humming a tune as we worked; I was home from school with a slight fever, but had been feeling better already.

The thump came again, louder and more insistent this time, conveying urgency and something else, something darker.

Now, a knock on the door doesn't sound like something to worry about, but none of us locked our doors by day, none of us had anything worth pinching, so what was the worry? Children and neighbours poked their heads round into each other's flats as a matter of course. No one ever knocked, so if someone was knocking it had to be serious.

Then Ma's face froze in shock. She'd remembered it was rent day. I was usually at school when the rent man came so had never heard his fist hit our door with the kind of force that money created.

'Gawd I'd forgotten it was today. Don't know what's got into me,' said Ma, putting her pile of washing down onto the table and grabbing my arm. 'Oh goodness, 'ilda, now listen carefully to me,' and with that Ma pulled me into the bedroom and held my shoulders, looking into my eyes to show me what she had to say was important.

'Now, you've got to be a good girl an' do what I say. Can

you do that, 'ilda?' she asked, her eyes flitting to the door as the sound of knocking striking the door came again.

'Course, Ma, what is it?' I replied, nervously. Were we in trouble?

'That's the rent man at the door, an' I ain't got it this week. It flew out of me 'ead an' what wiv your Pa not workin' much this week I ain't got the money. Now, I want you to open the door a crack an' say, very politely, that Ma ain't 'ere an' you don't know when she'll be back . . . Can you do that?' she whispered.

I nodded in assent and, faster than I'd seen her move in a long time, she knelt down to hide under the great iron bed, pulling the blanket down to cover herself and shooing at me to open the door. I clutched the door handle and opened the kitchen door that lead to the hallway. There was a man with his cap pulled low over his face, holding a small book and a pencil.

'Rent day. Where's your mother?' he said perfunctorily. I stared at him into the gloom of the hallway and swallowed nervously.

'She ain't 'ere,' my voice squeaked like a little mouse and I thought of Ma hiding under the bed and how uncomfortable she must be. 'She ain't 'ere, an' I don't know where she is.' I said this more confidently and jutted my chin out to brook no argument. I hoped the rent man didn't see the slight tremor of my arms as I held onto the door frame.

The man stood watching me for a moment, and I stared back at him, daring him to call me a liar. 'All right, darlin', you tell your Ma that the rent man came an' 'e wants 'is money,' he said, pushing the front of his cap up so he could meet my eyes square on. His face looked cold and hard or maybe that was how it felt to know the insecurity of not having the money to pay for our home, however mean and small it was.

'Tell 'er yourself,' I replied, sharply.

'I'll be back, don't you worry about that, an' I might even tell 'er in ways that don't need words, you get me drift,' he said, leaving his threat hanging in the air between us.

I slammed the door shut and stood with my back to it, gripping the handle for support, my stomach clenched and feeling slightly queasy. I staggered back into the room, feeling like I'd gone two rounds with Pa in a boxing ring, and I raced through to find Ma under the bed. We looked at each other, our eyes meeting in a mixture of shared guilt and relief, and just as suddenly we both started to laugh.

Ma was trying to get herself up again. She wasn't the smallest woman. Homely and plump, she was clearly struggling to pull herself out, using the iron bedstead as a lever. The moment of fear and anxiety instantly became pure comedy. A minute earlier I was almost peeing my pants with fright, and now there was nothing we could do except howl with laughter. I clutched my tummy it hurt so much, and I wiped the tears that rolled down my cheeks, as I held out my arm to help her up.

Back on her feet at last she dusted down her apron, re-adjusted the turban she always wore to keep her hair off her face, and at that moment Les, Joanie and three-year-old Ron clattered in from wherever they'd been playing, two of their friends trailing in behind them to see what was going on. They took one look at us, and started laughing themselves.

'What the 'ell's got into you silly buggers?' asked Les, and neither myself nor Ma could reply for laughing so hard. We gave each other a final look that translated as 'it's our secret' and both turned to the children.

'Who's 'avin' what for supper, then?' I said, changing the subject to the only one the youngsters were ever really interested in, and with that the bad business was closed.

All four of us tramped outside to play in the street before our dinner was ready. Nellie was there waiting for me, as were a couple of other friends from down our road, Margaret and Jean. Jean had found a long piece of discarded rope from the dockside and we used it to play at skipping while the evening drew in. Les was crouched over an old pram wheel, while Ron, who adored his older brother, crouched next to him, desperate to join in his games. Joanie had sloped off with her friend Ivy who lived five doors down, on the first floor of her tenement. We were all slum children and yet our imaginations were given free rein. Without much adult supervision, we could create our games out of the little or nothing we had.

When Ma shouted from the front step that dinner was ready, we all looked up, reluctant to go in. Ma was already chatting to Margaret's mother, Mabel, who had wandered out to find her daughter, and her three other boys, who were nowhere to be seen.

Mabel sighed, and grabbed her daughter by the collar to march her off. Ma stood with her hands on her hips, the dark circles under her eyes showing even more keenly.

'Come on, you littl' ragamuffins,' she said, fondly.

'All right,' we replied, promising to meet our friends after school the next evening. We trooped in, complaining as we made our way to the sink to rinse our hands and dry them on a clean rag before sitting up at the table.

Later that evening, after the pubs had shut, That Man returned from his night drinking, clutching a swollen hand and complaining that he'd lost a fight at The Ring in Blackfriars. Ma had shushed off the younger children earlier, saying they'd have an early night and be up 'like larks' in the morning. Pa could see that she wanted to say something but he wanted to drag out the moment, so he slumped himself down in his usual chair by the hearth and demanded his dinner.

Despite it being past 11 p.m., Ma ladled out the stew made of scrag end of mutton, carrots and a dumpling onto a plate and put it on the table without saying a word. The clock ticked as Pa eased himself up, wiped his mouth clean and demanded a drink, claiming he was 'dry as a bone'. Ma got up again, and wordlessly poured him half a cup of ale from a bottle she'd kept by for him. He said nothing, downed the drink in one and picked up his spoon to shovel the stew, the largest portion of which she'd saved for him, into the black hole of his mouth. Once finished, he shoved the plate to the middle of the table and sat, sniffing once and clearing his throat loudly.

While Pa was putting on this show of his power, I busied myself tying up bits of twine we'd saved into a makeshift ball to use again, all the while feeling my stomach clench tighter and tighter. The silence grew more intense, broken only by the wheezing and coughing that came from Old Mackintosh in the flat above ours, and the sound of two men arguing in the next street.

'What d'you want, Em? Spit it out,' said Pa, ungraciously.

Ma took a deep breath, but before she could speak Pa turned to pull off his coat and cap, knowing he was breaking her moment. Again, with the infinite patience she possessed, Ma waited for him to stop fidgeting. I don't know how she did it. I could feel the anger rising in me again and I could no more stop it than I could pummel this evil sod into the ground.

'Ted, the rent man came today an' I didn't 'ave the money,' she spoke calmly but I could tell now she was worried as her face frowned in the cheerless light of the gas lamp. 'I need you to give me the money, or I can't pay 'im an' then what'll 'appen to us?' she spoke again, her voice rising up an octave, sensing the impending explosion, perhaps.

There was silence.

Then came Pa's response. 'I gave you twenty shillin's this week, Em. Now what the 'ell 'ave you done wiv it?' he spat, turning his face slowly to hers.

'That was last week, Ted. This week you've given me nuffink. I need that money... please,' she replied, her voice trembling slightly.

'D'you question me in me own 'ome? Are you fuckin' questionin' me in me own 'ouse?' Pa's voice rose as he spoke, his questions becoming shouts that all the neighbours would hear.

It was a wonder none of them ever complained, but then again, knowing how quick Pa was to use his fists to settle an argument, it was no mystery. Pa had a reputation in these parts and was popular in the pubs and with the bookies' runners. He wasn't so popular in here, and maybe that's what irked him so much. He was used to having minor celebrity status out there on the streets of south-east London because of his boxing, but at home he was just our father, and a lousy one at that.

'I owe the rent man eleven shillings an' I ain't got it. What are you goin' to do about it?' said Ma, firmly this time. After all, she knew she was in the right.

She also knew that work was harder than ever to find. These days Ma would light a single candle at night rather than put a penny in the gas meter. She'd say, 'Isn't it more cosy?' but I knew there were harder economic reasons for doing it. Two children from my class at school had started attending on alternate days. Harry and Bill (twins) from three doors down were two of a family of 11 children. How they managed even to have a roof over their heads I'll never know. Times were tough for all of us who relied on the dockyards for work, but with that number of mouths to feed it must've been near impossible. Harry and Bill now came to school separately to cover for the other being sent begging up in the West End. It was the only way they could add desperately needed income to the depleted wages their Pa was bringing home.

And now, we owed money for our rent. Pa had also been up to his old tricks, stealing food from East Street Market over near Kennington. I was ashamed that he'd had to resort to taking food that wasn't ours from hard-working stall owners. It wasn't right, though I ate the food gladly enough to fill my hungry belly. Obviously he'd never thieve from his own patch, there were too many people who'd take offence. So instead, he'd set off, whistling at each passing lady as if he hadn't a care in the world, and returned home after dark with pockets full of stolen tins of cold meat and packets of tea. Once he even brought home a raw chicken, stuffed under his shirt. How much lower could our lives go?

Pa responded with snarling force. 'I ain't goin' to do nuffink about it. I told you I gave you money an' so you must've gone an' spent it all. It's your own fault there ain't no money, so don't come snivellin' to me about it.' Pa was furious, he stood up and threatened Ma by shaking a fist in her face.

Ma put her hands up to protect herself and I leapt into action, stung by the injustice of his words. 'Leave 'er alone,' I cried, not caring if I woke the others. I knew they'd stay cowering in fear in the back bedroom, and best they did. There was no point anyone else getting hurt. 'She's done nuffink, nuffink I tell you. You're the one who eats your dinner an' then goes out and spends your money on drink an' the like. It ain't fair, Pa!'

My voice had become a sort of wail. I could hear the desperate need for That Man to be someone different, a father who cared what I thought, who listened to his wife and kids and who kept the rent paid and the butcher sweet, instead of making our lives a misery by pouring our cash down his big, fat throat. I knew I was in for it, but I couldn't stop myself. I was driven by the relentless hardship and the many ways we concealed it on a daily basis. I was fed up with watching him eat his dinner and sit back while Ma worked day and night to keep us warm and fed. Us kids lived in fear and I was downright bloody sick of all of it. I stood up and raised my fists, which made Pa bark with ironic laughter.

'You dare to put your fists up to your old man? I'll give you that, 'ilda, you got balls,' he sneered, before assuming the pose he did most nights, his eyes fixed on his opponent, his body suddenly taut with focus, his fists raised, one slightly forward of the other.

I was screwed. So I went for him first. I tried, I really did, to whack the bugger so at least I got one punch in before he did his worst to me. I missed, of course. Pa laughed again and started dancing on his feet, mocking me as he did so. I lunged again but he was too quick, even with a night's beer inside him. In a flash he gave me a right hook, catching the side of my face close to my eye. I staggered, but grabbed at a chair to steady myself.

I heard Ma give a soft sound, like the air coming out of a punch bag. In another attack, he landed a punch straight to my face and at that point Ma raised her voice. 'Stop it, Ted, you've made your point. Can't you see you've 'urt 'er?' And with that she rushed to me.

I instantly dissolved into tears, grateful to be in her arms, but with a face full of pain.

'Oh you cry baby, I didn't 'it you 'ard. You should've seen that slow bastard this evenin', I got 'im 'ard on the left cheek. Shame I couldn't 'ave finished 'im, I'd 'ave made a packet.' Ted threw a few punches into the air, reliving his fight earlier, utterly oblivious to the distress he had caused. He poured out the rest of the beer while Ma marched me to the sink and began dabbing gently at my face with cold water.

'There, there, sweetheart, it'll all be alright, I promise you. You'll still be me beautiful 'ilda,' she crooned.

It was almost worth the injury to be loved so completely by my mother. Pa had lost interest, and at least the argument had fizzled out, but I went to bed that night feeling as low as I'd ever felt in that dingy, filthy bed, in that soot-ridden street.

Before my eyes closed, I whispered a prayer to God, asking Him to hear me, unlike my father, and to please find a way of rescuing me from the slums. 'Set me free,' I pleaded, with my hands held in the prayer position, tears streaming down my swollen cheek and settling into the greasy pillow. I felt like a prisoner in my own life, and I was sore as hell for the trouble I'd brought on myself.

The next morning dawned chill and grey. There was a thick quality to the smog as it hung over our borough, masking the towering cranes and warehouses at the dockside and distorting the chaos of sounds on the riverside. Les, Joanie and Ron said nothing about the state of my face, though it must've looked black and blue. All of them avoided my eyes, instead talking softly to me and being better behaved than usual. It was obvious they'd all heard the row last night, but I knew they must've been scared, so I was extra kind to them as well.

We all dressed in our damp clothes and headed into the kitchen for breakfast. Ma was still in bed again. She found mornings tricky these days and often complained of feeling tired, but that was nothing out of the ordinary for the women of Bermondsey who worked all the hours God sent, cooking, cleaning, mending and haggling for meagre supplies at the grocer's and butcher's.

I brought her in a cup of tea and she kissed me softly on my swollen cheek.

Suddenly there was a shout from the kitchen. 'I'd better go an' see what's 'appenin' out there,' I said with a grimace, as the sound of Les hollering something about his shoes cut into my moment with Ma.

'I'll be out in a minute, luvvie,' she said, sipping her tea.

Back in the kitchen, Les and Ron were on the floor, the remains of the bread and dripping lay as crumbs on the table while Joanie looked down at them, clearly enjoying the brouhaha.

I sighed. 'What's goin' on 'ere then?'

'It's Ron, 'ilda, 'e won't polish 'is boots an' they're filthy, look!' cried Les, as he tried to wrestle Ron's boot from the little boy's firm grip.

'Get off,' said Ron, his squeaky little voice rising in indignation. 'Not cleanin' 'em, already clean!'

'Oh you littl' fibber, I ain't seen you clean them boots for days!' said Les indignantly.

'Now, now what's the fuss? Ron you've got to clean them boots before you leave this 'ouse,' I said. 'You ain't showin' us all up by goin' out lookin' like a pauper. We've got more pride than that!'

Ron looked at me, mutinously. He still held one of his boots aloft, as if by gripping it he could stall the inevitable.

'Les 'as cleaned his boots. Look 'ow they shine. Come on,

55

I'll 'elp you,' I said, this time more gently. After all, Ron was the baby of the family, and we all indulged him because of it.

'I ain't cleanin' 'em!' replied Ron, his face a picture of injured pride, and he grabbed the boot brush with his free hand and flung it into the corner of the room.

'You'll clean those damn boots, Ronald Johnson, or I'll beat you wiv the brush you've just thrown in temper,' I said, reaching for the brush and losing my patience in the process. We were all going to be late for school at this rate.

Ron leapt to his feet, and held out his boot defiantly, wobbling slightly with the effort. I grabbed the boot brush, wiping the hair from out of my eyes and causing my bruised face to ache again.

'You'll give me that blinkin' boot, Ron, or I'll give you a beatin', I mean it,' I swore at him, stepping towards him in as threatening a manner as I ever was able to achieve.

Suddenly, Ron burst out laughing, and, pointing to my face, laughed, ' 'ilda, you look like you're goin' down the mines!'

I stopped moving towards him, and dashed over to the small, cracked mirror on the mantelpiece to see what he was laughing at. And there it was, a huge, great big streak of black polish on my forehead. The combined effect with my black eye and bloody nose was comical, I really did look like a miner!

'Oh Gawd, what a state I am,' I said to the mirror, before turning towards the boys, who by now were beside themselves with laughter. Les was doubled up, with tears running down his face; Ron was back on the floor, giggling as he lay on the floorboards. In a second we were all helpless with laughter. Ron knew I'd never beat him with a brush, I loved him and Les too much to do anything like that. I was known as the family 'soft touch'. In acknowledgement of this I threw the brush jokingly at Ron, who dodged it, then reached to grab it before starting to clean his shoe.

'From now on, I'm callin' you Boot Brush Lil,' said Ron cheekily, and we all dissolved into giggles again, our troubles forgotten, for now at least.

CHAPTER 5

Moonlight Flit

1933

Pa's face was shifty, his manner agitated. He kept looking over his shoulder as he talked. Suddenly he ducked out of the kitchen and into the black corridor, with a swift, ' 'Old up.' We watched him warily, knowing he'd been in the pub all evening, but also aware he wasn't as drunk as normal. Goodness knows what this strange mood would bring.

Ma and I sat in tense silence, with the tick of the clock being the only sound in the room. Outside we heard the shouts of drunkards messing around, hollering and calling out obscenities as they wended their way home, and the shifting backdrop of the tides of the Thames as they lapped against our bit of dockland. Every now and then we heard a great horn from the ships that lined the docks, but generally at night the docklands were black and quiet, the stragglers, the drunks and the prostitutes who worked this section of the riverside, cooing their trade with low voices, were the only sounds that disturbed the silence.

With a start, the door to the corridor slammed open. Ma and I both jumped out of our skins. We should have been used to Pa's need to create an entrance but we weren't. He was too cunning, too unpredictable in his ways. His back came in first, followed by his arse, which stuck out and moved with the effort he was making, trying to drag something heavy into the room. Ma and I gave each other a swift glance. Was it fear we were feeling? Trepidation? Or was it a weary recognition of yet another 'drama' to chalk up against all the others that followed Pa wherever he went. As we sat wondering what new scheme he was up to now, I repressed the urge to giggle when I saw his backside clad in trousers that were shiny from use heave into the room.

The other day he had come home, rip-roaring drunk, shouting about 'that bastard 'oo done me in, by Gawd I'll skin 'im alive, I will, I promise you that. 'Ow dare 'e, 'ow fuckin' dare 'e,' and with that his arms flailed and his legs kicked out and he eventually wrestled himself into a chair, knocking over another in his attempts to sit down. Pa had been fighting in one of London's dodgiest pubs off the Old Kent Road, which was more of a flea pit than a place to drink, and was where bare-knuckle fights were held. Pa had beaten a man to top place, knocking him out with one great blow from his hammer hands, or so he told us. Clutching his winnings, he held them aloft to the crowd around the ring, proudly boasting his success, or so he said, and his infamy among London's hardened pugilists. It was a brief moment of victory over the bleakness of his life, or so I imagined. I could see him in my mind's eye, punching the air, then waving his money at the publican and calling that the drinks were on him.

It was later, after Pa had sunk enough of the victory beer to fell a lesser man, that he was weaving his way home along St James's Road and was jumped upon and his winnings, or what remained of them after his evening standing drinks for all his 'friends', were taken. Even though we needed the money, even though we were worrying what we would put in our mouths and stomachs each day, I still took low pleasure in knowing Pa had lost the lot. It was worth the hunger to see the look of upturned, hurt pride on his red face.

Pa was convinced that the man he'd beaten 'fair an' square'

had done the dirty on him, but he would never know. Instead he was left with sore knuckles, a hangover the size of Bermondsey the next morning and a pocket lighter than he'd started with the day before.

With this in mind, I was nervous about what Pa was doing now. He grunted and puffed a bit more and then the object he'd been pulling into the room was revealed. It was a barrow, an enormous, two-wheeled costermonger's barrow that was probably used to ferry enormous sack-loads of fruit and vegetables from the cold stores to market, or to sell wares on the street. It had large wooden wheels and a flat wooden base that filled most of our small room. I wasn't foolish enough to ask where or how he'd got hold of it, though. Ma and I looked at each other again. This wasn't what we'd expected, though Lord knows what we'd thought it might be. Nothing good ever came from Ted Johnson, especially at this time of night.

With a flourish, Pa turned round and said, ' 'Ere it is!'

We turned our faces up to him, neither of us daring to ask what the significance of a probably-stolen barrow might be. His face twisted into a great shout of laughter.

'I ain't never seen the likes of you two – you look like a pair of simpletons!' he exclaimed, clearly enjoying the moment, and looking like he'd scored some kind of triumph, which made him generous with his mood.

'Tell us then, Ted, cos we ain't got a clue why there's a barra' in our 'ouse at this time of night,' said Ma in her quiet way, barely stopping to speak as she pummelled dough with one hand in the great bowl that she had on the kitchen table.

'Listen, luv.' It was the first time I'd ever heard Pa use an endearment when speaking to Ma. It caught me by surprise and made me wonder about their relationship – that, perhaps, there was more to it than met the eye. 'This is our ticket out of 'ere. I never liked this 'ovel anyway. We ain't got no rent money, that's a fact, and we can't pay that filthy old bugger who wants to take money off 'ard-workin' people like us.'

With that, I fidgeted in my chair but kept silent, not wanting Pa to remember I was there witnessing this extraordinary exchange. 'We've got to go, Em, and we've got to go fast. The rent man knows we can't pay and 'e's told Reg down the Dog 'n' Gun that unless we pay up it's goin' to be worse for us. It'll be bad, d'you understand me, Em?' his tone was almost soft as he spoke to his wife. Their gaze met.

It was truly the first time I'd seen them talk about anything other than where his dinner was, or whether he'd be spending his money down the pub again. I was struck by how little I knew about adult relationships and how young I was, even though I considered myself very grown up at the age of 12. I watched my parents with fascination. Something about this exchange was part of the reason they were together and kept having babies, though I don't suppose Ma had much of a choice in the matter. I squirmed a little, feeling in turns uncomfortable, and yet mesmerised.

Ma breathed in deeply and gave a sigh before nodding her head slowly. 'I understand, Ted, and that thing there, that barra you brought in from Gawd knows where, that's to carry our stuff, is it?' she murmured, looking him straight in the eyes.

I don't know how she dared. Pa frightened me so much I rarely looked directly into his face for fear of what I'd see. He nodded his head slowly.

The brief glimpse of that unfamiliar understanding between my parents was gone as quickly as it arrived. Pa pulled his cap off his head and pulled his hand through his greasy dark hair. He called for a drink, and Ma nodded to me and

I got up on the chair to fetch the single bottle of ale that sat there alongside the remains of today's bread, several jars of condensed milk and a box containing the Reckitt's Blue carbolic. I poured the frothy, pale liquid into a cracked cup and handed it to him.

He gulped it down in one, and then held out his cup for more. He didn't say a word, he didn't even look at me, I was as inconspicuous as a fly. After he'd finished, Ma told me I could finish my chores for the day and go to bed. I was almost reluctant. My curiosity had been piqued and I wanted to watch them to see if more of that strange relationship would be revealed. It wasn't to be though, and I sloped off, loath for the first time in my life to be away from That Man in that room with my beloved Ma.

Maybe that was it. Until that point, Ma had somehow belonged entirely to us children, or that's how we'd seen it. Tonight was the first time I had a sense she belonged to someone else, despite the fact that Ma and Pa shared the same bed as us and we often heard them doing what grown-ups do when they're married. Somehow this made me feel rather like I did when I ventured onto those barges on the riverside, slightly queasy and afraid of losing my footing.

I knew that Ma and Pa had had trouble paying last week's rent, and the week before that, so it was no surprise to me to learn that we had no option but to move. Mulling on how complicated the world suddenly seemed, I eventually drifted off to sleep, with Ron snoring at the foot of the bed, Les's feet touching my back and Joanie's hair tickling my nose as she lay beside me.

The next morning we were up as usual but everything was different. Instead of laying out the breakfast things, Ma was wrapping her bowl up in an old rag and stuffing socks and drawers into the cavernous depths of it.

'Get yerselves a bit o' bread 'n' jam, and then get your bits 'n' bobs an' 'elp me pack 'em tight as you can into this 'ere barra,' she said, wiping her face with the back of her hand, and looking round distractedly.

All the plates and cups had already been wrapped carefully and were in there, along with the old tin bath, Ma's pegs, her soaps and matches, and what looked like Pa's best suit.

'What's goin' on, Ma?' demanded Ron. 'What's happenin'? I don't like it. Where's all our stuff?' His voice sounded like the little boy of four he was. I forgot they were babies really, and clearly this turn of events had startled them into unease and confusion.

'Now, don't you look at me like that, Ron darlin'. There ain't nuffink bad happenin'. Your Pa an' I just decided we could do wiv a change, somewhere new to live. You'd like that, wouldn't you?'

Ron looked doubtful.

'We're movin' and that's that, but by Gawd I don't want any of you tellin' anyone. This is our littl' secret, you got that? You got that, sweethearts?'

'It's a secret,' said Ron, half as a question, and half a statement of wonder.

We didn't get to have many secrets. There was no such thing as privacy in our Bermondsey slums. Secrecy was a luxury and this fact didn't escape us that morning. The idea of sharing a secret was simply too thrilling to pass over just because we felt scared and upset to move away. We all nodded at Ma, as serious as if we'd been given a state secret to bear. She nodded back with a finality that said there was no more discussion on the subject. We were moving and that was that.

'Now, you've got to remember at school, you tell no one what our plan is, no one. D'you think you can all can manage that?' and with that she looked straight at Ron again, and I hid a little smile, knowing his excitement often spilled out over the most inconsequential things. How was he going to keep this one under his flat cap?

But Ron, bless him, nodded back as gravely as a spy undergoing a dangerous mission. He'd taken it to heart and in a trice he dashed into the bedroom, pulling out his pride and joy, the cart he played with every day come rain or shine. Him and Les had created their 'car' out of a couple of discarded wooden veg crates, some old pram wheels and a piece of rope. They'd built a pulley system with the lengths of wood and string that meant they could steer it. Les and Ron were proud of their creation, and Ron was particularly fierce about playing with it, refusing to share it with any of the other children who played in our roads each day.

Most evenings he was out in the street sitting in it, pretending he was driving a real car, the likes of which we only saw occasionally, especially on our road. Ma and I could normally hear Ron making beeping sounds as he shouted and hollered with the other ragamuffin children. He had little else. Just the clothes he stood up in, his cap and boots and some bits of old twine and driftwood that he had scavenged from the muddy Thames shore.

Once he'd gathered his treasures, he sat down at the table, good as gold, and started munching on his bread. We all took his lead, gathering up our bits and pieces, and putting them in the barrow, wondering where this next adventure would take us.

All throughout the school day we were fidgety and unsettled in turn. Even I got my knuckles rapped with a ruler for not concentrating during 'rithmetic. We walked home slowly, each of us savouring this, the last walk along Jamaica Road and into Bevington Street.

I wondered if we were leaving the borough altogether, but every time I thought that my heart gave a jolt so I stopped – leaving this patch of London would be inconceivable. Life without the clatter of horses' hooves on the cobbles; the smell of spices, jam and rank leather tanning; the lines of washing hung out in each yard and the gossip of our neighbours as they went about their business was simply too much to bear. It might be unsanitary, overcrowded and noisy but it was home, the only one we'd known.

My friends Margaret and Nellie lived in our road, as did Les, Ron and Joanie's friends. What would happen to our friendships – our shared jokes and secrets, our giggles and our fun – if we lived somewhere else? I couldn't imagine not seeing them every morning, and skipping into school together. And what about Mrs Mackintosh? Who would bring her her dinner on days she had nothing to eat? Moving away from our patch of south-east London would be like being transplanted to a different planet, and the thought made me dizzy with sadness.

That night we ate in silence. Ma watched us with eyes that seemed to know what we were feeling, but she stayed silent as well. We all knew there was no other option because Pa had said we were going, and if he made a decision it was the final word on the subject. None of us would've argued with him for fear of the belt on our hides. The little ones didn't know why we were moving, only I knew that, and I didn't let on to Ma that I knew how desperate things were with money. That would've broken her heart.

At bedtime the younger children kissed Ma on the cheek and settled into the bed. Ma spoke softly as she told a story about a happy family who travelled all over the world, none of them ever knowing where they'd be the next night, and wasn't that so exciting? She said that this family, imaginary though they were, often had to leave their beds in the middle of the night and with a hop, skip and a jump they'd be off on another adventure, towing their worldly goods behind them in a gaily painted barrow. I listened as she settled their nerves until I could hear Les, Joanie and Ron yawning, and I went in myself.

I suspected we may not be here next morning to wake up in our iron bed with the old, stained mattress, in the bare, dimly lit room. I was right.

It was pitch black when I felt the rough shake of my arm and heard the sharp whisper from Ma to 'get up, 'ilda, it's time to go.'

Blinking awake, I nodded my head and slowly dragged my body from the warmth of the blanket. My feet felt cold on the floorboards but I pulled my socks and drawers on, then my skirt and blouse, shivering slightly with the cool night air. My coat came next and I was glad of the warmth.

'Wake the others, won't you, 'ilda. I've got to get me bits together,' said Ma, in a slightly louder voice.

'Alright, I'm comin,' I said, feeling grumpy at being woken, and also scared for the first time as this imaginary adventure became a sordid reality, running from the rent man; a moonlight flit. I'd heard of others on the street fleeing in the middle of the night but I'd never thought it would be us one day.

With a sinking feeling in my stomach I started gently shaking the others awake. With lots of rubbing of the eyes, and yawning loudly, they all woke up and I started the process of dressing them to keep them warm. I could hear Pa now, scrabbling around with something in the scullery, his boots making the only real sound, except for the constant movement of the river, so familiar and yet strange that we barely noticed it. Would we ever hear it again? In a jiffy we were all awake, assembled in the kitchen, trying not to look as scared as we felt. Our faces looked white in the moonlight that filtered into the room through the small window.

'You ready?' said Pa, gruffly. His face had the shade of a night's stubble already, even though it was only just past 1 a.m.

Ma nodded and we all suddenly looked at our feet, not wanting to go, not knowing where we were going. Pa picked up the two handles of the barrow and lurched incongruously towards the door. How the hell were we going to get it down the steps? Out of the shadowy hallway, Pa pointed at the three of us and said to grab the end and to keep our mouths shut. We heaved and puffed, and the barrow made its juddering way down the few stone steps that lead onto the cobbled street.

At times like this we were all silently grateful that Pa was so strong and sturdy. He may not have worked every day, but when he did, he carried loads heavier than this up and down the dockside, unloading ships and carting sacks full of grain into the cold stores for storage, working for up to 18 hours a day in all weathers. He was hardened by his tough life, and no more so than at this moment when he lugged our life's possessions down our stairs and into the night.

We made it out onto the street and he gestured for us girls to wait while he, Ma and Les went back into the house to bring out the iron bed. It would've been funny had it been any other circumstance, seeing them dragging and pitching that great heavy thing out from the bedroom into the road. They did it though, and Pa finally manoeuvred the frame onto the barrow, tying it down with a piece of old rope so it wouldn't slip off. He went back in again and brought the table, then the chairs. We really were taking everything with us! He piled them on top of the barrow's contents making a precarious tower of our worldly goods, then it was time to go.

We struggled this way and that to the end of the road, the barrow threatening to capsize several times, and turned right onto the main road. Almost immediately we turned again, down into Spa Road, and found ourselves under the railway arches that straddled the street. We all shivered at the inky blackness but kept marching on, all the while wondering where we were going.

We were too afraid to ask That Man, of course. And no doubt he loved how vulnerable we all felt. It wasn't good to show fear to him. At moments like that he took an almost visceral pleasure in our distress, so we all kept quiet and kept our heads down.

The streets were almost deserted. Cars were a rare sight, and no horse and cart would be out at this time. There was a sense of disquiet at seeing everything so strange and still. Our days were such a cacophony of sights, smells and sounds that this new London, so unlike the one I thought I belonged to, was a surreal version of our daytime environment. It was almost dreamlike, and I thought of Ma's story again. From somewhere close by we heard a woman's sharp laugh, which disappeared into the darkness, then a shout from somewhere up ahead.

We all started walking that little bit faster, pulling our coats round our little bodies, all following in the wake of Pa like he was a down-at-heel version of the Pied Piper.

We stumbled further down Spa Road and then Pa suddenly stopped outside number 42, in a line of terraces opposite the town hall. They were as grim and grey looking as I'd ever seen. He pulled a key from his trouser pocket and opened the door while we stood watching in amazement.

'Stop gawking, will you. Get yerselves inside,' he said, looking round to see if anyone was about. The street was empty. Pa's teeth gleamed almost white in the glow of a gas lamp. He had a roll-up in the corner of his mouth, chewed up yet staying obediently in place. We didn't need telling twice.

Pa, Ma and Les unloaded the bed and the other furniture and shuffled it inside. We heard the bump, bump of the metal frame making its way up a set of stairs, and now and then soft swearing in the blackness. Once the furniture was in, we stumbled in behind it, taking in the peeling wallpaper. *How many others live 'ere?* I thought with weariness. *Who else are we sharin' this space with?*

'This is it, your new 'ome, all ours. Now, what d'you say to that, eh?' Pa said, spitting his cigarette into the dust of the doorway and shutting the door.

We looked at him, a mixture of tiredness and questions that needed answering. A home of our own, now that was something new. Could we believe him? Or was this one of Pa's nasty little jokes? Cautiously we all stepped further into the house and began our inventory, scoping out the boundaries to our lives.

Even though we'd travelled less than half a mile, we felt like we'd arrived somewhere entirely new. We were far enough away to outrun the debt collectors, but we were still in our beloved Bermondsey, with our friends within walking distance, as long as we kept an eye out for the rent man so we didn't get caught.

Slowly, I started to relax and look about me, as did the others. As our courage grew, we split up and ran into the rooms. There were two rooms downstairs, one of which was the scullery with a range set against the back wall and a door to the yard out back where the lavvy was. There was a small cupboard that Ma would use as a pantry and a small, grimy window that looked out onto the yard, which was backed onto by a row of brick buildings behind. The front room must be a parlour. We'd never had one of those. I'd heard of people who had parlours that they kept for visitors, but they were the posh folk and we didn't speak to them. Suddenly we were one of them, and already I felt myself walking a little taller!

There was a set of steep wooden stairs, our boots made hollow noises as they trampled up. At the top we found two bedrooms, one for Ma and Pa, and one for the rest of us. The walls were grimy with wallpaper peeling in damp furls. A grey net curtain hung in tatters from the window of the larger room at the front. On the floor there was a threadbare rug, which must once have been brightly coloured, and an iron bed left behind by whoever lived there before us. It was a great old thing with a brown-stained mattress that sagged below the frame. The second bedroom was completely empty except for an old tin bucket in one corner. The floorboards were thick with grime and dust. Whoever had lived here had left a while ago.

Downstairs, the parlour had a dirty net curtain and little else except for a pile of old newspapers dating back to 1932. In the kitchen there was a broom, a coal shovel and broken crockery lying in a heap at one end. At the other there were two wooden chairs and a child's cap sitting on one of them. We gazed around the rooms in delight. There was so much space!

I wondered how Pa had come by this bit of good fortune. I guessed it was through one of his old cronies in one of the pubs he drank in but I never asked, and he never told me. It was none of my business how Pa wheedled his way through life and, secretly, I was grateful that his drinking pals might have come up trumps at last. Amazed by the turn of good luck, and exhausted by the magnitude of what we'd achieved, I suddenly felt more tired than I'd ever felt in my life.

'Come on, you saucy littl' monkeys, get yerselves to bed,' I heard myself saying. I could hear Ma unpacking downstairs and I knew that she wouldn't go to bed till she'd got everything how she liked it. I knew I should have gone and helped her but my limbs wouldn't comply.

'All right, Boot Brush Lil, we're comin'!' said Les, rubbing his eyes. Reluctantly the others clambered into bed, still wrapped in their coats. I kissed them all and told them to go to sleep 'or the bed bugs'll get you'. It was pretty likely there were bed bugs, and lice, waiting for us in that house but I was too tired to care. *Anyway, we are used to scratching our way through life. A few more bugs won't stop me sleeping tonight*, I thought.

Within seconds, the sound of the others' breathing came steady and rhythmic. I settled down, pulled my coat around me and waited for sleep to come. After all, who knew what tomorrow would bring? Ron, who hadn't quite dropped off yet, piped up in his little voice, 'It's a palace. We're livin' in a palace!' and we all sighed with happiness. He was right. This house was beyond all our expectations, and we finally felt we were going up in the world. Maybe God had remembered we existed after all.

CHAPTER 6

Ma's Sacrifice

'Oi, mister, let us onto your ship,' shouted Ron, as the side of a barge towing in the wake of a large steamer came into view. His brown hair was swept off his face by the sea breeze that coated everything in salt and brine. He waved his cap at the men on the barge as it rode into view.

'Go on, mister, I ain't askin' for much, just a littl' go on your boat,' Ron shouted again, and we all laughed, knowing that his cheek usually worked wonders with the sailors.

Les, Ron and I were standing on the muddy foreshore of the murky Thames, watching the ships coming into dock. We'd managed to sneak past the lines of quayside workers and casual dockers who were smoking and hollering as some ships unloaded their contents and others were packed tight with goods for export. Seaweed lay in glistening piles at our feet amid the driftwood and discharge from the vessels, while the tidal churning of the Thames water threaded the shoreline with white salty residue along with the muck and oil of the boats. We were watching the lightermen as they stood on board the small barges that carried loads between the ships and the quay. It was a haven of industry, brash, busy and incredibly exciting to watch.

Sometimes, if we shouted loudly enough, the smaller ships would take pity on us and lower the rope ladder that meant we could climb aboard. Today was our lucky day. One of the barge men was pointing to the landing strip which jutted out further along the dock eastwards. With a 'luv-a-duck we're in!', Ron led the charge to scramble up the dockside and out onto the landing area, where our friendly sailor was waving and pointing to us. Weaving through men carrying large sacks over their shoulders, past old coils of rope that stank of grease and fish, through rows of dockers who hung about looking for their next load, and through the noise and chaos, we finally found our barge and with shrieks of delight we clambered aboard.

My heart was in my mouth every time Ron or Les scaled the sides of the boats, oblivious to their own safety, just thrilled to be part of the action, but today I had decided it was my turn to join in the fun too. One of the men patted Ron on his head and tousled his hair, while Ron clutched his cap between both hands and started asking questions at a rate of knots. Les was the next to get on board, and I followed, laughing as I lifted my skirt hem to jump on.

'Alright, darlin', always nice to see a pretty face on board me barge,' said one of the three men on board. He winked and pulled his threadbare cap, his face creased into brown wrinkles. I smiled shyly, and sat on the small wooden slatted area in the middle of the vessel, which couldn't have been much bigger than an omnibus, gripping the sides as the boat heaved up and down sideways in the wake of the larger ships coming in.

'Now then, boys, are you goin' to be sailors when you grow up? Bet you'd like to see the world, eh?' chuckled one of the men as he smoked a rolled-up cigarette out of the corner of his mouth.

'I'm goin' to join the Navy when I'm grown up,' said four-year-old Ron firmly, his chest puffed out as he spoke even though he was also gripping the side of the boat. 'I ain't hangin' around 'ere to be a docker like my pa. Too much like 'ard work,' he grinned.

'Me too. It's a life at sea for me!' grinned eight-year-old Les, waving his cap at a passing vessel. The men laughed at that.

While they were joking and chatting, I turned my attention to the river that coursed through all of our lives. I'd never seen it from this angle, out on it, while the docks either side stood sentry. The thick brown sludge that the river spewed onto its shores each day was less apparent here. Even though the day was cold and fresh, there was some weak sunlight that had made it through the smog and coal dust that coated everything, including us. The rays of sunlight danced on the surface of the water and it suddenly looked prettier than I'd ever seen it. Along the river's edges I could see the great cold stores, the warehouses for timber and fresh food stuff, which had to be kept cold until it could be reloaded to journey wherever it was going.

Then there was Tower Bridge, or the Tab as we called it. The ancient shape that straddled the Bermondsey stews, linking it to the other London, the one north of the river, the one we hardly ever made it to in all the years I lived there. It might as well have been another world, for all us kids knew of what went on there.

Suddenly, the wash of the Thames announced another large ship that steamed slowly into port, making our small boat rock alarmingly.

'Gawd, I wish I'd never got on 'ere,' I exclaimed in horror, my eyes as round as saucers, no doubt.

'Oh you don't mean that, Boot Brush Lil,' shouted Ron, full of glee at the movement and danger.

'I feel sick,' I moaned, clutching my stomach. 'Oh let me off, will you? I've 'ad enough of this,' I pleaded with the men. For a moment they pretended we were going to set sail to India, but then soon relented as they saw my look of wild terror. I scrunched up my eyes which were smarting from the moisture whipped off the wave tops by the wind.

'Don't you go cryin' wiv those big brown eyes, girl,' one of the men said, taking pity on me.

I inched along the side of the boat towards the landing dock, the spray from the river settling on my face and arms. One of the bargemen held my hand, the other gave me a shove on my back, and I was off the boat and onto dry land again.

Ron was waving and Les staring out at the tumult of activity, so I left them in seventh heaven as the barge moved outwards, away from the dock and towards the larger of the boats that was moving steadily towards its mooring post. For a second my heart swelled with pride for those two boys and their fearlessness, though I knew Ma would call it recklessness.

'Tell Ma I'll be back for me dinner,' called Ron as the wind whipped his hair again.

I waved back then turned on my heels, knowing if Pa caught me here at the docks, surrounded by working men, he'd thrash me within an inch of my life. Dodging past the workers bent forwards with the weight of the sacks they carried on their backs, I started the long walk back along Rotherhithe Street, swerving down Marigold Street to avoid our old road, just in case the rent man was around. He didn't work Spa Road so we knew we were safe from him there, but I wasn't going to do anything stupid like getting caught going too near Bevington Street.

At the end of the street was a discarded newspaper, a copy of the *Daily Express*. I glanced at the headline 'Judea Declares War on Germany' and frowned. Not another war, surely not? I picked it up, first checking there was no one who appeared to have dropped it, before following Jamaica Road home, back under the railway arches to Spa Road, where our house was sat squat and ugly.

Spa Road was busy all the time with horses pulling carts, the rag and bone men calling out their trade, the lady with the milk churns and the coal men carrying their wares in great urns and sacks. The tanneries sat on one side of the library, then there was a custard powder factory at the other end that emitted a wonderful sugary vanilla smell. When the wind was up we could also smell the tart vinegar being made at Sarson's Vinegar in Tower Bridge Road, not far from the Hartley's jam factory that created a distinctive sweet-sour smell that wafted through our homes, overlaying the brine from the river and the big oily deposits made by the docking ships. It was a hive of activity, our road, and we loved it.

Opening the door to home, I was greeted by yet another pungent smell, this time another cobbled-together dinner. Inside, Ma was cooking on the range, which was fuelled by driftwood collected from the stinking embankment, or coal if we could afford it that week. It was some kind of stew, made from the gristle and scraps begged from the butcher.

I dropped the paper onto the table, saying, 'Ma, is there a war on? Are we in danger?'

Ma turned round, wiping her hands on her apron. 'Now what's got into that pretty 'ead of yours, 'ilda? Course there ain't a war on. What are you on about?' she replied.

' 'Ave a look 'ere, it says the Jews 'ave declared war on Germany!' I said, biting my lip. Even though I wasn't old enough to have lived through the Great War, there were plenty of people who had, and the trauma and chaos of the bloodshed still seemed too close for comfort.

Ma read the article. 'You've got it wrong. It's a boycott, that's what it means. When you don't buy fings made by the

Germans. It says 'ere that them Jews 'ave been gettin' cross because someone called Adolf 'itler 'as come to power there and don't like 'em.'

'Oh,' I replied. The adult world seemed ever more complex. Before I could ask any further questions, I noticed Ma kept touching her left hand as she talked, but it wasn't till later when I was pegging out the washing and thinking my own thoughts (an act which was hard to do surrounded by brothers and sisters who needed feeding, cleaning, brushing and shooing!) that I realised Ma's wedding ring was missing. Once back in the house, which now smelt of cabbage and a kind of greasy, boiled smell from the combination of nappies and cheap meat, I ventured to ask her why she wasn't wearing it.

'You're too bright, 'ilda, ain't you,' she sighed; obviously she'd been hoping I wouldn't notice. 'It's down at "Uncle's",' she said through tight lips, and shook her head. 'I don't need to tell you that you don't say a word of this to your Pa, d'you 'ear me, 'ilda? 'E's not to know an' I ain't goin' to tell 'im.'

'Down at the pawn shop?' I said incredulously. 'Uncle's' was what we called it. I knew that Pa's suit often made it down there but Ma's ring was special. It was the only piece of jewellery she possessed, the only thing of value she'd ever owned in her own right. I couldn't imagine how she must have felt to hand that over.

'We're a bit short this week, that's all. Things will look up soon, 'ilda, I promise you. They're 'irin' labourers down at the docks again, an' Pa says 'e'll be workin' into the night wiv the Deal Porters who unload the timber ships down in Surrey Docks.'

'But your ring, Ma. What if Pa don't get the work? What if 'e spends it all before 'e brings it 'ome to you? What if—'

At that point my mother cut me off. It was rare she

77

was ever sharp with us children, but this was one of those moments, and I reacted like I'd been slapped on the cheek. Her voice was calm, but authoritative.

''Ilda, I've told you it'll be all right. Now I won't 'ear anyfink against your pa or against the work down the docks. We don't want to jinx it. I don't want another word said about this, d'you 'ear me?'

''Course, Ma, 'course I won't say a fing. But what are you goin' to tell Pa when 'e gets in? 'E's bound to notice, ain't 'e?' I said, feeling deflated, like I'd been punctured with a pin.

''E might notice, 'e might not, dependin' on 'ow lively 'e is when 'e comes 'ome tonight.' I knew that the word lively actually meant drunk, but I was too afraid of upsetting Ma again to say it out loud. 'If 'e asks I'll say it's at the mender's for a clean and polish. That'll keep 'im off the scent for a while at least,' she continued, warming to her theme.

I sighed heavily, knowing this could only lead to trouble but respecting her decision.

Times were hard for everyone down our way as the Depression hit harder still. There were rumours of rent riots being planned as people, sick of living in appalling conditions, started to revolt against the absent landlords who refused to clean up their tenements. Rats were becoming a huge problem, and there were Chinese whispers of rats being boiled in the nightly stew, for want of any better meat, and even of babies' faces being eaten by scavenging rodents.

The local pawn shops were filling up with the little jewellery the women of the borough owned. Jobs had been cut at the dockyards, casual labourers were laid off halfway through a working day. Pa was working less and less, some weeks he was only managing a couple of days, and it was the same for others down our street.

My morning walk to school was now punctuated with gossip by housewives worrying over the cost of gas and paying the butcher, rather than who was running off with whom. Yet we weren't the worst off in our road.

We hadn't been in our new house for long, but already we'd met most of our neighbours. I'd made friends with a family living two doors down from us. Helen was 12 years old, the same age as me. I met her when I started at the school closest to us: St James's on Thurland Road. She'd let me sit next to her in class and we'd become firm friends. Even though I missed Nellie and Margaret, I settled in quickly. Each evening after school we'd dawdle home, which was only round the corner and under the railway arch.

Helen had four older brothers and a younger sister. Her father worked at the tannery, and drank every night in the pub at the end of our street. Feeding six children must have been impossible on a tanner's wage, and Helen was often hungry, scavenging around the streets and warehouses, looking for dropped fruit or potatoes. Ma often invited her in for her tea, and we shared what little we had with her. Her mother Mary was grateful to us for having one less mouth to feed, and she became friends with my Ma. They often nipped in and out of each other's homes to borrow a cup of flour or tea.

I knew we had to be grateful for what we had, but I also knew we were pitied by the other housewives and children because of the way Pa treated us. His rages could be heard the length of the road when he got going. And, of course, neither Ma nor I were able to hide our bruises after each beating.

Mary would pat me on the head when she saw me, and tickle Ron and Joanie under the chin, though they both hated it! But they all turned a blind eye to the beatings, however much they sympathised with us.

Pa's violence towards Ma and me continued unabated. In one particularly bad beating, he'd taken his belt to Ma and, when I'd rushed in to protect her, he'd turned it on me. He rarely gave a reason for his attacks, but that evening he'd left the pub early, saying that one of his mates had said Ma had been seen with another man. It was all nonsense of course, but Pa was the type to hit first, ask questions later. He'd stomped in, slamming the door behind him. Ma had asked him, in that calm way of hers, what the matter was, and he'd called her a whore. Without waiting for her response, he'd unbuckled the black belt we'd all learnt to fear, and he'd launched at her, the strap making a whistling sound as it moved sharply through the air.

Ma screamed and covered her face. He beat her till she was crouched on the floor, all of us children wailing and crying around her. The others ran upstairs to hide from his temper, but I stayed. By God I wasn't going to leave her alone with that brute. I got a fist in my face for my trouble, along with a new black eye and a swollen lip to add to all the rest he'd given me over the years.

On another occasion, Pa had rolled in from the bar just after 11 p.m., demanding his dinner and cursing one of his 'pals' for refusing to loan him money for beer. Ma was upstairs sleeping, suffering with her swollen legs again, so I'd offered to stay up and give Pa his dinner.

I watched him warily, stifling a yawn. I dished out the remains of the stew Ma had cobbled together out of scraps of meat and potatoes, hoping he'd eat up quickly and fall asleep. I was tired, and had to get up for school the next morning.

Pa took one look at his meal, and pushed it away. 'That ain't fit for an 'orse. I ain't eatin' that!'

His voice was mean-sounding, his eyes piercing me. I stood with my back to the range, silent, waiting.

Pa got up out of his chair and walked up to me, slowly. He bent down and grabbed me under my chin with one of his big, veiny hands.

'Where's me fuckin' dinner?' he snarled.

I gulped, my face pulled up to his. He stank of his usual stale beer and cheap tobacco. My nose wrinkled in disgust.

He might have been drinking, but he saw my reaction. Quick as anything, he drew himself up. His frustration at the lack of beer money, and his hurt pride at being let down by a drinking mate melted into boiling hot anger aimed at me.

I could see the flash of temper in his eyes. I blinked. He roughly pushed away my face, bruising my chin. A sob escaped from my mouth, filling the quiet room, feeding his hostility.

He drew his fist back and I saw it before I felt it. With a hammer blow, he punched me. My nose exploded with blood. I screamed, then slapped my hand across my mouth, crying out with the pain. I didn't want to wake the others but I couldn't help it. I cried again, tears mingling with blood.

'Let that be a lesson to yer,' bellowed Pa. 'Now get out of me fuckin' sight.'

He turned away from me. I turned and fled into the bedroom, grabbing a kitchen rag as I went to stop the flow of blood. I was sure he'd broken my nose again, the pain was unbelievable and my head was dizzy. Eventually I drifted into a half-sleep, my face throbbing.

The next morning, Les, Ron and Joanie looked at me in horror, but I refused to answer their questions. I would have to go to school with a bruised face, a bloody nose and a soul that felt diminished with every punch That Man rained down on me. Ma took one look at my still-bloody face and hugged me tight to her. She wiped away a tear as she looked at me. We had no words to say. What difference would they have made? Her love was all the salve I needed, but I agonised over the pain Pa's beating of me caused her.

Our neighbours would have heard every word he shouted, every scream from Ma and me, and yet no one came to help, no one dared interfere with a man and his family.

They showed us they cared in other ways, though. After that beating, Les was given an extra couple of apples by the grocer when he went to pick up the veg for Ma. It was a small gesture of kindness, and though it didn't go anywhere near fixing the problem of Pa and how he treated us, it bought a lump to my throat.

One morning I'd opened the front door to go to buy milk and found a package lying on the reddened doorstep. Curious, I took it inside, and Ma opened it, to find a loaf of bread and a few potatoes inside from an anonymous donor. She stared at it for a long time, and I swear I saw a single tear drop onto the package but Ma wrapped it up and said we weren't forgotten by God, or our neighbours.

And where better on this earth could we be living but our beloved Bermondsey? The kindness of strangers was what kept our community going. The women of the borough looked out for each other, even though there was little help they could give except to offer a cup of hot tea, some sympathy and the occasional loaf of bread. It meant the world to us though.

'Look, 'ilda, things are bad down at the docks an' Pa 'ain't 'ad much work. 'E's been up the Labour Exchange, an' got food from the Relief Office. You might as well know that we're strugglin' to make ends meet,' Ma said. I looked up at

her. Things must be worse than usual if she was pawning her
wedding ring and we were relying on handouts. As far as I
knew, we'd never had to go to the Poor Relief before, even
though we'd had to move because we couldn't afford our
rent, and we'd been living on the scraps of meat in thin soups
for as long as I could remember. Pa refused to on the grounds
of his pride. I knew the amount of food in the handouts was
barely enough to feed a family as I'd heard other housewives
complaining about how they would manage.

The relief food consisted of a tin of golden syrup, a pound
of margarine, one long tin loaf of bread, two pounds of flour,
one tin of condensed milk and two pounds of beef. It wasn't
nearly enough to feed us all for a week. I had a million more
questions, but the look on Ma's face silenced me. I bit them
back, my mind whirring. If the Labour Exchange gave us
29 shillings a week, and our rent was 11 shillings, then how
would we manage?

'Go 'an get the littl'uns in for their supper,' Ma said briskly,
tying her apron round her waist. Was it my imagination or
was she looking thinner these days? I walked slowly out the
front door and onto our street, worrying about how we'd
survive.

The gas lamp was flickering on as dusk fell, casting a
small pool of orange light nearby. I could hear Ron's voice
now, back from the docks and shouting loudly at another
child, while Les was kicking at a stray stone and Joanie was
whispering closely with a little girl from down the way.

'Your dinner's ready,' I shouted, with my hands on either
side of my waist, looking for all the world like a mini version
of Ma. My brown hair was scooped back behind my ears just
like Ma, and I was wearing a flowery blouse and plain skirt,
even though I was only 12 years old.

When I'd finally rounded up the children and got them

to the table, bellowing for Ron to wash his hands and Les to stop scuffing his boots on his chair, we finally sat down to eat. Ma doled out the stew and passed a plate to each of us. She then sliced the bread into four thin slices and told us to help ourselves.

'But there's only four plates, Ma. Aren't you 'avin' any? You'll be 'ungry.' I said, looking at the plates on the table and recounting them.

'Oh, duck, I ate earlier. Don't you worry about me, 'ilda, I'm right as rain,' Ma said, patting her stomach as she did so and settling into the remaining chair by the range, picking up an old jumper she was unpicking so she could use the wool to make a new jumper for Ron.

'I didn't see you eat. When did you eat? You said that yesterday,' I blurted out. Slowly, I started to realise that maybe Ma was lying to us, and hadn't really eaten at all. I looked up at her, half-wanting reassurance and half-wanting the facts. Had she eaten or not?

'Don't you worry, girl. I'm perfectly fine. Just eat your dinner and you can go out an' play again,' she repeated, wearing a smile on her face as she spoke.

I wanted so much to believe her. The others were completely oblivious. The boys were wolfing their food down and squabbling over the last crumbs of bread, before tucking into a home-made roly-poly that Ma had seemingly magicked out of thin air.

'Stop fightin', you two,' I said wearily. I was still trying to work out what was really going on in the adult world where things weren't always what they seemed, and I found it confusing and tiring.

I ate my supper. I'll admit I felt guilty for the first two mouthfuls but was then driven by hunger and I ended up wiping my plate clean with my bread and licking my fingers, guiltily. It wasn't much to sustain us children, but it was better than nothing, and we were always grateful for our dinner even if we didn't show it.

After we'd all finished, Ma stood up and started collecting up the plates to rinse and put away. 'Go on, out you go,' she said with a smile, and the three others raced off out the front.

'You too, 'ilda, go on and 'ave a bit a fun,' she said, not looking me in the eyes.

I turned round towards the door, frowning as I went, then decided suddenly I wanted the truth. I turned back to challenge Ma and find out what was going on. But I didn't need to say a word. I caught her in the act.

She had scraped a finger round one of the plates, hoping to pick up the remains of the gravy, and was lustily licking it off her finger. We both froze as we realised I'd seen what she'd been hiding. Seconds passed, the moment elongated into its awkward shape, leaving us both unable to speak. I knew that Ma had bought cheap sausages for Pa's dinner, we'd had the stew with off-cuts of meat, but there was nothing for her, except the wipings from our plates. She was giving it all to us. Her heart was so big she'd see herself starve rather than watch us go without a meal.

I couldn't say anything, I didn't trust myself. And what could I say anyway? As suddenly as I'd discovered the truth, I realised I didn't want to see it anymore. I turned round and walked out into the street, hearing Ma say, ' 'ilda,' in a small voice that it broke my heart to hear.

I turned out of the house, feeling my feet take me the length of the road, past the baths and That Man's new drinking hole, the Queen's Arms, hearing the quizzical exclamations from Les and Ron saying, 'Where are you off to, 'ilda?', and ignoring them as well.

I kept walking, turning right onto Grange Road. I turned

right again and found myself in the road I was born in: The Grange. I don't know why I needed to be there but it felt familiar, though I was only a baby when I left. I kept going, turning down the smaller streets, dodging the kids out playing and the housewives chattering, the carts carrying Pears' soap. I didn't stop till I'd reached Tower Bridge Road and found myself on the Tab, staring out at the river, trying to make out the sea on its winding horizon.

I felt pain, real physical pain, at the thought of Ma missing her dinner. And she very often missed breakfast too. My heart felt like it would burst, and I stayed there for a long, long time, till my breathing calmed down from the shuddering, gasping for air from the exertion, and the overwhelming feeling that I was drowning in my sadness for this lovely woman. I knew I'd be in trouble when I returned, but tonight I didn't give a rat's arse, as Pa would say.

I watched the factory workers as they streamed across the bridge, making their way home after a ten-hour shift most likely. Sighing, I realised I could stay on the bridge no longer, that I had to go home eventually to face the horror of our existence. It was dark now, Ma would be worried and I didn't want to attract the attention of the dockers, the lucky ones who'd had a back-breaking day's work and who were already deep into their nightly drinking bouts.

Ma looked up as I came in and clutched her chest, looking at once relieved and some other emotion I couldn't name. I was just too young to understand the turbulence we were both experiencing. She didn't shout or ask where I'd been and I was, at least, grateful for that. Instead she fussed over me, bringing me a scalding hot cup of tea and pouring in my favourite Carnation milk as a treat, as if I was ill. I looked up at her, and her eyes were wet where she must have been crying.

'No 'arm done, eh, 'ilda?' she said quietly, and I nodded my response, looking into my tea cup as if it contained the answer to all our worries.

CHAPTER 7

Black Mog

1935

'Now then, Ron, take that winkle out of your mouth and wait till Pa gets in,' snapped Ma, as she busied about setting the table for our Sunday high tea.

All four of us children were seated round the table in the kitchen, eyeing the food with undisguised greed. We were waiting for Pa to return from the pub so we could eat together, the only time our family ever really did so. As such, it was an important day for Ma, and she marked it by putting on the best spread she could manage, saving her pennies for the man who carted round winkles and shrimps each Sunday afternoon so we could eat them with bread and marge.

Each Sunday morning, Ma would tie on her apron as if she meant business, then she would proceed to make us a cake or a treacle pudding. The smell inside our home was heavenly, the sweet aroma of a sponge or seed cake or the smell of treacle as it warmed through, stayed with us all day.

When I turned 14 I had started work at the Peek Frean biscuit factory, and the extra 11 shillings I brought into the household had made all the difference to our way of life. My wages had come after nearly two years of barely making ends meet as we lived on Poor Relief and handouts from our neighbours and friends, while Pa scratched around for the dwindling work at the docks.

The day I started my job was one of the best days of my life. I was thrilled to see the look on Ma's face when I handed her my brown packet containing my first week's wages. She counted it out carefully, and gave me a shilling back to spend on myself! Well, I knew exactly what I wanted, I'd seen a dress stall down the Blue, as we called Bermondsey Market. I'd already spent a happy morning searching through the second-hand clothes. I wanted a skirt, with no patches and no darning, and I'd seen just the perfect one, but I'd have to save hard to afford even other people's cast-offs.

My wages now paid for our Sunday high tea. It was on those afternoons that we forgot the strain of living day to day, we forgot scraping together the odd pennies to put in the slot meter for gas, or only being able to afford to pay off one of our creditors. It was the only time we felt like a proper family, with a mother and a father, and our brothers and sisters around us. Or that was how it was for me, anyway.

'Ron! If I've told you once, I've told you a thousand times, keep your 'ands to yerself an' leave that food alone! It's not just your stomach we'll be fillin', there's others as well as you,' said Ma again, raising her hand as if to slap Ron.

Luckily for my cheeky youngest brother she was quickly distracted by the sound of the kettle boiling. 'Don't you move a muscle, Ron Johnson, I mean it,' she half-chuckled now, knowing what a rascal he was. We could hear the love in her voice, which always betrayed her attempts to tell him off.

Ron, who was six years old, looked guiltily up at Ma and said 'sorry' in his best, most polite voice, then the minute her back was turned he reached for a shrimp, cramming it into his mouth with sheer delight.

I made a tsk sound, and Ma turned round and arched her eyebrows, knowing what Ron had done. He stopped chewing and tried to look innocent, at which point we all burst out laughing.

It was a sunny summer's day, as far as we could tell from

the little daylight that reached past the smog. But our windows were fastened shut against the overpowering smell of dung left by the horses that pulled the carts as they rumbled down our street. We sat, therefore, in itchy, sticky impatience as sweat dribbled down our backs, pausing only to flick away the flies that hovered over our meal.

The whole of Bermondsey suffered like this in the heat. There was no such thing as public sanitation and so we lived with the vermin that tracked the greasy walls and the outside lavvies, which became infested with diseases like dysentery. There'd even been tales of cholera in nearby St James's Road less than 30 years' ago, which wasn't that far behind us. All in all, you had to have a strong constitution and an iron stomach to live here, though Pa reckoned it was the beer that kept him healthy, and he might have been right, the amount he drank.

Ma looked again at the kitchen clock. She sighed and said, 'I don't suppose you should wait any longer. I don't know where Pa's got to,' though I'm sure she could hazard a guess. 'Tuck in, go on, or the food'll spoil.'

And with that we descended on the piles of bread and delicious Thames winkles with relish.

Starting work was my first taste of freedom, though I'd loved my school days. I left clutching my School Leaving Certificate and the reference from my headmaster Mr Stein at St James's, telling my prospective employer that I was 'a girl of excellent character ... honest, truthful and trustworthy, willing and obliging, courteous and polite, and clean and tidy'. I blushed at those words. I couldn't believe they were about me. I felt proud that day.

The morning after saying farewell to my school days, I was up early getting ready to go in to the biscuit factory in the hope of landing a job there. Peek Frean's was seen as one of the best places to work in the area, because it was clean, it smelt biscuity and sweet, and it offered all sorts for the workers, such as dentists and amateur dramatics clubs.

I knew I had to look my best and act like a proper lady to get one of the coveted jobs, and who knew how many other young girls were hoping to work there too. I took great care in dressing myself. I scrubbed my face till it shone pink and ruddy in the mirror and tied my hair back. Only then did I take myself to Ma for inspection.

'You look spick and span,' beamed Ma. 'Just keep your 'ead 'igh an' your wits about you an' you'll be fine.'

I kissed her goodbye and, with a tummy that felt like it was doing somersaults, I started the short walk between Spa Road and Clements Road to the big factory nudged up against the railway arches.

I smiled nervously at the receptionist, who sat at a plain desk with a huge typewriter in front of her. She had neat, brown hair swept back off her face and a kind demeanour. She gestured for me to sit and wait my turn to be taken up for my interview. There were already two other girls there, waiting to be seen. I said 'hello' and my voice echoed in the large space that was lined with windows.

I fidgeted for what seemed like hours, till eventually another woman, with a severe face and a clipboard, pushed open the doorway and gestured to the girl at the end. The girl looked like she was going to pee her pants with fright and I thought to myself, *She ain't no competition*. Years of living with Pa and the ticking time bomb of his moods and rages meant I felt I could tackle anything that came my way. The lady with the clipboard may frighten the life out of that girl, but she had no such effect on me. I was made of sturdier stuff.

The second girl seemed more self-assured, but her boots were dirty and she didn't look like she'd made much of an effort, so I thought I could beat her to a job too.

Finally it was my turn. Feeling fairly confident, I walked down a long corridor, the floors gleaming. I could hear the sounds of voices and machinery, the clatter of metal against metal, and there was a strong smell of vanilla. I took a good long sniff of it, determined that I would be back to breathe it in every day. The place had the air of a busy, efficient factory and I can honestly say I couldn't wait to work there.

I was ushered into a small room and told to wait again. This time a man wearing a long white coat came in and introduced himself as the floor manager. He was carrying a box with the Peek Frean label on, which he solemnly opened, placing a stack of different types of biscuits on the table.

'Right, Hilda, you've got a minute to pack up all those biscuits into the right places and seal the box. Are you ready?'

And with that, he held his hand up, one finger extended, one eye on the wall-mounted clock, the other fixed on me. 'Go!' he said.

Without a thought, I sprang into action, quickly eyeing the inside of the box, which had sections of different shapes and depths. It took me just under the allotted minute to finish. I barely had time to draw breath before the man in the coat said, 'Stop!'

He wrote something down, then said, 'Take a seat, young lady. The doctor will be along in a moment.'

With that, he picked up the box and left the room, leaving me feeling puzzled. Had I completed the task correctly? He'd given me no clue at all. And why did they need to get me a doctor? I didn't have anything wrong with me, that I knew about anyway, except of course the bites from the bed bugs that covered my legs, and the hair lice that made all of us Bermondsey kids scratch like crazy. At that, I gave myself a good itch so I didn't have to do it when the doctor came, smoothed down my hair and tried to look elegant.

Within minutes the door opened again, and another man in a white coat introduced himself as the company doctor. His hands were cold, but I submitted to his prodding. He looked inside my mouth and down my ears, and he turned over my palms, checking my fingernails before he finished.

'Are you a healthy girl?' he asked.

'I ain't never been sickly,' I replied. 'I 'ad a few days off school wiv a fever, but apart from that I've always been lucky wiv me 'ealth.'

'Good,' was all he said, before he too made some notes on a piece of paper and left the room.

I sat there, tapping my feet against the floor, wondering what else could be next.

The severe-looking woman reappeared and congratulated me, as I had passed the tests and could work at Peek Frean's packing the biscuits into fancy boxes.

I was thrilled! I couldn't say 'thank you' fast enough.

All the way home, I nearly skipped for the joy of it. My own job! I felt like a grown-up at last. It was my first taste of independence.

Ma's face lit up with an enormous smile when I told her the good news. 'I start on Monday,' I said, and that was that. I was a Bermondsey Biscuit Girl and proud of it.

By now the shrimps were fast disappearing from the table, mostly going into Ron's open mouth.

'Shut your mouth when you're chewin' your food,' said Ma, crossly.

At that moment, Joanie, who was now an attractive, dark-eyed young girl of nine, leant over next to me and nudged my arm. 'Cover for me, won't you, 'ildy? I'm off out tonight an' Ma'll never let me go unless you say it's alright,' she grinned, popping a piece of seed cake into her mouth. She'd chosen a moment while Ma was distracted to ask me.

'Why should I?' I whispered back. 'Where the 'ell are you goin' anyway?'

'Nowhere, just out an' about. Go on, 'ildy, please?' said Joanie, pleadingly. 'I won't be back late, I promise.'

I nodded my head in reply. 'Just don't get into any trouble, Joanie,' I said a little sternly. Joanie was only young but she was a lively girl, who was so much more carefree than me.

'Fanks, 'ildy,' she said, finishing off the last of her cake and getting up from the table.

She skipped off to get ready for her outing, saying, 'Ma, I'm off out. Won't be back late, just meeting some friends.'

She looked at me pointedly, and so I added. 'Yes, Ma, Joanie's just popping out. That's alright, ain't it?'

Ma nodded, too distracted by Pa's whereabouts to notice when her two girls were cooking up a pack of lies. Joanie gave me a quick smile and dashed out before anyone could say another word.

'Well, I thoroughly enjoyed that, thanks, Ma,' I said brightly, and got started on clearing up the dishes.

Several hours later, Ma and I were having a rare moment sat down together, while Ron and Les were undressing. Pa had appeared earlier, staggering slightly from drink, but in one of his happy drunk moods and had regaled us by vamping on the piano in the parlour, which had made us all laugh. He'd been given the piano by one of his mates from the pub. None of us dared ask what he'd done to get such a prize.

Pa could turn on the charm when he put his mind to it, it

was the reason he had so much success with other women. We rarely saw that side of him at home; he usually reserved his likeable self for his pals in the boozer, or the constant stream of floozies he dallied with. If only they knew the real Ted Johnson, they'd be a lot less impressed, I reckoned. But in the rare moments when he did play the fool at home we enjoyed it as a respite from his wicked temper, all the while wondering how long it would last. I could never relax around him, even when he was smiling and joking, and singing loudly with his coarse East End voice.

The afternoon had become another sultry evening, and there was still no sign of Joanie. 'Where did you say she'd gone, 'ilda?' said Ma with a worried frown.

'Oh, she said she was just meetin' friends at the Rialto, I fink,' I replied, fidgeting a little, hating the lie. I didn't know who Joanie had met or where she'd gone.

'Was she now? Hmmm,' said Ma, and I could tell the game was up. She was looking at me steadily. I blushed and averted my gaze, my head down while I found a scratch on the table intensely interesting.

It was at this point that Pa, who had fallen asleep after his afternoon's exertions, woke up with a start. There was a line of dribble on his chin, and he blinked, looking around and getting his bearings. He yawned, stretched, and looked at us before rubbing the stubble on his face. 'What was that about Joanie?' he asked, gruffly.

There was silence for a second. We all knew that Joanie was Pa's favourite. From the minute she was born he took to her, and I couldn't remember him ever belting her one. Ma and I exchanged a glance.

'Nuffink to worry about. She's probably 'eld up by the omnibuses,' said Ma, placatingly.

I glanced at the clock. It was gone 9 p.m., and she should've been back by now. The sun had set and night was falling. The street outside, which was usually so busy by day, was becoming quiet. Ma watched at the window, pulling open the curtains a crack and peered outside as if by doing so, Joanie would suddenly appear.

Pa yawned again. He took out his tin of tobacco and started rolling himself a cigarette. When he'd finished he stepped outside the door to smoke it and exchange pleasantries with the neighbours.

Time was ticking on. Joanie still hadn't appeared. Pa was now swearing at someone in the street, and I could hear that his grandiose happy mood of earlier had slunk away, leaving the embittered, dangerous man we all knew. Ma was openly fretful now. She didn't push me on where she'd gone. She knew I hadn't a clue and I was just sorry I'd lied to her.

Pa came back in and started pacing the room. He told me to get him a drink as he was 'bone dry' and so I did, scuttling to fetch it while the tension around me built up. That Man was staring at Ma as she worked her darning. I could tell he was gunning for a fight as the minutes ticked past, slowly.

Then, at half-past ten, the sound of the front door opening greeted us. Joanie crept in, looking like she'd been caught robbing a bank. Ma was the first to react.

'Where the 'ell 'ave you been? We was worried sick,' she said, standing up with her arms on her hips.

'I did nuffink, Ma, just met a few of me pals, that's all, no 'arm done,' Joanie said in a wheedling way.

She turned to Pa and looked at him pleadingly, 'I didn't mean to worry you, Pa. I'm back now. I won't do it again.'

With that, Pa looked back at Ma, his face turning redder by the second. 'What the 'ell were you playin' at, Ma, lettin''

Black Mog 'ere out on 'er own? She don't know no better but it's you who's at fault 'ere,' he said with mean spirit.

I opened my mouth to defend Ma, but she hit back at him with surprising force. 'Don't you go blamin' me, Ted Johnson. You 'ad as littl' idea where that girl was as I did. Don't you dare go blamin' me!'

Joanie, who at this point felt it was safer to disappear quietly up the stairs to bed, had been called Black Mog since the day she was born. Pa's father Harry took one look at her mop of unruly black hair and her big dark eyes and christened her Black Mog. Pa almost always called her that, and I noticed his voice always became softer when he said it.

But at this point his temper finally burst, like water from a dam. He stood up, raging at Mother, his face contorted, his chin jutting out at her, aggressive and frightening. 'You fuckin' bitch, 'ow dare you talk back at me in me own 'ouse.' He shouted his oft-repeated refrain about this being his ''ouse', with the assumption we were bit parts, side-players in the drama of his life. 'If you can't control the fuckin' kids then you're no good as their mother, you lazy cow,' he spat, leaning in to her, blocking her exit from the room.

To my surprise, and horror, Ma launched a verbal attack back at Pa that almost matched his own. 'Don't you dare tell me I ain't a good mother, Ted Johnson. I'd give me life for me kids. I keep 'em clothed an' fed 'owever much money there is in me purse, an' wot do I get for fanks from you, eh? Nuffink! Nuffink is what I get. Nuffink or a slap round the face. That's what you're best at eh, Ted!'

There was a momentary pause in the fight, while Pa absorbed the fact his normally placid, God-fearing wife was finally standing up to him, and loudly at that. God knows if the boys heard this racket, I expect the whole neighbourhood could've heard them at it by now.

Then Pa did what he knows best, almost without thinking. A boxer's instinct. He raised his right fist and drove it into Ma's face. I leapt up and grabbed at Pa's arm, my fury making me braver than I had ever felt. How dare he say those things to the woman who had brought us all up, and done a damn good job in the circumstances.

Pa then turned round and I heard the slap before I felt it. Delayed reaction. Staggering back in shock, I touched my face but all I could feel was the hot tears that came.

'Don't you get involved. This is between me and yer Ma. If she can't keep control of 'er kids then she ain't fit to be their mother,' he said harshly. Looking round at both of us, he picked up his coat, despite the heat, slapped his cap onto his head and, with a grim expression, strode towards the door.

'That's right, you go back to the pub, you spend our food money on beer, why don't you? You're goin' to anyway,' shouted Ma after him. I don't know how she had the courage.

That Man slammed the door so hard it jolted on its hinges.

Then there was silence. Ma sat down slowly, as if the effort involved in giving as good as she got had exhausted her. I hurried over, both of us crying, and she folded me into her arms.

There was no sound from above. Joanie always managed to avoid the repercussions of her actions where That Man was concerned, and I doubted she would ever mention tonight's events, let alone apologise. Joanie simply wasn't like that. I loved her for her cheek and her wilfulness, but she could also be thoughtless, and was undoubtedly Pa's favourite. I sighed as I thought about my little sister. So young, and yet so forward in her ways.

There was a little blood running from a cut by the side of

Ma's eye, but she'd escaped quite lightly. My face was scarlet with the impact but, again, it could've been worse. Despite that, and despite the fact I was now a young lady with a proper job at the biscuit factory, I still needed my mother's comfort after yet another run-in with That Man. Would it ever end? Would we ever be free of his bullying ways?

CHAPTER 8

Terror at Home

1936

The stinking heat that permeated the walls and rooms of
our line of houses left us breathless. It was the end of May
but the heat was already building up into another hot, long
summer. I was upstairs in the bedroom Les, Ron, Joanie and
I shared, making sure the littl'uns were in bed and getting
ready for sleep.

'You said your prayers?' I asked Ron, who grinned at me
cheekily.

'I don't need none of those, Boot Brush Lil,' he said, flop-
ping his head onto the pillow and pretending to snore loudly.
Ron was such a cheeky monkey but we all adored him, even
when he got into trouble, and, strangely enough, he was the
one who was regularly beaten with the stick by Mr Stein, the
headmaster at our school. Somehow he never took it to heart,
though, and was always a happy, adventurous boy, so unlike
me in many respects.

I loved a good laugh, always have done, but I also knew
that there were duties and responsibilities in life. I suppose
being the eldest I had no choice but to know about that.
Tonight was no different. Once Joanie and Les had settled
down as well, I whispered, 'Good night, see you tomorrow,
please God,' which I did every night without fail. It was my
little way of making sure we were all safe and sound.

I crept down the stairs and found Ma in the kitchen,
fanning herself with an old newspaper. There was a picture
on the front page of a line of German athletes at the Berlin

Winter Olympics making a funny gesture with their hands, in a kind of regimented salute. Us kids all thought it was comical till Ma pointed out that they were making Nazi salutes, and that was a bad thing because they did terrible things to Jewish people. The newspaper was months old, yet somehow it had survived being cut up into squares and placed on the nail on the lavvy door to be used to wipe our backsides. Most other bits of discarded paper or newsprint ended up that way, but for some reason Ma had kept it, probably to light the range with.

It was obvious there were things going on in the wider world. Pa had mentioned Germany a few times. He seemed to think there might be trouble again. That confused me. Wasn't the Great War the war to end all wars? If that was so, then why was everyone so worried about this Adolf Hitler and his gang of Nazis? And what did any of it have to do with us?

My thoughts were interrupted by Ma getting up from her chair, her darning spilling onto the table.

Ma was eight months pregnant with her fifth child, and she looked ill and tired, no more so than tonight. She stood up to ease her back and walked round the small room, backlit by the gas lamp on the street outside, revealing the silhouette of her misshapen body and wrinkled stockings.

As she shuffled backwards and forwards, I told her to get herself to bed. I was worried about her. She looked exhausted, there were dark rings under her eyes and her hair hung limp in the airless room. 'Don't you worry about me, girl, I'll wait up for Pa. 'E's been workin' today by all accounts so 'e'll need 'is dinner an' a bit a comfort when 'e gets in.'

Ma cared for all of us, including That Man, with steady devotion, but tonight her resolve dissolved with my protestations and she shuffled up the steep stairs. I heard the bed creak under her as she guided her hot, heavy body onto the mattress.

I yawned a little and looked at the clock. I might have several hours to wait before my father got home so there was no point sitting idle. I picked up my knitting, squinting as I moved the wool between the needles, scratchy against my skin. The hours passed slowly.

The night was sticky with the torrid heat. Then, just after the pubs closed, as the streets became busy with staggering, braying men, I heard the thud of Pa's boots on the street outside ours. They stumbled slightly. I put down my knitting and braced myself. The door opened and Pa's short, dark frame covered the doorway. I stood up and faked a smile, waiting to see what mood he was in tonight. He cast his eyes around the room then settled them on me.

'Where's your Ma?' he asked, throwing his cap onto the table and walking unsteadily to his chair.

'She's restin,' Pa. She's not well wiv the baby, but I've got your dinner 'ere,' I said, all the while breathing shallow breaths.

'What's this?'

I could feel the air thick against my skin. I gulped and replied, trying to placate him before his sour mood turned worse. 'It's what we all 'ad. There weren't much at the butcher's for us this week. It's the leftover roast made up into stew. It's tasty, Pa, I promise,' my voice tailed off, sinking beneath the weight of his displeasure.

The feeling I always had with him, like my stomach was drawing in tighter and tighter, was making me feel giddy. Why did it always have to be like this? He drew in a big, long breath. He raised his head up, and his small eyes, as black as shards of coal, looked as mean as I'd ever seen them. He licked his lips, then carefully, slowly, he pushed one hand across the table, sweeping the plate off onto the floor. It shattered into pieces, shards of china lying jagged and sharp.

'When I get 'ome from work, from workin' my arse off for the likes of you an' that lazy cow wife of mine, I expect a proper dinner.' He emphasised the last two words as if I was a simpleton and hadn't realised the meaning of them. 'I don't expect much in this world. I just want a beer an' a hot dinner inside me an' I'll work all the 'ours God sends, but this, THIS,' and he jabbed at the mess of stew that smeared across the wooden surface. 'THIS ain't a PROPER DINNER. Now if you know what's good for you, you'll get yerself up them stairs 'n' get Ma up out of her bloody bed.'

With that he rose out of his chair, his posture leaning towards me aggressively. I'd already starting backing towards the wall, but seeing him so hostile, I shook my head.

'Not tonight, Pa. She ain't well, it's the baby makin' 'er tired,' I trembled, feeling my knees shake in fear.

'She ain't the bloody King, she can't try an' fuckin' abdicate from bein' my wife!' barked Pa and laughed at his own wit. There were rumours that our monarch Edward VIII intended marrying his lover Wallis Simpson and could abdicate as a result. London was agog at the shocking turn of events. It was the only news worth debating in the alehouses and markets, factories and on the docksides. 'Go and get 'er, NOW!'

With that, Pa kicked back his chair, shoved me aside, and strode up the steep stairs. He marched into their bedroom. I could hear their voices, urgent and combative but in whispers, so they didn't wake the others. I didn't dare go up those stairs, though I felt a coward, but I saw the mean streak in him tonight and nothing could've made me put one foot in front of the other. I was frozen with terror. Then I heard the reluctant sound of the bed creak again and Ma's slower, softer footsteps as they left the bed. There were more exchanges, though I could make out nothing of what they were saying.

Then there was a sound that chilled my blood. Stopped it in its tracks. There was the noise of a heavy object as it crashed down the stairs, a noise that shuddered to a halt as it hit the floor. Time arrested as the lump of flesh and bone lay for a moment, unmoving.

'Ma!' I screamed, and ran over to where she lay. My heart was pounding. The bastard had killed her.

I could hear his footsteps as he came down the stairs behind me but I didn't care about him anymore. 'I didn't touch 'er, I swear it, 'ilda,' Pa said, almost pleadingly.

I looked up at him, his face covered by shadow and I felt sick to my stomach. I had no doubt in my mind that he'd pushed my frail, heavily pregnant mother down the stairs, even though I hadn't witnessed it. I didn't want to hear his excuses or his guilt. I wanted to spit out my anger but I was too scared that Ma had been badly hurt, or worse.

'The silly cow took a wrong turn...' he added, his voice trailing off.

This time I turned away from him. I didn't want to see him beg. We'd been at his mercy for so long, how dare he now plead with me? As if that would make anything better. I didn't reply. My whole being was focused on this woman who meant so much to all of us as she lay on that floor.

'Ma, can you 'ear me? Please, Ma, please say sumfink!' I begged. My whole body was shaking violently.

'You've killed 'er, you've bloody killed 'er,' I shouted as I grabbed her shoulders. I could feel no movement from her. I couldn't hear her breathing. Time took on an urgency I'd never felt before.

I wanted to shake her awake, but I was terrified I'd do her more harm. Bending over her face, I put my ear up to her mouth, hoping against hope that I'd hear a faint breath. There was a slight flutter of her eyelids, then a short gasping breath. I felt the warmth of her breathing against my ear.

'She's alive, thank Gawd, she's alive!' My voice wobbled with a swoop of relief, which almost immediately became a fear she might be paralysed or injured.

'Ma,' I said, my voice broken, 'please wake up, Ma, please get up.' I swept back her hair, shaking her, planting kisses on her cheek.

There was a slight movement, then a soft groan. 'Ma you've come back to me!' I said, turning and gesturing wildly to Pa, who looked on. His expression was one of intense relief. For a moment he must have wondered if he would feel the sharp tug of the hangman's noose around his neck.

His neck may have been saved, but I had no idea if my beloved ma was badly injured or not. I eased my hand under her head and brought her up to sitting position. She was still floppy and her weight surprised me.

'' 'Elp me wiv 'er, let's get 'er up,' I said to Pa, who hovered uncertainly behind me.

For once he didn't argue. He seemed to accept my authority. We both took hold of Ma's body under her arms, and half-dragged her onto a chair, sitting her down like a rag doll that sagged forwards slightly. As we moved together I could smell the foul stench of beer and cigarettes on his breath. I recoiled, though I was still holding Ma's arm to steady her. Ma was blinking, like she couldn't work out where she was.

'It's alright, Ma, you took a bit of a tumble,' I whispered.

'' 'Ilda, is that you?' she said. I could barely hear her over the frantic beating of my heart.

'It's me, Ma, don't tire yerself. You've 'ad a fall down the stairs. When you can, tell me if anyfink 'urts . . .' I uttered, making sure I spoke slowly in case she was confused.

'I fink I'm alright, darlin'. Me arm's a bit sore and me 'ead feels a bit peculiar but I'm okay, I promise,' Ma said, a little more certainly.

'Get the pot on an' boil us up a cuppa,' I commanded Pa.

Without a word, he grabbed the kettle and poured water from the jug into it. He was silent, in relief or concern I couldn't tell.

'Now then, Ma, what's the name of your firstborn son?' I asked, thinking as she'd taken a knock to her head she might have lost her memory. I'd heard tales of people thinking they were children again, after bad accidents.

'Les, 'e's my eldest boy, then of course there's Ron, the littl' bleeder. Such a cheeky boy, don't know where 'e gets it from,' and with that Ma chuckled to herself.

I breathed a huge sigh of relief, and turned to Pa.

'Where's that cuppa? I reckon we all need it.' The set of my face was grim. I wasn't going to forgive him in a hurry. I wanted him to know how close he'd come to killing my poor Ma. I don't suppose he'd ever have taken notice of what I thought, but I couldn't have him feeling everything was now okay. I wanted him to suffer a little bit longer in the hope he'd feel something like remorse for his violence.

I could barely look at him as he placed two steaming cups of black tea on the kitchen table then added the last of the sugar to both of them.

'You'll need sumfink to settle yer nerves,' he grunted, pulling out a chair for me to sit on next to Ma.

Ma was now sitting upright, the only sign of her fall a great bruise on her arm and a cut on the right side of her face.

Suddenly, she gave a loud moan and held her hands to her belly, which was round and full with the baby.

'Ma! What's wrong? Is it the baby? Is the baby alright?' I barked, scanning her face for her expression.

She rubbed her tummy again, then patted my arm.

'Just a twinge, 'ilda, nuffink to worry about. I'm sure of that,' she replied.

I bit my lip and said nothing. There was no use worrying her with questions. I watched her closely as we sipped our tea. Ma's hands shook at first as she held the cup, but slowly she seemed to come right.

She didn't have any more pains, and eventually she turned to me and smiled.

'I'm right as rain now, girl. Don't you worry about me,' she said. 'Now Pa 'ere will 'elp me to bed once I've finished this. Time for you to go up. I'm fine now. Just a littl' shocked but the tea's done me a world of good, luvvie.'

I wanted to believe her. I couldn't believe how close we'd all come to losing her. I threw Pa a black look. He had the decency to look momentarily ashamed.

'Get to your bed, sweet'eart,' Ma finished. She let go of my hand which she'd been holding.

Reluctantly I agreed, casting a final look at That Man before I headed up the stairs. Pa didn't meet my eyes, instead he ran his hands through his oily hair and darted his gaze away to the kettle on the range. The subject was clearly closed, and I knew then I'd probably never know the whole truth. I slunk into the bedroom and got into bed, trying to keep as much distance between myself, and the tangle of limbs that belonged to the boys and Joanie.

I needed space to think. My head was buzzing with the night's events. I was worried about Ma, and the unborn baby. I knew in my heart of hearts that That Man had pushed his wife down the stairs, and no one would convince me otherwise. I'd seen the look of horror on his face and I knew. I knew he'd come within a hair's breadth of killing her.

I didn't know how I would ever face him again, and yet

I lived under his roof. In that moment my hatred for him seemed to solidify. The wash of feelings I'd had for him since I was old enough to know the beatings were wrong seemed to set into a permanent mould. He was a wife-beater, a thief, a womaniser and a drunk. Those were the shapes that formed the hard stone of anger that settled within me, never ever to leave me.

I got home from the factory shortly after 6 p.m. The littl'uns were out in the street. Joanie skipping with a pal who had a long old piece of rope, while Ron and Les shrieked with delight as they played at being soldiers in Southwark Park.

Ma had looked pale that morning, but none the worse for the night before. I'd done the children's breakfast, and gone to work relieved. But now, inside the front door, I instantly knew something was amiss. Instead of Ma standing at the scullery sink scrubbing clothes or washing plates, there was, instead, a low guttural moan coming from the bedroom. I dropped my coat where I stood and darted into the room, blinking at the gloom of the curtains that were still pulled shut against what little daylight there now was left.

'Oh, 'ilda, thank Gawd you're 'ere. I think the baby's comin',' she said in between a long deep breath and that low, awful moan again.

'Blimey, alright, Ma, it's okay, I'm 'ere,' I said, hoping the terror I suddenly felt didn't show in my voice.

Ma was sitting on the edge of the bed, gripping the iron head with one hand, while the other rubbed her back. Then, with a stifled cry, she gripped the bed harder and bent her head lower.

'Them's contractions, Ma,' I said, rubbing her back and thinking I should find some clean sheets and rags. Her body was rigid, then she slumped back a little, her breaths coming shallow and short.

' 'ilda, be a dear, go an' find yer father. I've got to go up the 'ospital an' I need 'im,' Ma pleaded, her voice urgent. Her face was twisted in pain. I couldn't help but wonder if her fall had brought this on. My face must have been a picture of worry because she managed a smile.

'Jump to it! This baby won't wait for the likes of you!' With that, she let out another moan, this time through clenched teeth. 'This is the last baby, I swear it,' breathed Ma and she laughed, which had to be a good sign.

My heart sank. Dragging Pa out from a pub meant trouble, even if his wife was giving birth. I had no choice though, so I ran out, first checking to see where the others were to tell them I was off on a mission to find our father but they'd all disappeared off in the muddle of streets.

I ran into the Queen's Arms on our road. He wasn't there. I checked a couple of other dives in Jamaica Road, and he wasn't there either. I sprinted along to Canada Wharf, arriving at the Bricklayer's Arms in a flurry of sweat and bent over like Ma, fighting for breath. There he was. When he didn't get work he was usually found hanging out on street corners around Rotherhithe Street or in one of the pubs that sat in squat fellowship with the brick warehouses that towered over them. I could hear him before I saw him. He was telling some kind of joke loudly and with the help of a day's worth of beers inside him.

'Pa,' I said nervously, walking in, cheeks flushed and fidgeting with the fear of the dark, dingy wooden room. There were about 15 men inside, some sat in pairs, the rest sitting on what looked like upturned beer barrels. There were discarded betting slips in crumpled heaps on the low, dark wood tables, and the smoke from pipes and rolled-up cigarettes formed a silently seething fog that curled and drifted in the light from the open door.

'Ma's 'avin' the baby an' she wants you to know about it,' I said, my voice coming out like a squeak amid the shouts and laughs in the room.

''Ere, Ted, it's your daughter. She's a right good-looker, eh?' said one man, who took off his cap with a mocking flourish, before turning to a mate and nudging him in the elbow.

In unison, the men all turned to look at me, and, mortified, I shifted from one foot to the other, wishing I could be anywhere else on this earth than in Ted Johnson's drinking den. It was dark and stank of old beer and the ciggies they were all puffing away on. I couldn't for the life of me think why they all wanted to spend their days in such a place. My eyes slowly grew accustomed to the gloom and I made out Pa's shape as he swivelled his head round to see what the disturbance was.

'What are you doin' in 'ere, 'ilda? This place ain't for the likes of a young lady. You'll put me to shame,' he said, his voice low, but I could hear the threat within it.

I swallowed nervously, and raised my head up to reply. No use showing fear in here, they'd eat me alive. 'I ain't here for fun, Pa. I've been sent by Ma. She's havin' the baby an' she 'as to go up the 'ospital.'

What I didn't add was that I couldn't work out why she needed this low-down drunkard to help her in the business of childbirth, but I kept my mouth shut and my eyes fixed on Pa's. I wasn't going to back down, I'd run too far to get here.

With that, there was a great shout from one of the men, and cries of 'Fine excuse to wet the baby's 'ead' and 'We'll help you celebrate, Teddy'. I thought then of all their wives and children dependent on such a bunch of men and I shuddered.

'Alright, keep it down. I'll be back to stand you all a round. I don't forget me duty,' Pa swaggered, picking up his brown wool docker's coat and flipping on his cap.

'I'll see you back at the 'ouse, later,' growled Pa to me.

I turned back and fled into the relatively fresh air of Rotherhithe Street. I ran all the way back along the river, my eyes peeled for Ron and Les as I went. I ran past Bevington Street and kept going until I saw the gigantic arches of Tower Bridge. It was a sure bet that the boys would, by now, be watching the ships come and go from their patch of 'sandy beach', as they called it, on the Thames foreshore. I swooped up great lungfuls of briny air and raced on, turning just before I got to the bridge and taking the steps down to the beach, which was littered with detritus from the ships.

The river moved with a heavy pull from the oily deposits left by the vessels that rose upon her daily. I couldn't see the others so I looked up at Tab and saw Ron, Les and Joanie leaning over the edge, pointing at a ship as it sailed beneath them. They looked so innocent, so lacking in guile, that I stood for a moment watching them. The world was becoming an increasingly confusing place. Adults acted in ways I didn't understand. Men threw their wives down stairs then sat with them while they drank tea. Other women in our street walked around with bruises and worse, yet had baby after baby. I didn't understand grown-ups at all.

I shook my head to clear my thoughts, and shouted up at them, 'Oi, you three!' before running up the steps and onto the bridge. At least here today they could be children for a while, waving at seamen and imagining their adventures in the world out beyond our Bermondsey borders.

'Look at this ship, 'ilda. I swear I'm goin' to sail on a ship like that one day,' said Ron excitedly when I got up to where they were standing.

'That's nice but listen 'ere. It's Ma, she's havin' the baby an' I reckon we best 'ang about 'ere a bit longer while she's doin' it,' I said, leaning over the edge as well, and giving myself over to the freedom of being there, watching ships, not worrying about the washing or the dinner, or even the pain Ma was going through. It was best to be distracted. We all knew women who hadn't made it through the birth of their babies, and plenty more whose babies had died before they had breathed in the stale London air.

Only the other month, we'd heard that Flo from Bevington Street had died giving birth to her second baby. The little girl, who'd made her appearance into the world backside first, had also perished. There'd been no midwife present, just Flo's aunt and mother. She'd laboured for days, trying to bring that poor baby into the world, and by the time they'd called in a local woman to help, it was too late.

Then there was the dirt and disease, which always took its toll on the weakest of the babes. Helen's mother Mary had lost two babies, one, a little boy, just days after the birth. Childbirth was a dangerous business in the borough. Later people would say that mothers were four times more likely to die in childbirth than was a coal miner going down into the mines. At least out here, with the wind pulling our hair into tangles, I could forget for a moment how powerless I felt over such momentous events. And besides, Ma was probably now on her way to St Olave's Hospital in Rotherhithe, so she would soon be in the best place. We just had to play a waiting game.

'Pa's gone to 'elp so best we keep our distance till 'e's back out at the pub,' I murmured, feeling the guilty pleasure of having this time to ourselves so I could feel like a kid again and not feel like I had to take on the adult world of responsibilities.

With that, Les pointed to another steamer, saying it was bound for Greenland and we gazed in rapture, unable to conceive what Greenland was like, but knowing it was unbearably exotic and exciting.

'An' there's another, 'eadin' for Sweden. I know that because it's got a big badge on it,' said Ron, his face alight with happiness. 'An' guess what?' he added, reaching into his threadbare pocket.

'What, Ron Johnson?' I replied, with mock seriousness, resisting the urge to smooth down his wayward hair in a maternal gesture.

'The barge men gave us these,' and with that he brandished a small brown paper bag with a bounty of liquorice drops inside.

'You lucky things,' I smiled. 'Can I 'ave one?'

Ron looked down into the bag again and decided he could spare me one. I hid my smile as I popped one into my mouth. We all did the same and we stood there sucking happily, watching the great cranes lift and soar along the riversides while an army of what looked like worker ants fetched and carried loads from the barges, scuttling about with shouts and waves and general clamour.

By the time the sun started to set we were all chilly and ready for home and supper. We walked back slowly, and I made dinner out of the leftover mutton stew and Ma's sponge pudding for afters. Pa arrived back just as we'd finished eating so I prepared him a plate of dinner, and we all watched him, eyes wide as saucers, till he'd finished.

'No news yet,' he said, wiping a slice of bread round his plate and licking his lips with relish. His short frame was hunched over the table, both elbows resting on the scarred wood.

The next day he was back in the evening with a smile on his face. 'It's another girl, an' you can all go and see Ma tomorrow,' he said in an uncharacteristically generous offer.

We literally counted the hours till the following afternoon. The littl'uns ran out of school, panting and out of breath with excitement, and I had never left the factory with such haste. Pa was at home, as promised, and together we walked, skipped and ran along Jamaica Road, till we reached Southwark Park. Scampering across the grass, we whooped with the feeling of freedom and happiness, a new sister and an afternoon at the park. What could be better?

Eventually we reached the back of St Olave's and Pa told us to wait a moment while he fetched Ma, as children weren't allowed in the hospital. We kicked our boots and tried putting grass down each other's necks until there was our Ma, coming down the back stairs with a little bundle of blankets in her arms.

'Shhh,' she gestured, holding her finger to her lips. We crept up to her, one after the other, and saw a little black-haired baby cradled in her arms, wrapped in a confusion of clean, white sheets and cotton blankets, and mewling like a kitten. 'Come an' meet your sister,' Ma said gently. The boys hung back but I went and gazed into the little face.

'What's 'er name?' I whispered.

We were struck dumb with fascination and the newness of this tiny person who was going to be our new baby of the family. For a second, I wondered how Ron would take it, but he was a good-natured boy and hadn't seemed to mind that he was losing his 'baby' status with the arrival of this little one.

'Say 'ello to your new sister, Patsy,' said Ma, and with that the baby opened up a dark eye and started pouting her lips, making gentle smack smack noises as she did so. 'She's 'ungry. I'd better give 'er a feed. Your Pa's gone to celebrate wiv his mates so you've got to get yerselves 'ome. 'E won't be 'ome for 'is supper most likely, so leave sumfink out for 'im, won't you, 'ilda?'

'Course, Ma,' I answered, and kissing her on the cheek, I gathered up the others and started the walk home, while Les and Ron skipped around Joanie and me.

The baby seemed perfectly healthy, just small on account of her coming a month early. I hadn't wanted to worry the others so I'd said nothing, but I'd secretly been worried that Ma's fall might have damaged our sister in some way. Seeing Patsy complete and whole made me happy. Pa hadn't broken his wife, nor his baby. Patsy seemed lusty enough, though, hungry for her feed and sniffing the air in the park like a little creature. My heart warmed to the memory of her as we ambled home.

We picked daisies as we went to make into crowns to wear in our hair. The evening felt soft and benign. Pa would be out for hours, and if we were lucky he'd be in a good mood from the drinks he'd have been bought as a new father, so I didn't fear his return. Not tonight, anyway. That evening we ate our bread and dripping supper in silence, all awestruck by the magic of the day's events.

CHAPTER 9

Christmas Party

1937

Slam! The front door crashed open. Pa ran in, his face wild. 'There's a bloody riot goin' on out there!'

We were sitting round the kitchen table. It was a cold October day. I was peeling spuds ready for that night's dinner before leaving for work, while the others were in various states of undress.

'What, Ted?' said Ma. 'Slow down. I thought you said a riot.' She folded up the dry sheet ready for sleeping on tonight.

'I tell you, Em, there's a bloody riot on the streets of Bermondsey, there's coppers left, right an' centre, there's fightin' and it's all because of them fascists. Blackshirts they call themselves, an' a right lot of dodgy geezers they are, I can tell you. I won't be in for me dinner. I'm goin' back out there wiv Reg to teach them fascists a lesson they won't forget in an 'urry!' Pa roared, then turned and flew back out of the door.

'I'd 'eard a rumour there was goin' to be trouble down our way, but I never thought it'd kick off so badly. You'd better all stay at 'ome today. I don't want you goin' into the streets if you'll be in danger,' said Ma, as we all rushed to the parlour window to look into the road.

We'd noticed there seemed to be more people milling about this morning, and now we knew why. Ron and Les cheered. Ron instantly said he wanted to go out and join in the fighting but Ma gave him such a stern look that he didn't mention it again.

*

The day passed in a state of anxiety. I was worried that if I didn't go into work, my boss would think I was a slacker, like my Pa. What if he docked my pay or, worse, sacked me? We needed that extra money, but there was nothing I could do to contact the factory. Ma was determined none of us should leave the house. As the day passed, we heard the swell of a great crowd, and the sound of horses' hooves and things being thrown. It wasn't until the evening that Pa returned with the smell of beer on his breath and an excited look on his face.

'All the dockers were there 'elpin' to fight the Blackshirts. There was a queue of 'em a mile long stretchin' back. I ain't never seen nuffink like it. We got 'em. We put 'em to rights, but, Em, I tell you, it ain't safe out there tonight. It did us dockers the world of good though, 'avin' a proper punch-up! Those Nazi buggers got it, ha!' Pa laughed. He drew his hands through his hair.

'It gives me a mind to celebrate,' he added, winking at Ma.

'What d'you mean, Ted?' said Ma, frowning.

'I've decided, in honour of beatin' up them fascists, we're goin to 'ave a Christmas booze-up,' he declared. Pa sat down heavily on his favourite chair and rolled himself some baccy. He took a pinch of snuff from an old battered metal box and sniffed it off the back of his hand.

'Oh, are we now?' replied my mother, putting her hands on her hips and looking at That Man, barely disguising her sarcasm. 'An' where are we goin' to get the money for that?' she added, looking pointedly at Pa as he got up to check his reflection in the rusty mirror above the fireplace.

He looked at his face, this way and that, licked his fingers and smoothed his hair back, black and gleaming, taking his time to reply and enjoying the feeling of power that gave him, no doubt. *He must have another fancy woman*, I thought to myself, my heart sinking for Ma. He always made this effort when he had another on the go, as he did most of the time. I didn't know how Ma stood for it.

'Well. Don't you worry yerself, Em. We're 'avin' a party an' that's that. I'll get old Bill from the pub to let us 'ave a barrel of the good stuff, I'll twist 'is arm I'm sure of that,' he finished, obviously liking what he saw in the mirror. He was cockier than usual tonight. The riots had obviously fired him up.

He hitched up his belt, and pulled on his coat. 'I might just go an' 'ave a word wiv 'im. Don't wait up for me,' he said, and with that he sloped towards the door, checking his visage one last time, winked at me then headed outside, whistling a ditty as he went.

I didn't dare look at Ma. She knew as well as I did that when Ted Johnson behaved like that, he was up to no good. There was little she could do, so what was the point worrying? 'What the eyes don't see, the 'eart don't feel', or that's what her mother said to her as a girl. Didn't make much sense to me. You didn't have to see him with his floozy to know he had one, and that had to hurt Ma. Still, Christmas was a few weeks away and he was sure to forget all about it by then. He'd most probably be too busy stealing what he could from East Street Market again to think about a knees-up. I don't suppose he'd ever bought a turkey in his life. He'd thieve that, and more besides, for our Christmas dinner, but at least it put food on the table.

But he didn't forget all about it. The next thing we heard was that the whole of the local pub was invited, as well as our neighbours. Ma spent the next two months worrying about whether she could put on a decent 'spread' or not. I hadn't lost my job after that day spent hiding from the riot, my pay hadn't been docked by the factory either. So, to help out, I gave her back the shilling she allowed me from my weekly wage packet, saying it was 'worth it to see you stop your worryin''. The extra money was enough to get extra bread for sandwiches, a pack of cheap Stork margarine and three eggs for an extra cake.

Christmas was always a struggle. Each week through the year, Ma put away a few pennies into the Christmas Club, like most people round here. Each week the club man would knock at the door and she would give him what she could, and he would write it in her book religiously. It meant that by the time the littl'uns got excited about Father Christmas and presents, she could afford to put some nuts and an orange in our stockings, and there would always be a present for each of us on Christmas morning, alongside whatever spoils Pa managed to bag.

The date of the party, Saturday, 18 December 1937, finally arrived. All of the children were excited as they'd been told by Pa they could stay up as long as they wanted, even though they rarely got to bed early. Pa had been practising some of his favourite songs on the piano in the parlour, and the table was set with a small fruit cake, a pile of bread and marg, some scones that Ma had made for the guests and a Victoria sponge cake. It wasn't much, considering how long we'd been putting by a bit extra.

Pa was as good as his word and had acquired a barrel of beer, which was already going down a treat. By the time the first guests arrived, in the early afternoon, he was already tipsy. His voice was loud as he made jokes and laughed. We loved seeing him like that, because for a brief moment we could believe he was the jovial, loving father we'd always wished for. Seeing him smiling and joking with the littl'uns,

I almost forgot the many bad times, so desperate was I for a glimpse of kindness from him.

It never lasted long. And today would be no different... But for that moment we forgot all his bad ways and got caught up in his burst of infectious good humour.

The party got under way. The front door was left open – there was no point in shutting it as everyone was invited. Ma's face got redder with the little beer she drank and the bustle of the party in full swing. Dad was regaling the crowd with jolly songs that became ruder the more he drank. His was a rough London voice, there was no grace in his singing, but he knew how to put on a show. The beer was flowing, and it wasn't long before the mood started to change.

Voices became rowdy, and none more so than Ted Johnson's. He shouted above the crowd, and then suddenly it all went horribly wrong. I don't know the exact moment when the atmosphere turned, but turn it did, and it went bad for all of us.

The first I knew of it was when Ma's voice could be heard above the din of voices and the clatter of out-of-tune piano keys. 'I saw you, Ted Johnson, don't you deny it! I saw you an' your girlfriend there, don't you DARE deny it...' Ma was clearly half-cut herself, as she never normally raised her voice. She hardly ever drank either. Maybe my father had finally driven her to drown her sorrows.

Then Pa's voice boomed back at her. 'What are you on about, you nosy cow? You're seein' fings. I ain't got no girlfriend. So wot if I like the look of a pretty girl and want to talk to 'er? Ain't nuffink wrong with that. And anyway, what's it to you?'

He was starting to build up steam. The crowd started to register confusion, and then we heard a wail from little Patsy, who was still a babe in Ma's arms. The crowd parted as I walked towards the source of the disturbance, my heart pounding in my chest. Ron and Les were there too, both of them looking as upset and furious as I felt.

'Put the fuckin' baby down, you cunt, an' I'll giv you what's comin' to you,' shouted Pa, brandishing his fist, and giving Ma the hardest stare I'd ever seen. With his clump of greased black hair shining with the boot polish he'd applied to it, and his features twisted into anger and his stocky, muscled frame ready for a fight, he looked terrifying.

'Oh, you're goin' to threaten us in front of all your pals, are you?' she shouted back.

I admired her courage, but knew this was only ever going to end up one way. *Don't put the baby down*, I kept thinking. *Just leave the room, Ma, an' let Pa 'ave 'is fancy woman. It ain't worth the bother.*

Pa shouted again, this time more menacingly, 'If you don't put that fuckin' baby down I'll give you both what's comin' to you!'

Ma looked startled, and then, clearly moved by maternal devotion, she turned to one of the neighbours and handed over the baby.

We all looked at Ted Johnson, waiting for his reaction. The air in the room at once became thicker, swollen with expectation. The crowd of roistering friends and neighbours was suddenly frozen with expectation. We looked on, hushed, standing round my parents like we were round a boxing ring. There was a sense of unreality as we all watched Pa to see what he'd do next. Even though most of us were scared of him, no one could take their eyes off him. I prayed in that moment that he wouldn't really carry out his threat. *There must be a good 'art inside that black canker of a body*, I thought to myself and pleaded with God. But there wasn't. And God didn't hear me.

With a move of swift economy, That Man felled his wife with one hammer blow to the face. He hit her the way I've seen men hit each other while queuing for work at the dock gates. It was fast and efficient. Time seemed to slow to a stop. I saw Ma's cheek wobble as she reeled back from the impact. A line of spittle escaped from her damaged mouth. Pa toppled Ma with one mighty blow. I looked up at him, briefly. I saw the look of intense concentration on his face, then his leer as he watched her go down.

Ma gave a sudden outbreath. Time righted itself and sped forwards. She lay crumpled on the floor, blood tracing down the side of her jaw from her open mouth. Her eyes shut, her hands clutched her face.

By now us kids were all in tears: Ron was sobbing and even Les had tears running down his smut-ridden cheeks. None of us moved. We didn't dare. Pa stepped back, satisfied with what he'd done. He drew his fingers through his hair, pulling it out of his eyes and looked around at the room. There was silence for a brief second, then the hullabaloo broke out. All at once everyone scattered, knowing that once Ted Johnson had got a temper on him he was likely to go berserk. The room cleared, leaving us children wailing in fright, and Ma still in a daze from the blow that had knocked her down.

Then, just as suddenly, That Man strode out of the room, grabbing his flat cap as he went. His hand reached for his pocket and we heard the jingle of coins, and with that the door slammed shut. Ma was already pulling herself up and touching her nose gingerly. Blood dripped down onto the floor, making puddles that sank into the floorboards.

'I'll get you a cloth, Ma. 'Ere, Black Mog, take the baby while I get this mess sorted,' I said, as briskly as I could manage, trying to arrest the shock we all felt with some good, old-fashioned stiff upper lip.

'I'm alright, 'ilda, I'm fine. Pa's 'ad one too many, that's all it was. 'E'll be alright when 'e's 'ad a chance to calm down,' Ma said.

I looked doubtful, but said nothing. Pa's moods came on him in fits and starts and it was their unpredictable nature that made him so frightening to us kids. If he'd won a fight down in Blackfriars, or won a bet on the dogs, then he'd buy anyone a beer, and sometimes if he was feeling generous, he'd even bring home a small bar of chocolate, for us to share while we listened to him regaling us with his victories. But when it went bad for him, it went bad for us too. There was no accounting for it. His emotions changed in a flash and left us reeling. It wasn't just his temper, it was his way of dominating us so completely that we had to feel whatever it was he was feeling. It was that I could never forgive him for.

He'd had a hard life, though, had Pa, there was no doubting that. His father had beaten him, much like he beat Ma and me. Imagine that, his father used to make him walk two miles on his own from Spa Road, where dad's Ma and Pa also used to live, to Blackfriars Road to beg in the street for ha'pennies, at the age of six. If he didn't bring home enough money then Grandpa Harry Johnson would beat him with his belt. His mother Annie Smith died in St Thomas' Hospital when Ted was only a year old, in 1902. He lived with his grandma until his pa got him, and he was brought up by him and his stepmother. By Pa's account, he became the housewife, doing the housework, scrubbing the floors, cleaning the knives and forks, and getting hidings from his father to boot. I could barely believe that Pa knew how to clean, I saw little enough proof of it in our house, but he swore it was true. He tried to run away to his grandma's but his Pa went and fetched him back. He always said his stepma beat him as well, even saying she'd poured boiling hot water on him as a child as a punishment. He'd also seen his pa regularly beat her until he went off to fight in the Great War, returning in 1916 so badly shell-shocked he lost his sight for a year.

I suppose Pa didn't stand a chance. His world was one of chaos and violence right from the start. His life was set from the minute he was born. Pa had nothing, and nobody ever gave him anything.

By the age of 15 he was working on the dockside as a lighterman on a tug at Hays Wharf for 25 shillings a week. He fled the violence at home not long afterwards, joining the Army Service Corps, working as a cartman driving a horse and van for 30 shillings a week. It was the Army that first gave Pa his taste for boxing. Suddenly, all the beatings he'd received as a boy could, in his twisted way, be revenged on countless, nameless opponents. He soon began winning medals at the Regimental Boxing Shows, boasting of his triumphs to his fiancée Emily, my Ma. He married her on discharge from the Army, and before long Ma was pregnant with me so he was looking for work. Ma's father put in a good word for him at the Port of London Authority Docks Committee.

Ted was granted a Brass Tally (dockers were given an oval-shaped brass tally to hand in whenever they were given work and they would collect it at the end of the day with their pay. If they didn't get work, they would have to sign on at the Labour Exchange with their brass tally as proof) that meant he could work in any dock around the country, so he started at Tower Bridge Wharf earning 10/6 a day. From there he moved to Butler's Wharf, working aboard ships, loading and unloading their exotic wares. Pa's life was a grinding mix of queuing long hours for work, fighting off other men down at the dock gates, then working up to 18 hours a day hauling the goods off the ships and into storage. It was a life of drudgery, broken only by the bouts of heavy drinking in the pub and the hard-won limelight of his pugilist infamy.

There were plenty of men like Pa in the East End – working for a pittance, knowing their life was the lowest of the low, and then going off the rails with the rage and despair of poverty. My face bore the telltale signs of his rampaging, he had broken it many times and it became permanently swollen and red. I only had to look in the mirror to understand Ted Johnson's frustrations. I was lucky that my employers and friends chose to ignore my many injuries. There were many other girls at the factory who came in to work with a black eye, or worse, so it was not that unusual. He was legendary down at The Ring, where all the local hard men and crooks used to go to watch or take furious illegal bets in the makeshift ring made of rope, but to me, he was a failed man, a brute who cared little for those he should protect and love.

And now we had to wait for his return, no doubt with more grog inside him, and the leftover threat of his temper tantrums. While Ma recovered, I swept the parlour. I put away as much of the food as I could salvage, and washed down the table. I then filled the enamel kettle with water from the big jug and set it to boil on the range. Once it was hot, I took the scrubbing brush and set to work on the floor, removing all traces of the spoiled party, including the bloodstains, and giving me something to do rather than sit and fret over Pa's imminent return.

About an hour later the door went, and his dockers' boots announced his arrival. It wasn't yet closing time at the shops which lined the end of our street, and Pa took out a penny and handed it to Leslie.

'Les, d'you know what that penny is for?' he said with a leer.

Les shook his head. I stopped my scrubbing and stood up, brush in hand, waiting for the inevitable bad news.

'That there's for a ruler. I want you three to go down to the store and buy one for me,' he said with relish. He'd planned this, whatever it was.

'Then you three are goin' to come straight back 'ere an' you're goin' to get a beatin' from that there ruler, d'you understand?' he said, almost softly.

Les's face went white. He nodded in resignation, turning away from the spite in Pa's eyes.

Me, Ron and Les put on our coats and walked slowly down to the general store. I could feel my palms sweating in fear, and the three of us were silent as we walked. At age eight and twelve, Ron and Les were normally as badly behaved as any boys, whooping with fun and creating mischief. But today was different. Today they were scared little boys, and my heart bled for them.

We bought the ruler and walked back home, barely saying a word, steeling ourselves for the inevitable punishment that awaited us. Inside the house, once the door was shut, Pa did his worst. He told us all to line up in front of him, all of us except Joanie of course. She had disappeared out after the party exploded and still hadn't returned.

' 'Old out yer 'ands,' ordered Pa. We could do little but obey.

'Turn yer palms over,' he added. His voice was full of sneering contempt.

We stood in front of him, our bare, pink palms held flat, naked. We waited.

Pa took his time. He liked to revel in his power over us.

Then came the stinging of the first slap from the ruler. It slapped onto my right palm and I jumped, squeezing my eyes shut.

It came again, this time harder, then again. My palm was red raw and burning. He then hit my left hand. I jumped again. Ron started crying. Les was silent but I could feel the hurt and rage coming off him in waves.

Pa hit me again and again. I refused to cry. I didn't want to give him the pleasure of seeing me weep like a little girl. Then Pa moved to Ron, who trembled as he stood next to me. There was nothing I could do to stop what was coming. I prayed hard for Ron to be brave, for Les to contain his building anger, so that this would be over as quickly as possible.

From the corner of the room, Ma was watching. Her face an agony of pain for us. I couldn't bear seeing her looking so distraught, but there was nothing I could do.

The ruler swished through the air, again and again. The sound of the sharp smacks filling the room. Ron sobbed. Les stood, surly, receiving his punishment.

But what were we punished for? Because we'd witnessed Pa beating Ma? Because we'd refused to wipe the horror of what we were seeing off our faces, perhaps?

Pa didn't say. He grunted when he finished. And the three of us shuffled upstairs to add our tears to those already shed by Ma.

The Christmas party became a legend in our road, for all the wrong reasons. For a while, neighbours refused to catch our eyes, instead patting us on the head or touching our arms in a show of sympathy, and, perhaps, even solidarity. Mr Brown, who ran the general store at the end of the road, gave the littl'uns each a biscuit when they next went in. It was the place we'd bought that bloody ruler and it made them sick to our stomachs to have to go back.

But we didn't have long to lick our wounds. There were darker forces at work outside of our borough. Pa came home each night with the news, relaying the rumours that swirled like dust in the ale houses. Germany had annexed Austria. Chamberlain was suing for peace. Britain was doing everything it could to keep peace in Europe. But that just meant that if we failed, there could well be a war on the horizon, and we all went to our beds each night with the same prayer. Please, God, keep us safe. Please, God, no more fighting. Please, God, no more suffering. We'd had plenty of that already.

CHAPTER 10

'Oppin'

1940

'Come on you lazy so-an'-so's, get yerselves out the 'ouse!' cried Pa from the wheel of a great big truck parked up outside our doorstep. His face stuck out of the side window and he was beaming, his cap sitting at a jaunty angle on his head. He always knew how to make an impression, did Pa, and on days like this we were glad of it, despite his many, many faults.

Pa had somehow borrowed himself a vehicle so we could all go hop picking down in Faversham, in the far reaches of Kent. It was the first time we'd ever left our little corner of London and we couldn't have been more excited were we going to the moon.

'Alright, Ted, we're comin'. It would 'elp if you gave us an 'and!' shouted Ma, with a huge smile on her face, as she hurried round checking we hadn't forgotten anything. There was a pile of our things stacked carelessly by the front door. We had to take with us everything we'd need, including the enamel cooking pots, blankets, clothes and tinned food.

Pa jumped out of the truck cab and started loading up the truck, throwing in our stuff and whistling a tune as he worked.

'Now, 'ilda, what 'ave I forgotten?' she said with a sigh and a wink.

'Nuffink, Ma, we've got everything we need,' I replied, giving her arm a quick squeeze.

It was a relief to see Ma look happy. More and more frequently she complained of feeling breathless and tired, she looked pale, and her feet and legs were swollen with dropsy by the end of her hard-working day. I was worried about her, but knew there was nothing I could do to help, except take on more of the chores and look after my younger siblings. I'd have given anything to see her smile, and so we were all in high spirits, buoyed up by her good mood, which shone a light over all of us.

Today she was bright as a button. Her ubiquitous apron was packed in her string bag, and she looked like a proper lady with her simple blouse, skirt and hair tied back off her lovely face.

Despite being old enough, at 11 and 15 years old, to know better, Ron and Les were still behaving like street urchins. They'd wandered off this morning, narrowly escaping a belting from Pa because they'd been late back from the 'sandy beach' on the Thames where they still played most evenings. They'd caused a fracas earlier when Ron, in an act of mischief, tied up Les's shoe laces while he wasn't looking, causing Les to fall flat on his nose and giving him a nose bleed. Ma wasn't happy about that, but Les didn't seem to mind too much, and once the blood stopped flowing, he was able to continue helping with our packing

By the time we were all set for the off, it was already midday, and Pa was impatient to get going. With one last look round the house, Ma finally shut the front door with a slam. It was the start of September 1940, and it had been a hot summer. The streets of Bermondsey were dirty and dusty, there were flies everywhere and the sweet-sour stench of our neighbourhood was overpowering. By day the children all hung out on the streets, playing games and running wild. By night, the pubs were full of men slaking their thirst and escaping the cramped, overheated rooms they all lived in. All of us longed to leave behind the piles of horse dung, and the smell of carbolic from the lines of washing that hung in zigzags across the yards, rows and rows of nappy squares drying in the heat.

Les and Ron were fighting over who got to sit up front, so Pa put a stop to that by raising his fist. They both fell silent and settled in the back, then a minute later were squabbling over something else. Both were scratching their heads, and I shouted at Ron to, 'Stop itchin' your 'ead, you're showin' us all up,' knowing they'd probably got nits again.

I had dressed four-year-old Patsy earlier, and made sure Joanie was ready to go while Ma had packed up some food supplies, a huge pile of sandwiches made with lard and a pinch of salt. At last we were ready. Ma got in the back and I lifted Patsy onto her lap. Joanie went in next and I followed. Only the men ever sat at the front of the truck. It was always women and children in the back. But at last we were in and ready for our big adventure.

'Are you all ready?' said Pa with spirit, flicking his cigarette end out of his mouth onto the dusty road.

'Yessss!' we all replied.

'I didn't 'ear you. Are you all ready to go 'oppin'?' he hollered.

'YES!!' we all shouted back. 'We're off 'oppin'!' added Ron with a flourish of his cap.

And with that, Pa pulled off from the kerb and drove the truck down past the little line of shops, past the town hall and out of Spa Road.

What a novelty it was, watching the familiar streets of our borough from so high up, and we squealed and squabbled until we finally left London behind. From narrow streets, with dark tenements and crowded rooms, where the sky was only ever a small square of grey above us, to then be greeted by wide, blue skies, punctured with streaks of cloud which soared into the heavens, was amazing. We couldn't believe our luck!

For the past couple of years we'd been living with the fear that the threat of war had brought into our lives. For months we'd been discussing Prime Minister Neville Chamberlain's attempts to appease Germany and its Nazi dictator Adolf Hitler. We'd held our breath as the Munich Agreement was signed, hoping and praying it meant war could be averted. There was little other talk on the street. Ma would be out reddening her steps, chatting with the other housewives about whether our nation would be sending its sons and fathers out to fight again. None of us really believed it was possible. Yet as time passed, the sense of a storm approaching grew and grew. It was almost a relief when, at 11 a.m. on 3 September 1939, war against Germany was declared.

We were barely aware of the political and social turmoil that surrounded our little island, but we all knew there was a war on. You couldn't miss the posters that popped up as if from nowhere on our buses and walls, telling us to 'Dig for Victory' and 'Take Your Gas Mask Everywhere'. At first, we quite liked the colour they brought to our streets, then, as the messages started sinking in, we realised how serious our plight was. Food rationing had started earlier in 1940. Gas masks had been distributed and each of us carried our brown cardboard box on a string containing the rubber mask, which was stuffed with cotton wads. It became second nature to take it with us.

We feared gas attacks, of course we did, but the question on everyone's lips, from the dockers to the Lord Mayor himself, was, when would the Germans start the bombing raids they promised us Londoners? So far, the start of the war had been a bit of a letdown – nothing had really happened.

We knew of families who had sons and fathers out fighting, we even knew a few whose loved ones had already died, but somehow it hadn't touched our lives in any significant way yet, apart from the inconveniences of shopping for food.

Conscription hadn't stopped Pa from dodging his patriotic duty. Pa got out of being called up by visiting a back-street doctor in Blackfriars, who sold certificates for a few shillings saying he was unfit to be enlisted, so life carried on for us pretty much as normal. It was just another example of That Man shirking his responsibilities, and all the more despicable because he was a fighter and more than capable of armed combat. He would never have risked his fat neck for King and country. He acted only for himself, as he proved time and time again by his selfish actions. Dodging the draft was simply another way of him wheeling and dealing his way through life for the benefit of Ted Johnson and no one else.

Each week the papers predicted that German bombers would tear up our grey patches of sky and drop bombs on our city. At first we'd believed them, and then as time went on, and nothing really happened, we all settled back into our routine. All in all, the war seemed a long way off to us.

Suddenly the truck lurched forwards. We'd left the narrow streets of London and were somewhere in the country, where the skies looked huge and there seemed to be barely any people in sight. We blinked at the sight of trees and tall rows of hop bines that towered along the country lanes. We'd reached our destination, nearly 50 miles away from Bermondsey. It had taken us almost three hours. The road became a pot-holed track, flinging us to and fro in the back. We clung on for dear life until we ground to a halt.

I got out first then helped the others. It was only after dusting down our skirts and readjusting our turbans that

Ma and I could get a proper look round. There seemed to be hundreds of families, many of whom we recognised from our road. Whole streets were given hop cards, sent by the farmers in August to allocate us our spot, despite the fact there was a war on. There was a line of makeshift tin huts leaning into the field, which was rigid with lines of tall hop plants that seemed to look over us like giants.

Pa gave us a shout and we turned to see him with the farm foreman. 'Your hut's over there. You'll find everything you need in there. The water pump's out back of the farm, and there's milk and eggs for sale.

'You start work at 7 a.m. tomorrow morning and finish at 5 p.m.. No picking after 5 p.m., that's the rule around here,' said the – to us – well-spoken man with a slight Kent burr to his voice. I ogled him like he was an alien. I'd never heard anyone speak posh like that who wasn't on the wireless!

We gathered our bits and Pa marched into the hut, with us trailing in his wake. The hut had earthen floors and long wooden pallets called 'duck boards', upon which were our palliasses made of old linen that we filled with straw from the farm. There was little else.

Ma got busy with unpacking and I helped her as best I could, while the others, bursting with excitement and the frustration of the long drive, skipped off into the fields to greet the other children. Pa shouted after them to fetch firewood while they were at it. We set the huts to right, filled the pitcher with water from the farmyard pump, and set out the food for our dinner. Pa busied himself making the campfire, and we put the pot on to boil up some water.

'A cuppa will see us right,' said Ma. She sounded tired.

'I'll see to that, Ma,' I answered as she yawned and gave me a grateful smile.

'Blow me, there ain't no lavvies 'ere. Some bloke just said

we've got to use an 'ole in the field!' exclaimed Pa, who'd been in and out of the hut, looking for his mates and 'gettin' adjusted', as he put it.

'I ain't usin' no 'ole in the woods,' said Ma, her face set with a grimace. 'It's disgustin', that's what it is,' she recoiled.

Pa and I laughed in rare fellowship.

The next morning we were up early. None of us had slept well on the straw bedding as it was prickly and uncomfortable. Pa stood outside the hut with his first morning fag while Ma sliced bread for breakfast. By 7 a.m., all of us except Patsy, who was still too young to pick, were ready with our hop carts and off we went.

Of course, hopping wasn't a holiday, we weren't daft enough to think that, but the money we would earn from our week spent hopping would be a vital part of our yearly income. From early morning we worked hard, picking and sorting the hops from the leaves, though there were a few leaves left in those carts to weigh them down a bit. We got paid in bushels – five bushels made a shilling. Each bushel contained eight gallons of hops. It was back-breaking work, and boring too, but it would earn us a small fortune.

There was just enough room between the hop bines to work two abreast, but by lunchtime I realised it was just Ma, Joanie and I picking; the boys had disappeared off exploring again, while Pa had sloped off to the pub saying he had 'a docker's thirst'.

When the hop carts were full of the bristly hops, we'd add them to the bushels and they'd eventually be added to the poke, the cloth bag used to transport vast quantities to the oast house. Our bushels would then be added into our book, logged by the foreman, and at the end of the week we'd be paid our wages. What didn't get spent by Pa down the pub would be squirrelled away by Ma.

The warm, hoppy smell was a welcome change from the squalor of our streets back home, while the children with their pale skin and stick-thin legs were half-wild with excitement at this chance to run free in the surrounding fields. It was like heaven, even though it was hard work, and it was an extra bonus for Ron and Joanie as they were taken out of school to go hopping. I'd been given permission by my boss at Peek Frean's – they were better than most employers for giving occasional time off.

That evening, Ma and I made dinner, with the potatoes we'd brought from home and a little meat bought from the farmer, all cooked on the paraffin heater. Our fingers looked black in the light of the flame from our day's work stripping the vines. The stew was thick and hot, and we all ate in companionable silence around the fire. There were people milling about, chatting and laughing; some were singing hopping songs that we didn't yet know the words to. It was a spectacle, and even Pa stayed jolly, only getting up to leave for a drink after dinner.

Later, Ma settled the younger ones down into bed while I rinsed the plates. The children went out like a light after all the fresh air and exercise. The sounds took on a murmuring quality, and Ma and I spent the rest of the evening watching the fire and chatting now and then.

Ron was first up the next morning. He shook us all awake as he was desperate to get out and play. The day started much as the day before: breakfast then the beginning of a long working day, bending and reaching for those hops. We ate our lunch, finished the milk bought earlier from the farm, and set about stripping the bines through the afternoon. For some reason, Ron had decided to stay with us, picking and chattering non-stop, as he did so.

Then the world as we knew it changed, irrevocably. The sky seemed to go darker. There was the heavy drone of something above us, something that sounded like low, deep thunder. The noise built and built.

All of the pickers, as one entity, looked skywards. Above our heads were the unmistakable shapes of hundreds of planes, spread as one huge mass above us. There was silence for a brief moment, then a woman somewhere further down the line screamed. The sound of her cry set off a feral fear in me, much like a cornered animal might feel.

'Oh Gawd, Ma, what's 'appenin'?' I spoke without moving my eyes from those big, black planes that covered the sky as far as we could see. My voice sounded unreal, tense as tripwire. The planes were moving as one great beast, across the sky, moving steadily towards London, leaving vapour trails behind them.

Then, in an instant, the crackle of gunfire sounded. Instinctively I ducked, as did many others. We'd all stopped picking and were standing with our eyes shaded against the afternoon sun.

'It's started,' said Ma, with a finality that made me shiver.

All of a sudden, more planes arrived in formation, tacking through the airway with gunfire blazing in retaliation.

'Must be ours,' said a man behind me. 'Yeah, them planes, they must be our boys,' he said louder, and with that a cheer rose up from the line of pickers.

'Get the bastards!' shouted another man, punching the air with his fist curled round his cap.

Another, joined in, 'Do your worst! Knock them Jerries outta the sky!'

There were jeers and shouts from others, but we watched spellbound as the normal fabric of our lives rent into pieces.

'They're 'eadin for London,' said a woman to my left. Her voice was flat.

There was nothing else to say. They were heading for our home with only a small battery of RAF pilots to stop them in their tracks.

With a ratta-tat, one of ours swooped from high up in the clouds, roaring through the skies. Suddenly the sky was filled with a dense stream of black smoke as one of the Jerry bombers nosedived to the ground. A great cheer went up among the hoppers. Our planes ducked and dived around the vast mass of enemy aircraft, with sudden flames of gunfire rattling through the airwaves. But the German planes kept their path, staying in their formation as much as they could, one great man-made killing machine.

I shivered. The day was warm but the war had finally become a reality. Ron and Les went wild as another German plane was brought crashing down out of the sky in a blaze of red flame and thick black smoke. The boys were excited by the fighting above us, but I could only feel deep fear.

'Go on, giv 'im one,' yelled Ron.

'Go on, boys, get the bloody Jerry bastards,' added Les, delighted to be able to use the swear words he'd spent his life hearing from his father.

'Ron, Les!' Ma's voice was sharp. 'I don't ever want to 'ear you swear again, d'you 'ear me?'

'Sorry, Ma,' they both said, keeping their eyes firmly on the skies, hopping from one leg to another with the agitation and excitement of it. They were so young, I thought, just little boys really, even though there was only four years between Les and me.

One by one, the RAF planes were picked off by the

German fighter planes as they charted their direct course to our city. A plane came down, careering low over our heads and we all ducked, involuntarily. 'One of ours,' said a man in front of us, and several others leapt after it, hoping to get there in case they could help whoever was unlucky enough to be inside that death machine of twisted, melting metal.

As we watched them go, a great wail set off: the air-raid siren had started.

There was immediate panic. Shaken out of our fascinated torpor as we gawped up at the skies, suddenly the threat from the planes became very real. Some people ran to the nearby woods for shelter, others stayed to watch the skies. All of a sudden there was a great yell from one of the tin huts and the door burst open. Joanie was as naked as the day she was born, and she came running out, trailing water from the bath she was taking, screaming in panic! She didn't seem to care that every red-blooded hopper was now staring at her with delight despite the fact we should be running for shelter.

'Joanie, get yerself covered up! My Gawd, girl, what's got into you?' shouted Ma as she ran towards Joanie and directed her into our hut. The rest of us ran for the woods, but no bombs fell on us. They were saving them for our beloved city.

Our hearts thumping, we ran through thick undergrowth into the thicket of trees and vegetation. It had dawned on us that all our friends and family were in danger. With a wail, Ron started to cry. I tried to comfort him but what could I say? Our pals and neighbours were in the direct line of those bombers and there was nothing any of us could do to help them, except pray.

Gradually, we crept back to our campfires. None of us could bear to work any more. We sat round in groups warming ourselves by the fires and talking in low voices. The enormity of the day's events had made us feel small, and very scared.

The sun began setting. The sky flared orange then sank into darkness, yet there was a glow of red on the horizon.

'They're bombin' our city,' said Pa, and none of us could say anything to that.

We tried to carry on as if it was a normal evening. I tucked up Joanie and Patsy in bed, and looked round for Ron. He was standing at the door of the hut looking out at the distant city, which looked almost pretty with flares of red light. It was the sight of London burning.

He turned his small face to me and said, ' 'ilda, what does it mean?'

I could only shake my head in reply. We stood there, watching the distant flames devour our city. 'Will we 'ave an 'ome to go back to?' he asked in his small-boy's voice, and I couldn't answer that either.

Days later, we woke to find Pa loading up the truck. It was time to head back home, if, indeed, we still had one. Our journey back to London couldn't have been more different from our departure. Gone was the jollity and the laughter. As every mile passed, I wanted to shout at Pa to turn back. I didn't want to see my beloved Bermondsey in flames.

Driving through the outskirts of London was like driving into a film set. Gone were some of the buildings, instead there were the shells of houses and warehouses, and piles of brick and rubble that once housed people and industry. The closer to home we got, the more silent and watchful we became. There was a pall of smoke hanging over the streets. Firemen were still hosing down the places where the bombs had struck last night. There was twisted metal, pieces of furniture and even children's toys strewn across the streets. So many lives destroyed. So much devastation. I don't think any of us could really believe our eyes.

We had to deviate from our route many times as roads were impassable. Eventually we turned into Spa Road, and we gave a small, embattled cheer as we rumbled down the street to see our friends' and neighbours' houses were, miraculously, still there. Pa drew up outside number 42, our house. It was standing.

We jumped down off the truck, and were instantly met by people from the neighbouring houses bombarding us with questions. Did we know what had happened to old man Ernest? He'd copped a direct hit in one of the shelters under the arches. My guts seemed to twist inside me. I had never been so close to death. Old man Ernest was one of those characters I thought I'd see every day. He whistled as he hobbled up our street for his daily paper and small supplies of bread and milk. We always said ' 'ello', and he tipped his cap to Ma and me. Sometimes he would offer us kids a sticky sweet from a brown paper bag and we'd accept, grateful for the kind gesture. Now we'd never see him again. It brought death right to the heart of our lives and, suddenly, the world seemed an even more frightening place.

More questions followed from the huddle of people gathered around us. Was it true the vinegar factory had taken a direct hit? Did we see the bombers come over? How many of them were there? And we had our own questions in response. What was the bombing like? Where did we go if it started tonight? Had anyone else we knew been killed?

We stayed out talking for a long time, just milling about, getting to know this strange new London we lived in.

That night, Ma asked Pa if we should stay in Bermondsey.

'Where else are we goin' to go, Em?' he replied, and for once he was right. Where could we have gone? London was our home, bombs or no bombs. It looked like we were going to have to make the best of it, as usual. We could do that. We could get to an Underground if the siren went. Most of all, we could stay and carry on with our lives as best we could so that, in this small part of the borough, the Jerries hadn't won. After all, we all knew what it was to stand up to a bully. It hurt, but it had to be done.

Later, when the siren went off, we left the house and ran through the blacked-out streets to London Bridge station, where we joined the queue for passes to stay there overnight. We'd all gone to bed wearing our coats, boots and hats and so it took us only a few minutes to get up and out. It was a strange experience, holding hands with each other, wide-eyed in the darkness, hearing the drone of the overhead engines and praying we would make it to safety.

That night the docks, warehouses, wharves and factories in the East End suffered massive bombing raids, unleashing the aroma of burnt cinnamon and ginger into the air along with the smell of the great timber yards which became a furnace. We huddled together on the platform, Ron and Les curling round Pa's legs, while me and Joanie huddled against Ma, who was comforting Patsy. The baby of the family was inconsolable against the muffled noise of the explosions and chaos.

There was barely space to stand, but the atmosphere was upbeat. Some men sat around playing cards, while others sang uplifting songs like 'Roll out the Barrel'. We hardly had any sleep but we were together, and we were safe, despite Patsy's tears.

When the all-clear sounded, just after dawn, we stood up, brushing ourselves down. The first Tube trains had started drawing into the platforms, and workers were having to step over some of the sleeping bodies. It was a surreal and unearthly feeling, like the world had turned on its head. We were reeling as we stepped out into the early morning. There was a mixture of sights: people in uniforms making their way into work, nurses with pale faces riding on bikes, auxiliary firemen wiping their blackened faces and a woman kneeling by the empty space that used to be her home.

Ma put a protective arm around me and shooed us on. Some things weren't meant to be witnessed. Seeing someone lose their home, and most likely, relatives or friends at the same time, was too private to bear. I felt like I was looking at something sacred. The shattered homes looked exposed, somehow, like they were missing their outer wear. Fragments of walls displayed floral wallpaper, shredded into bits. There was a great iron bed hanging over the edge of one destroyed building, the blankets flapping in the breeze. It was like looking at hell. And it was only really the beginning.

CHAPTER 11

Powder and Paint

1941

The undulating wail of the siren rose above the noise of the street. Where a minute ago there was chatter and gossip, as us girls from Peek Frean's walked home together, arm in arm, there was now the silence of terror. Words froze in my throat. The sound was ghostly and yet terribly real. Alongside it was the deep throb of plane engines as the German bombers made their way across Kent and over the outskirts of London. We were under attack again.

The Blitz had become a way of life. Every night our homes and lives were subjected to the terror and bloodshed of the big German bombers. The evening was setting in and the blackout was in force, leaving us little light to guide our way through the dark streets to the nearest shelter. The lampposts and kerbs had been painted white to help us find our way. Me and my friends, Rita and Lily, grabbed each other's hands and started to run wildly, not thinking where we were going.

My thoughts were immediately for my family. I shouldn't have gone out and left them at home for the evening. How would I know if they reached safety tonight? Before I could think any further, a great booming noise came from the area to our right, near the docks, and the sound of buildings collapsing shocked us into moving yet faster. We turned left onto Tooley Street and ran towards London Bridge. As much as it pained me, there was nothing I could do about my family. I had to get underground, and fast. The shattering of buildings as they crumbled into dust, and the wail that seemed to rattle my bones played on and on.

The bombs were falling nearer and nearer. I could hear the engines as they carried the bombers closer: their guttural drone a warning of more bombs to come. Now there were flashes of red and orange as warehouses, shops and homes collapsed into flaming chaos under the incendiaries that rained down upon us.

Panting, almost retching from the hysteria, we stumbled into London Bridge Underground. People were arriving from everywhere like rats from a sinking ship. We pushed into the crowd, praying that we wouldn't be next. A great smash nearby made us scream. There were children sobbing as they were roughly carried down the stairs and into safety. Terrified white-faced women pushed their way through, shouting that they had babies. The crowd moaned in mutual horror as another wave of explosions surrounded us. There was the clatter of gunfire in retaliation, the sudden flaring of light as bombs landed before erupting into flame and black smoke.

Nothing would stop the German air force as they ripped down our city, brick by brick, life by life. My hand was clenched so tightly in Rita's that my knuckles showed white. It wasn't until we reached the platform that our grip relaxed and we could breathe again.

'Gawd, it 'ad to be tonight,' exclaimed Lil, choking with the dust that followed us down into the dimly lit Underground. 'I was on a promise wiv that geezer down at the dance,' she said crossly, her expression furious.

Rita and I looked at each other, then burst into laughter in the face of the adversity we all faced, and Lil's indignant tones.

'Blimey, Lil,' I said, between giggles, 'you'd be on a promise wiv a bigger bang than 'im if you stayed out there tonight! An' anyway the air raids 'ave been goin' on every night for Gawd knows 'ow long – it weren't exactly a surprise!' And we all dissolved into cackles again, releasing the panic of tonight's attack.

When we'd got our breath back we turned and looked around. 'There ain't much space in 'ere. Where the 'ell are we goin' to kip tonight?' pouted Rita.

'Come on, there's space over there,' I said, pointing to the side of the platform near the steps. 'It's not exactly the Ritz but we're together, and we made it down 'ere alive, so we'll make the best of it,' I tried to rally them, with moderate success.

The girls, Rita and Lil, were my best friends from the biscuit factory. We were thick as thieves, and had taken to going out in the evenings before the raids usually started. Tonight's wave of bombing had come earlier than expected, so we'd been forced to run for our lives. I was happy being with them though, even under these circumstances. Having friends outside of home, with all the violence and drama there, was a lifeline for me.

I'd blossomed into a young woman with a love of dancing and laughing, and it was all because of my best pals. I loved my family passionately, but it was this new, treasured freedom that had brought me out of myself. Ironically, since there was a war on, I was the happiest I'd ever been in my life. I was 20 years old, I had a little money in my purse and a new dress made from navy-blue cotton with puffed sleeves and a swishy skirt, which had earned me my first ever wolf whistle the other day. I reckoned life was for living, despite the carnage that surrounded us. In fact, it was the nightly onslaught from enemy planes that forced us to live life to the full. There was no point moping about when you could be dead the next day.

I squeezed Lil's arm and the three of us, arms entwined, picked our way through the bodies of those already crammed in tightly, apologising each time we trod on someone's hand or stray foot. People were already sitting or lying down with blankets. Children were crying or sleeping, some with their dolls or toys, some clenched tightly to their mothers while they waited out the storm being unleashed on our borough. Despite being far under the ground we could feel the earth shaking as bombs hit the homes and factories above us. The booms were relentless but the noise was diluted, which made us feel safe. Before long we were squabbling about who got to sit with their back against the step. Rita won, she always did, so Lil and I leant against her legs and wondered how long it would be tonight.

'I wish I could find out where Ma is tonight,' I worried. It was pointless to say it but I couldn't get my family out of my head. 'At least she's got an Anderson shelter in the yard,' I added, hoping the thought of Ma, Les, Joanie, Ron and Patsy all huddled inside there would make me feel better. There was a small patch of dirt out the back of the house and Pa had dug it out and fitted the corrugated iron shelter, in case the attacks were too close for us to have time to run anywhere else. It didn't look strong enough to withstand the force of an assault, but it was better than nothing.

'I 'ope Ma's in there wiv the others,' I said again, knowing I wouldn't know if they were all right until the raid was over, and that could take all night.

'There's no point in you worryin', 'ilda. There ain't nuffink any of us can do about it. We've all got family out there tonight. They'll be right as rain, you'll see,' said Lil reassuringly, patting my hand for comfort.

'Yes, I'm sure you're right. Sorry, of course we've all got family out there,' I replied, forcing myself to smile, but then wrinkling up my nose in disgust. 'It absolutely stinks in 'ere!' I held my hand up to my nose to try and shield it from the appalling stench of unwashed clothes, sweat and stale tobacco.

'Christ, yes it's disgustin', an' we've got all night to go,' said Rita with a resigned expression. The smells never bothered her. She had eight brothers and sisters and lived in two rooms, so didn't know anything better than overcrowded space and the mingling odours it created. I'd obviously gone soft by living in Spa Road, having four rooms between the seven of us. Even though we had as little money as we'd ever had, and the house was a wreck that we couldn't afford to patch up, I still felt like I was living in a palace compared to our rooms in Bevington Street.

I sighed as we settled down for the long night ahead. The chaos of so many people crammed into the space meant that sleep was virtually impossible. Some lucky buggers had grabbed the bunk beds that lined the inside of the station, but we weren't so fortunate. There was a steady drip, drip of water from the murky ceiling. We wrapped our coats more firmly around us and shared the only food we had, a few broken biscuits given to us by the foreman at the end of our day packing.

'At least we've got supplies,' I said, cheerily. 'That's sumfink – shows there's always a bright side.'

'Aw, 'ilda, you've always got something good to say. That's why I love you,' said Lil. 'Now, who's up for a game of cards?'

The next morning, a long high monotone sound announced that our night in the shelter was over and we'd survived to live another day. It was time to get back to being a worker. We queued and shuffled towards the stairs, fighting against the early morning workers coming towards us. We struggled up till eventually we made it out into the grey morning, gasping with the novelty of leaving behind the stale air and odours from deep inside the station.

It was still early, just before 6 a.m.. I'd caught a few minutes dozing on and off during the night but really we'd had no substantial rest at all. Despite that, I was desperate to see the others and to know they were safe, and so taking a bleary-eyed leave of my friends, I cantered the mile or so back to Spa Road.

The smell of burning was thick in the air. There were still great plumes of smoke rising upwards, covering the horizon with a ghostly pall. Flames licked the skyline. It was obvious that our part of London had taken a pummelling last night. Several buildings on the route were now just enormous piles of smoking rubble, there were puddles of water where water pipes had burst, and people were milling about, some crying, others too shocked to speak as they surveyed the wreckage of their homes, businesses and lives.

I stumbled over a glove, which I reached down to pick up, then recoiled in shock when I realised there was still a hand inside it. I retched at the side of the road. My shock at seeing bodies, and worse still, parts of bodies, lying in the streets we all called home was complete. London had become a place of nightmarish disaster, not the busy metropolis we all knew and loved.

I stumbled on down Tooley Street, past the charred buildings, past the pieces of those poor people lying scattered like rubbish. Now and then, bricks would topple from on high, falling from the wrecked buildings, making me dodge round, all the while breathing in the dust and smoke. I walked on, with my heart beating so loudly in my ears I thought I might burst. With every step I took, my sense of anxiety about my family and their safety increased. Every corner I turned revealed fresh horrors, which made me pant with fear. By the time I got to Tower Bridge Road I was pelting as fast as I could, running through the rubble of the city I adored, desperate to find out if my Ma and the others had survived. How could I have left them? Now, I was mad with terror, berating myself for not running through the bombs to reach them.

My thoughts were a cacophony of anxious questions and unspoken fears, but as I turned into my road, thankfully, they dissipated. There was no need to speak my darkest thoughts because the row of houses was still standing. Miraculously, there seemed to be little damage done to our street. All around us was carnage and despair, but apart from the smoke and dust that hung over it, our road felt like a little island of calm. Most of our neighbours were out on the street, looking up and down, sweeping their steps, hurrying off for work, carrying on with the business of life.

I felt a sudden, and warm, feeling of pride in my community. Whatever happened, we got through thick and thin. The lean times of the Great Depression, the shrinking work at the docks, even a whole load of German bomber planes didn't stop us in our tracks. We dusted ourselves down and we got on with life. I couldn't have been more proud to be a Londoner, and a south-east Londoner at that. The grit and determination of our community, carrying on as normally as we could, impressed me far more than those huge towering machines of metal that rained down death and destruction upon us. We'd see this war through, I could see that in the activity around me.

The town hall, which sat virtually opposite our house, was layered with sandbags, and yet people were starting to turn up for work, undaunted, eager to get on with the war effort.

The coal man was already touting his wares at one end of the street, while the milk lady with her vast milk churn was working the other end. There were dockers hanging around the Queen's Arms, waiting for the landlord to open early so they could have a smoke and a drink before setting off for Surrey Docks.

The men, all hardened, tough people with hardship and poverty etched into their faces, were all of them up and ready for work, as if they hadn't spent last night crouching in damp, cold Anderson shelters or under draughty railway arches. The women were sweeping and talking, shooing away ragged children, getting ready for the day ahead. I loved each and every one of them as I paused there, on my road, for the briefest of moments.

Shaking my head to clear my thoughts, I realised I had the important business of seeing if everyone was okay to deal with. I ran through the front door.

'Gawd, 'ilda, you gave me a start!' exclaimed Ma, holding the kettle and chiding Ron at the same time. 'Now, Ron, if I've told you once, I've told you a thousand times, get your 'ands off the table an' wait for the others to start eatin',' she screeched.

Ron was a handsome boy of 12 and Les about to turn 16. Neither was old enough to enlist, but Les had started saying he wanted to 'get them Jerry bastards', and I realised with a sinking heart it was only a matter of time.

'Now then, 'ilda, get your apron on an' giv me an 'and. I'm dead beat after last night. Patsy wouldn't stop cryin' an' I 'aven't 'ad a wink of sleep. That blinkin' shelter was full of water again. It's 'orrible in there. I don't know why we bother wiv it.'

With that, I grinned; it was business as usual here too. No one looked shell-shocked or frightened. It was an ordinary day in the Johnson household, and no Jerry bomber was going to change that. 'Alright, Ma, just let me get this coat off an' I'll be there. I ain't got much time as I've got to get off meself,' I bantered, grabbing my apron and tying it round my slim waist.

I brushed my tousled thick hair till it resembled a sleeker version than last night's conditions had permitted. I still wore it as a bob but curled it up at the sides as was the fashion. I gave myself a brief look over. There were dark circles under my eyes from lack of sleep, and my skin looked a little paler than normal, but all things considered I looked ready to face the day. I moved a curling tendril of hair back behind its pin and reached for the jug of water to wash with. I wiped a cloth over my face, rubbing away the soot and grime of the Underground, then turned with a cheery, 'Well, I'll be blowed, what's all this noise? You're all louder than a German plane.'

I chuckled as I put my mind to cutting bread and smearing it with marge and jam for Patsy.

Later that day, while I was standing on the factory floor, with girls front and back, all packing their boxes of biscuits, Lil gave me a nudge. She looked to see if the foreman was looking our way, and when she saw he'd wandered off in the opposite direction, she said, 'Pssst, 'ilda, you up for a night on the tiles tonight, if the Jerries don't get in the way, of course? There's a dance on 'ere at the factory, 'an it's only sixpence to get in. What d'yer say?'

I adjusted my hairnet, and smoothed down my white coat, all regulation uniform at Peek Frean's. I cocked a look behind me to check the miserable old git hadn't decided to come back this way, and shouted back, over the hubbub, 'No, I don't think I'm up for it tonight, duckie. Ma's on 'er

own wiv the others, an' I couldn't forgive meself if anything
'appened while I was out. I'd rather stay at 'ome tonight.'

'Oh you're no fun, 'ilda. What's got into you? We might
all be dead tomorrow, so what's the use stayin' in wiv your
mother? You've got to enjoy yerself,' said Lil, mouthing the
words with exaggerated expression so I could get the gist
above the factory's din.

There were men shouting and women talking, and great
sacks of flour being unloaded, huge milk churns upped and
emptied into vast vats. There were hundreds of women in
matching hairnets and coats picking biscuits off the moving
conveyor belt, packing boxes with diligent movements, then,
quick as lightning, checking, sealing and labelling their boxes.
It was a hive of activity, and we always used it as a chance to
catch up with the gossip and make plans for the evenings. But
after last night's panic at the thought of Ma in the Anderson
with the kids, I couldn't go out again.

'Not tonight. You go an' 'ave fun. See if you can't find your
young man again,' I hollered at Lil, one eye on my box, the
other on the garibaldis, which were travelling past me.

'I'll tell you what,' I relented, 'I won't go out but I'll pop
down the Blue wiv you after work so I can get meself that
skirt I wanted.'

'Alright, 'ilda, we'll go down the market, an' I'll bet you'll
look so pretty you won't want to miss out on the fun,' Lil
laughed.

I shook my head but smiled back. Working in the factory
had given me a life I had never dreamt of when it was just
me and Ma at home, looking after the littl'uns and bearing
the brunt of Pa's tempers. Pa was still quick with his fists,
but somehow being a working girl outside of home gave me
hope that in the future I might not always be at his mercy.
The work itself wasn't all that interesting, but being part of a

team of women my own age had opened my eyes to the wider world outside our cramped rooms. I'd always had friends at school, and playing away from home had helped me grab precious hours away from the intensity, and the chores. But I'd finally found friends who were more than just an escape. They made me laugh, and I felt like I had a new family, albeit one where music and dancing were the norm, not scrubbing and cooking!

I didn't neglect my home life, my family ties were too strong for that, but I had a new world away from the relentless darning and washing. A world of excitable chatter, flirtations with soldiers on leave in London, and, most of all, friendship.

When the home-time hooter went, we all trooped out as part of a great surging mass of men and women to wait in front of the factory gates. Every night we stood there, fidgeting and gossiping until they were finally opened and we could pour out into the streets. There must have been several thousand workers in that crowd each night, though the war had removed all the young men our age.

In a few minutes, Lil and I, arm in arm, arrived at the Blue, the main market place in Bermondsey, where I'd seen the skirt I wanted being sold by a man with a suitcase filled with women's clothing. It was nothing fancy. It was a plain brown wool skirt with a satin lining, but I thought it was the smartest thing I'd ever seen. It looked like it would fit me perfectly.

I ummed and ahhhed for a few moments, before reaching for my purse. I didn't need my tokens, I knew my skirt was for sale on the black market, but I wanted it so desperately I bought it anyway. Feeling pleased as punch, I waved goodbye to Lil and headed home.

Started training as usal then I got a
Post Card from the Ring Telling me he has
Put me on the Boxing Bill for the Saturdays
Proffessional Show I am to fight a
Boxer named young George Fox
of Bethnel Green.
So, to the Ring I went on the Saturday night
Show and I met this man Fox in the
Dressing Room he was about my Stamp—
any way I undressed waiting to be called this
being my first Proffessol fight. I could
hear the crowd all Shouting the other
Pair what was on. it Seemed ages before
it was my turn Knowing MR Dan
Sullivn would be looking for me My.
Turn to go into the Ring it came into the Ring
we Both went the announced our names
the Bell Sounded for the first Round
that Ended, out for the Second Round
Down went George Fox I knock his Nose
he was smothered in Blood they stopped
it, so Back to the dressing Room he said
you can Punch Hard. So that was my first
Proffessol Fight. the amatur Boxing Club

(*above*) 'Down went George Fox, I knock[ed] his nose, he was smothered in blood' an excerpt from Ted Johnson's diary with an account of his first 'professional' fight.

(*right*) Ted Johnson standing tall and showing his fighter's physique by the poolside of Tooting Bec open air lido.

(*above right*) A young Ted Johnson (right) in army uniform during the Boer War (1899–1902), throughout which he honed his fighting techniques.

A patriotic occasion with the family in 1922. Ted is dressed in a suit (far left) and the baby next to him is Hilda, being held by Emily.

(*left*) Hilda's home at No. 42 Spa Road in 1933. Hilda (aged 12) stands on the left beside her mother Emily. Ron is at the front and Les stands taller behind him.

(*above*) 'Oppin. The first time the family leaves the smog and squalor of London: hop picking in the fields of Faversham in 1940. Hilda standing in the middle (third from right), with Emily (far right), Ron (front far left) and Les (far right).

School Leaving Certificate

This is to certify that _Hilda Johnson_

of _42 Sha. Rd_ ....is exempt

from the obligation to attend an elementary school from
the date on this Certificate.

E. M. Rich.

Education Officer

Date............. 25 JUL 1935

NOTE.—Preparation for commerce and industry and instruction in home-craft are provided in the trade and junior technical schools maintained or aided by the Council, and in the Council's voluntary day continuation schools and evening institutes. The addresses of the schools and institutes in the neighbourhood can be obtained from your Head Teacher.

36510—(W. 19072-7)—7.11.34.

London County Council.

St. James' C. of E. Mixed School,
Thurland Road,
Jamaica Road, S.E.16

Ref...........

24. 7. 35

Hilda Johnson has been a pupil of this school for the past 3 years. She will be 14 years of age on the 29th of this month, and is now free to leave school and seek employment. Hilda is a girl of more than average ability. She has worked steadily and well during the time she has attended this School, and she is now a good all round Standard VII Scholar. She is a girl of excellent Character, and her Conduct has at all times been highly satisfactory. I have always found her honest, truthful, and trustworthy, willing and obliging, Courteous and polite, and clean and tidy both in person, and in her work. She is a tall girl, and can swim. I can strongly recommend her. Signed: J. D. Steen,
Head Master.

Hilda loved her school days, and when she left in 1935 aged 14, her headmaster stated that she was 'a girl of excellent character … obliging, courteous and polite'.

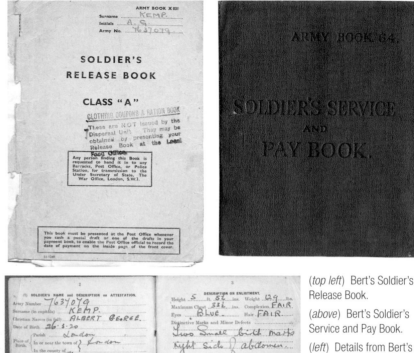

(*top left*) Bert's Soldier's Release Book.

(*above*) Bert's Soldier's Service and Pay Book.

(*left*) Details from Bert's Soldier Book.

(*below*) Bert and his army pals while serving in Cyprus, 1941. Bert is stood in the middle.

Making the most of an opportunity to enjoy the warm weather, this is Bert while serving in Palestine.

(*above*) Hilda's new family: Albert Ernest Kemp and Dolly Kemp, Bert's parents stand together in 1949.

(*left*) Hilda and her beloved Ma in the country-side in Braunston, while evacuated in 1943.

(*top left*) To her dearest Bert: Hilda posed for this photograph in 1943 to show her engagement ring to Albert who was serving overseas.

(*above*) As a young soldier, Albert Kemp in 1940.

(*left*) With her pale pink roses, Hilda with Albert on their wedding day in 1945.

'Hilda and Albie Good Luck – Dad': no wedding present, only a telegram from Ted before the wedding day.

(*right*) Celebrating the marriage of Albert George Kemp and Hilda Irene Doris Johnson on 4 August 1945.

(*below*) The happiest day of Hilda's life. From left to right: Albert Ernest Kemp (Pop), Dolly Kemp (Mum), Joanie ('Black Mog'), Joanie's fiancée Sid, Bert, Hilda, Ted, Dorothy (Bert's sister), unknown man, Patsy, Ron.

Hilda's little girls: Christine (left) and Brenda (right).

Me (aged 3) with my beloved grandmother Hilda (aged 54).

It wasn't long after we'd eaten our dinner that the siren went off. We scrambled about, grabbing the children and heading into the back yard where the Anderson shelter stood. Inside it was as dank and smelly a hole as you'd be likely to get. Ma had tried her best to make it look cosy, with a paraffin lamp and extra blankets, but we knew we were in for a cold, uncomfortable night. I wrapped Patsy in one of the blankets as she huddled with Joanie and Ron on one of the wooden benches and Ma opened a book and started to read bedtime stories. Pa had been out all evening, and he often didn't come back during the raids, preferring to shelter under one of the arches near whichever pub he was in or make a drunken dash to the Underground.

We could hear explosions and the rattle of gun fire but nothing came too close, and despite the discomfort we all managed a fitful night's sleep. The next morning we climbed out, grateful to be out of the tiny, claustrophobic space. By the low early morning light, I noticed Ma looked tired and ill. Her feet and legs were swollen with the dropsy. I'd scraped together the money to pay for a doctor a few weeks earlier, but there was little he could do, advising her to rest up now and then. Well, no woman in our neck of the woods ever had a chance to 'rest up', the thought was laughable. The only time Ma got any rest was the scant hours she spent sleeping, and even then Pa wanted his duty from her, and like all 'good wives' she had to submit to his clumsy, drunken advances or get a beating.

I'd heard Ma and Pa in bed since I was a little girl, when we all shared a bed. After we moved to Spa Road, the walls were so thin that everything could be heard through them anyway. It was a fact of life, and we didn't think anything of it. Everyone else had it the same. Ma and Pa just got on with it and we either slept through it or heard them at it. Privacy was a luxury none of us could afford.

The birth of Patsy seemed to have stopped Pa in his tracks, though. Ma was looking ill and maybe even he had noticed. Either that or he had a new fancy woman, which was more likely. He still treated Ma as badly as ever. He knew she was suffering with sore legs and tiredness, yet he resorted to violence at the drop of a hat, with the arrogance of a vain, insensitive man. She still submitted to his lusts occasionally, but his vigour seemed to have worn out with her as well, and the nights had been silent on that front for months now.

I made Ma go and have a lie down while I got the others their breakfast and shooed them out to school. The factory day passed. Ma had promised us all fish and chips for dinner that night as a treat because the younger ones had behaved so well in the shelter. It gave us all something to look forward to. A fish supper was something we all loved, and as it was the only food not rationed, it was readily available.

Rationing for food had started early in 1940. It didn't make much difference to us as food was always scarce in our home. The only thing that was different was that Ma had to register with the local grocer store and queue up for hours each week to get supplies.

That evening, Pa donned his trilby and went out in search of supper. We couldn't have been more pleased to see him arrive home with a stack of battered cod and freshly fried chips, all wrapped in yesterday's newspaper. It was a sign that some things carried on, despite the bombs and the sirens.

We all sat down together. Ma gave us forks and put the salt on the table but we all preferred to eat the oily treat off the paper it was served on, with our fingers. Pa had drenched the food in vinegar and the bitter-sweet smell sent me into a hungry swoon. I scattered salt crystals across the yellow chips and golden batter, then added more, my mouth watering in anticipation.

In sensual reverie, I finally lifted a chip to my mouth. Biting into it I could feel grease coat my lips then the fluffy white potato inside it as the perfect culinary counterfoil. I don't think a fish supper had ever tasted so good! I chewed slowly, and closed my eyes for a second to appreciate the moment. I licked the oil from my fingers in a wanton, and rare, lack of table manners. I applied liberal amounts of salt over my meal and bit into another golden chip. Despite the rationing of the rest of our food, despite the horrors of last night, there was something marvellous about the meal. It was as stubbornly English as ourselves. Fish was plentiful in the waters off our island, and potatoes were our staple diet. The combination spoke to us of homely comfort, and our refusal to be anything other than what we were: British and proud of it. It also meant that the heart of our community was still beating. We could still get fish and chips, so the world had to be alright. London was still in business, however many Jerry bombs kept falling.

The cod was white against the crispy batter. I sank my teeth into a large piece, savouring the luxury of it. The fish was light and fresh-tasting. The batter surrounding it peeled off in greasy, crunchy orange clouds. For a few minutes we all fell silent as we munched through our glorious dinner. Somehow, the meal acted as a salve. For a moment I could almost believe I had the father and the family life I'd always yearned for. We looked up as we ate, grinning in acknowledgement of the pleasure it afforded us. No one used a fork. We were all cramming the thick golden parcels of cod into our mouths.

Finally, sated, Pa sat back in his chair and rubbed his belly.

The rest of us took this as our cue to start chatting as if it was just another ordinary day. For a brief moment, the war faded away and we became what I'd always wanted us to be: a happy family enjoying time spent eating together.

Once Ma and I had cleared away the grease-stained newspaper, I went upstairs to try on my skirt. I had decided to go out for a short while with the girls, after checking it was alright with Ma. The dinner had reminded me that life had to carry on as normal, and I couldn't hide away from the Blitz trying to protect everyone, as none of us would be safe till this blasted war ended.

So I pulled on my new garment, relishing the feel of the material against my skin. I came back down the stairs holding myself like royalty, desperate to show it off to the others.

'You're a beauty. It goes lovely wiv yer pretty hair,' said Ma as I entered the kitchen, with love shining from her brown eyes.

'Thanks, Ma,' I said, giddy with her reaction. 'Can I please borra a bit of your lipstick to wear out tonight?' I blushed as I asked, knowing it was cheeky of me to ask her. She had one pink lipstick, it had lasted her years and I knew I shouldn't really ask to use it. But I wanted so much to look my best. After all, who knew who I might meet at the dance?

Ma scrutinised my face. Then, frowning, she said: 'Listen, 'ilda, this is what me mother always said to me: "A littl' bit of powder, a littl' bit of paint, makes a girl, what she ain't!"'

I giggled, but realised the message behind it. It was the message all of us slum girls heard from our parents and from school: to not get above yourself, to mind your station in life and be happy with it. It was a bitter-sweet moment with Ma, because I knew I didn't want her life of continual child-rearing and cleaning. I didn't want a man who treated me the way her husband did. I wanted more than that. Was that wrong of me? I looked away, not wanting to hear it.

Ma grabbed my shoulders and continued, ' 'Ilda, I'm not sayin' it to 'urt you, I mean it to be a warnin'. You don't need fancy clothes or lipstick to be beautiful, you're that already, because you've got the biggest 'eart of anyone I know. That's what makes you beautiful, not all that clobber like skirts and lipstick.' She smiled at me, eyes twinkling, then kissed my cheek.

'I love you, Ma,' I said, quietly.

Later that evening, before the night raid, I was wolf-whistled and winked at twice. Ma's words rang in my ears, though, and I didn't get above myself at all, just smiled to myself that life, though dangerous and chaotic at the best of times, also had its moments of pure beauty.

CHAPTER 12

Blitz

'You're an old bastard! I 'ate you, I 'ate you, Pa!' cried Les, caught in the iron grip of his father's burly arms.

Pa had lost his work down at the docks, but had somehow landed a job with Bermondsey Council, and so spent his days lugging sandbags and huge reels of blackout material down at the ARP depot in Rotherhithe. Therefore his strength still massively outranked that of his 16-year-old son Leslie, and he was out to prove it this morning.

'Christ, Ted, put 'im down! You'll kill 'im if you carry on like that,' gasped Ma, her hands in front of her face, holding them in a prayer position in shock at what she was witnessing. It was seven o'clock and we should have been getting dressed and out for the day, but something Les had said or done had sent the old man into a fury, and there was no stopping his rampage.

'Ted, you're goin' to kill 'im! Let 'im go,' sobbed Ma in fright.

Les really did look like he was scarcely able to breathe. Pa had him in a headlock and was casually, slowly smoking one of his cigarettes. He must've been flush with cash that week as he had a woodbine in his evil mouth, not one of his regular roll-ups.

' 'E cheeked me, Em, 'e told me I should've enlisted, like them posters out there say, an' I don't like 'earin' disrespect in me own 'ome. I won't stand for it, Em. It ain't none of anybody's business what I do, or don't do, so leave your fat mouth out of it,' he raged back at her.

Ron and Joanie, who had been messing around upstairs, making a right old racket themselves, went silent when they heard their father's voice. They knew it meant trouble and they'd learnt the hard way to keep out of it.

'Now get your fuckin' nose out of my business, Em. If you can't discipline your kids then I'll 'ave to do it,' and with that, Ted pulled his lit cigarette out of his mouth.

Suddenly, in those brief seconds before he did it, I knew what he was going to do. Even though it was Ted Johnson, the biggest, vainest bully a woman ever met, I still didn't believe he'd have the nerve, or the sadism, but he did, by God he did.

Slowly, enjoying the moment, Pa drew his cigarette end to Leslie's leg, just below where his long shirt ended and his skinny white legs began.

'No, Pa, no! Don't 'urt me! I did nuffink, I said nuffink to disrespect you, I just told the truth,' shouted Les, his face wild, his eyes swimming with angry tears.

I stood stock still as if I'd lost the movement of my legs. Time seemed to stop. The sounds of the street and the clear-up after last night's raids all melted away. There was only this black-hearted man with my beloved brother held prisoner, unable to escape from his twisted intentions. I couldn't watch, and yet I couldn't tear my eyes away from them. Caught together in this fearful dance, the boy and the beast, hunter and prey.

Then That Man gripped Les all the tighter and brought the burning ciggie to his leg. He held it there for several seconds as Les screamed a high-pitched sound that chilled me. There was the smell of his flesh burning. Pa gave a momentary sigh and then released Les, who ran from the room and up the stairs, a strangled sob escaping from him. I stared at Pa in shock. That Man had tortured my brother. He'd done it in front of us with no shame, no remorse at all. At that moment That Man became, not a troubled alcoholic with a taste for a fight, but a monster who took pleasure from his brutality. There was a look of satisfaction on his face, which was, to me, even more disturbing than the pain he'd inflicted on my brother.

I edged out of the room, not wanting to see any more. Ma had followed Les upstairs, and was trying to console him. I raced up to find him crying in her arms. 'I 'ate 'im. I can't stand another minute 'ere wiv 'im,' he sobbed.

Ma rocked him back and forwards, making shushing noises but he wouldn't be pacified. The wounds he suffered went far deeper than the cigarette burns on his young skin. He was a young man on the brink of adulthood. Pa was the main male role model in his life. What was Les to become if he couldn't follow his father's example? It was a difficult path he had to tread, and Lord knows how he would manage it. I could see that my brother was suffering from hurt pride as well. He'd been too weak to fend off That Man which left him feeling sore as only a young boy can. My heart ached for him.

'I don't ever want to be like 'im. I 'ear 'im beatin' you both, an' there's nuffink I can do about it. I can't stand livin' 'ere any longer.'

By now there were tears streaming down Ma's face. 'Oh, son, don't talk like that. Please don't go. It'll be alright, I promise.'

'It won't, Ma, you know it won't. There's nuffink in the world I can do to stop that bastard hittin' you an' 'ilda, I ain't strong enough, an' for the life of me I can't take it anymore.'

With that, Les shook himself out of Ma's arms and grabbed his coat and cap.

'Sorry, Ma,' was all he said before he turned and left.

We heard the sound of his boots hitting the wooden staircase on his way out. Ma and I looked at each other. Had Les left us for good? Neither of us could blame him if he had.

We could do nothing now but wait to see if he came home that night. With a weary sigh, Ma stood up and held her hand out to me. I grasped it, wiping away the tears that had made silent tracks down my face. With that, Ma and I came downstairs.

That Man was sat there, finishing off his cigarette with long slow inhalations, as if none of the uproar was anything to do with him. He finally ground the stub on the sole of his boot, picked up his cap and left the house, slamming the door on his way out. He didn't say a word.

My heart felt sore, like a wound that never quite healed. I picked my way upstairs to find Ron, Joanie and Patsy and see if they were okay.

Father was drinking more and more. Every night he was out till all hours, and even the air raids didn't stop him. He would meet his mates on Tower Bridge Road, and when the sirens went off they'd dive half-cut into London Bridge or Elephant & Castle Underground stations, without a worry for our wellbeing. On the nights they couldn't stagger that far they'd take shelter under a railway arch, not once thinking about what their wives and families were doing for safety.

'Come on, Ma, Les'll be okay. 'E's strong like you. We'll pull through this, you'll see.'

I knew I had little comfort to offer but she patted my hand anyway and took a big breath in, and said, ' 'Course we'll be alright, duckie. We always are, ain't we? Now I got to go shoppin' an' you'll be late for work if you 'ang about 'ere makin' me feel better.' And with that, she smiled a watery smile. We had to carry on, and she of all people knew that hard truth.

'Right now, where's me 'at, an' me basket?' she said in a livelier tone. 'An' them ration books, now where did I put those?'

'They're all in the kitchen, Ma,' I replied. 'Don't forget your gas mask again, will you?' She managed a chuckle at that. She almost always forgot it on her way out, and I spent my days worrying that if we had a gas attack then Ma'd be found gassed to death, trying to find it.

We both checked our hair and Ma adjusted her hat, and we were ready to go. Ma would spend an hour or so just waiting in line to buy our bread and tea rations, then again at the butcher's for our minced meat, now that meat had been rationed since last month. She wouldn't be back till lunchtime and she'd have little to show for it. We were allowed half a pound of breast mutton, half a pound of beef mince, half a pound of lard and the same of sugar. It wasn't much to feed a family of seven! Luckily bread wasn't rationed, or we'd have starved.

'Ready, girl,' she said, touching my arm.

We both knew how to put a brave face on. We weren't going to provide any more fuel for the local gossips, so we looked as bright as we could going about our business. We left the house at the same time, me going right to walk up to Peek Frean, her turning left to go and queue at the small line of shops down our street.

It was tough making the rations, particularly the meat ration, last for the whole week. We always looked forward to the start of the week as we knew we'd get a hot pot or shepherd's pie, and then the leftovers on the following night. Now that Pa was earning a regular wage, even though much of it ended up being pissed out of him each night, and I was in paid work too, we had a staple diet for the first time in our lives. Mum still put on a show for her Sunday tea, Blitz or no Blitz, and many a time we'd dived into the shelter clutching our precious plates of stewed apple or milk pudding.

I walked to work through the rubble-strewn streets, looking at the scenes of devastation that had become more and more familiar the longer the Blitz lasted. There were tenement houses sliced in half with ragged net curtains flapping in the breeze, the buildings looking like they had great bites taken out of them where once there were chimneys and roofs. Smoke hung on the summer air, creating a choking mist that seemed to hover all day.

The factory had survived the bombings, though, and it was business as usual. In fact, business was booming as Peek Frean's was supplying biscuits to the troops, so we were working harder than ever. Lil and Rita were there, gossiping and flirting with the boys who carried in the great milk churns, but I noticed there were familiar faces missing. Either they'd been evacuated with their families or, worse, they'd been killed in the night-time raids. I shuddered and tried not to think of the ever-present danger we were all in. Without thinking, I reached for the gas mask that I wore across my chest.

Looking around I said ' 'ello' to my friends, noticing the extra effort everyone seemed to be making with their appearance. Maybe I'd got it wrong, but it seemed to me that they were wearing make-up and taking more care in their hairstyles and dress. Was it because we never knew if today would be our last, and we were determined to go out in style? Or maybe it was the sudden shortage of young men in our midst that sharpened the minds of girls wanting to find a fella. Whatever it was, I was proud of them for looking so neat and pretty. It was a small revolt against wartime. A statement that life was worth living, and we'd fight the Germans on our own, good-looking, terms.

I packed biscuits till my arms ached. My back was stooped making my neck muscles tight. Now and then a broken one appeared on the conveyor belt and we fought over who would eat it. If we'd been caught we'd have been out on our ears, but we didn't mind taking the risk. We ate lunch in the canteen, where we didn't need to use coupons, so we thought of it as bonus food.

By dinnertime, I was tired but at least the day had taken my mind off Les and Pa. I bit my lip nervously as I walked home. Would Les be home? And, more to the point, would Pa be on the rampage again? I walked in, dropping my gas mask on the table, and instantly pulled on my apron. Ron and Joanie were outdoors. I'd seen Ron briefly running in the direction of his 'beach' and I'd managed to shout after him that dinner would be on the table in half an hour. Les was nowhere to be seen but that wasn't unusual, as he ran free most evenings with a pack of friends around the dockyards that were as compelling as they were dirty, noisy and dangerous. I made a mental note to ask Ron to go out searching for Les when he returned in time for his dinner.

All day, I'd been worrying about my brother, wondering if he would come home to us. Ma was down on her knees scrubbing the floors next to a bucket containing grey soapy suds and a great hairy scrubbing brush.

'I'll get the dinner on, Ma, don't you worry,' I said briskly, peeling the potatoes with a knife and dropping the peelings into the butler's sink.

Ma stopped for a minute, wiped her forehead which was

greasy with sweat, and arched her back. ''Ave you seen Les?' she asked, tentatively.

I shook my head in reply and Ma sighed. 'Gawd, 'ilda, I feel old these days, I tell you,' she said, a grimace on her face.

'Oh don't you go sayin' things like that, Ma, you've got years left in you,' I joked, hoping she wasn't feeling ill again. Ma was 40 years old, and I would never have admitted it to her, but she looked years older. Some nights she even struggled to get up the stairs to bed because of the swelling in her legs, and of course Pa was no help at all. In fact, her vulnerable state seemed to make him madder, more aggressive and argumentative, like he could see the life leaching out from her worn body and he was somehow enjoying the feeling of power it gave him. I didn't have time to worry about That Man, thankfully. I set the pot on to boil and the spuds bobbed in the water as it heated. Minutes later, there was the sound of the front door opening. Ma and I shot a quick glance at each other. There was a whistle, and a clump where someone's gas mask had been dropped on the floor, then, lo and behold, Les appeared in the doorway.

'You're back!' said Ma, struggling to her feet.

'Thank Gawd fer that!' I exclaimed, with a rush of relief.

Les looked awkward. His mouth was set in a line and I could see how much courage it had cost him to come home. His voice trembled a little when he spoke. 'I'm 'ere an' I'm fine. Now what's fer me dinner?'

It must have been terrifying for him to return, but he'd come home to us. For now at least.

''Ow are you?' Ma said softly, moving towards her first-born son.

Les looked at her, his brown eyes a liquid pool. There was sorrow written on his face, and fear, and something else I couldn't name.

He looked changed, different. Like he'd grown up in the few short hours he'd been away. Something in him had locked up tight. Shut away from us for ever.

Ma and I looked at him, Ma with unquestioning love, me with the sense that our Les had somehow changed. He'd moved away from us in his heart, no doubt to protect himself. He'd gone out of this house a frightened, angry boy and returned a young man, sharpened by grief and fear.

'I've found somewhere to live,' was all he said.

We both held our breath. So he hadn't come home for good.

'I'm startin' work at the tannery next week an' they've said I can sleep there as well.' Les looked at Ma as he spoke, and I watched as her eyes filled with tears.

Ma's voice broke as she replied, 'Son, you don't 'ave to live there. We're yer family. You can stay 'ere, just keep out of Pa's way an' it'll all be all right.'

Les shook his head.

'It won't be all right, Ma. You know it won't. The tannery's only round the corner. You can still see me every day, but I can't live 'ere no more.'

With that, Les looked at me. His face was pale but determined. This was the first act of a grown man and I wouldn't have undermined it for the world.

' 'E's right, Ma. Les'll be round the corner. It'll be better this way, you'll see. 'E can keep out of Pa's way an' still come home for his dinner,' I said, looking at Ma.

Ma nodded. She wiped away her tears and reached towards Les, pulling him into a hug.

He pushed her off with the tender pride of a newly formed young man.

'We'd better get this dinner on then, if we've got a chance of eatin' it before the sirens go off!' I exclaimed, lightening the mood that threatened to descend into more tears and upset.

We ate in silence. Ma, Les and me pushed the food round our plates though it was, by our standards, a feast of cottage pie made from our newly bought rations of mince. Ron chattered away as usual, barely noticing how quiet we were, while 14-year-old Joanie sat watching us in silence. As I was clearing away I heard Les announce his news to his younger siblings. At first there were wails from them, but then Ron warmed to the idea, demanding that he live in the tannery as well.

Ma chuckled at that, and we all smiled. How typical it was of Ron to be so excited and see the good side of everything.

It wasn't until much later, when we were all fast asleep, that the siren sounded. It never ceased to spook me, especially at 2 a.m.. Its insistent cry, swooping high then low, made my stomach clench with panic. Ma and I dragged Ron, Les, Joanie and Patsy out of bed, with a 'Get out of bed, NOW!' and hurried them into the shelter that took up most of the back yard. It was damp and smelly, and very crowded once we were all inside it and the hatch was shut. Pa was out with his mates, as usual.

It was dark, and so I lit the paraffin lamp and five scared faces flared into light before me. Ron, Joanie and Les were huddled together, crammed onto one of the wooden benches with its thin mattress. Ma was sat with Patsy on her knee next to me. The drone of the engines overhead grew louder and the sounds of the explosions more intense.

'Wrap yerselves up warm. Come on, Patsy love, there's no point getting cold,' said Ma, trying to inject some normality into the insanity.

Even though it was a warm May night, we all felt chilled

inside the shelter with its earth floor, which always seemed to be part-flooded whether it had rained or not. Almost immediately there was the sound of guns banging at enemy aircraft, and explosions followed soon after. The great throbbing noise from the bombers overhead was terrifyingly loud.

'They're right over us tonight, Ma,' said Les. He turned his gaze to her.

Our faces looked pale by the dim light of the lamp. I clutched hold of Ron and Joanie, as much for my own comfort as for theirs.

'There goes another,' said Les again.

Somewhere close by had been hit. A great boom rent the air around us. Too close for comfort. Far too close. The sound of shattering glass made us all jump. Joanie and I screamed with fright, Ron and Patsy started wailing. I shushed them, saying, 'Don't you worry. We'll be alright in 'ere, you'll see,' though I had no idea if it was true.

Ma and I exchanged a grim look. 'At least we're givin' as good as we get,' said Ma, cuddling Patsy up to her.

Then the world around us exploded. There was a thin long screech, a whistle that seared the atmosphere. Then the bomb hit with tremendous, deafening force, sucking the air out of our lungs. There was silence for an infinitesimal moment before a great roar of shattering glass. Then a boom as a building collapsed around us, or so it seemed. We all screamed. I had my hands over my ears and I was screeching and wailing. The sound of debris – bricks, mortar, guttering, stone and glass – rained down in sickening thuds, crashing down around our little shelter.

Les shouted, 'They've hit the 'ouse, the bastards!'

He tried to get out to see what damage had been done, but we all held him down as the all-clear hadn't sounded. There was, again, a split second of quiet, then we heard voices, high-pitched and strange, howling into the night. They joined our own cries in an animal-like high-pitched chorus. Then there was the sound of water being sprayed either from jets or from damaged water pipes. Ma was rocking backwards and forwards, clutching Patsy tight to her chest. Ron and Joanie were holding tight onto me, our heads bowed together, bawling in fright. For what seemed like hours we heard people crying, bombs falling and the rumble of heavy aircraft above us.

There were several more direct hits that sounded like they were nearby. Then the sounds started to fade away into the distance. The sharp bursts of gunfire stopped, and there was suddenly only the noises from the ground.

We waited, desperate to go outside, but frightened of what we might find when we did. Eventually the all-clear sounded, and we emerged from the earth like we were leaving the trenches. Les was out first, helping to pull the rest of us out of the hatch. Ma came last, grabbing the side of the shelter for support. We looked up as one, expecting to see our house a mess of rubble and glass.

I don't think any of us could believe our eyes.

The house was still standing!

We looked at each other, and for a brief moment we laughed with the madness of relief. I looked up at the heavens and mouthed a silent 'thank you' for saving our lives and our home, before clutching Ma's arm and telling her to wait as Les and I would go inside to see if there was any damage.

Les and I exchanged a grim look before pushing open the yard door. Inside, the scullery was as we'd left it. The kitchen was the same. Opening the front room door, our boots crunched on the glass that had sprayed over the floor. It glittered orange from the flames reaching into the sky opposite us. We moved towards the gap where our window once was, spellbound by the sight in front of us.

The town hall had taken the hit. The beautiful big town hall that had stood proudly in front of us was a fiery, smoking wreck of rubble. It looked like it had been part demolished, which I suppose it had. There were flames shooting into the sky, and firemen were already battling with feeble jets of water, attempting to stem the inferno.

'Lord in 'eaven, what did we do to deserve this?' I asked as I gazed at the enormity of the chaos.

Les climbed out of the window and into the street. I was standing, peering through the window as if it could protect me from the sight of such carnage. There was a body lying in the street. At first glance I didn't recognise the man who lay dead or dying feet from our front door, and I was grateful it wasn't one of our neighbours or friends at least. Such scenes had become familiar in these dark days. It was odd that everyday life had broken down so quickly that it had become almost normal to see such sights.

There were firemen and ambulance women running from side to side, their bodies silhouetted against the flames. Two women struggled past, carried a stretcher with a woman's body lying motionless upon it. Huge billowing smoke trails curled into the sky. We were lucky to be alive. My God, we were so lucky.

I was aware then of Ma standing next to me. 'Come inside, 'ilda,' she said softly. 'There's nuffink you can do for those poor people, come inside an' get warm.'

I hadn't realised I was shaking, with cold or shock I couldn't tell. There were flames and crumbling brickwork everywhere. All the windows at the front of the house had been blown in. If we'd have stayed indoors we'd have been killed for sure, lacerated by the shards that littered the floorboards. We were okay though. We had to be thankful we hadn't suffered worse, like those poor people on the street and on the stretcher.

Within minutes rescuers arrived to search for bodies in the wreckage. Les rushed out to help, but there were no survivors. We ate our breakfast in silence, knowing how close we'd all come to meeting our Maker that night.

A neighbour caught my arm as I left the house to go to work, pulling me to the side of the street to tell me that the Peek Frean's shelter had been hit too. Without a second glance, I threw off her hold. Frantically, I ran through the grim streets, the warzone we called home, to the factory where my friends worked. I could barely contain my sobs as I pelted down the damaged roads, past the leaning structures and smoking ruins. When I got there, the clock tower was still intact, but the shelter was a furnace of flames. Fire crews ran everywhere. They had been fighting the fires most of the early hours of the morning but still it burnt. I grabbed hold of a passing girl's arm.

'Are there many dead? Do you know Rita or Lil? Were they in there?' I shouted.

The girl looked at me with dark eyes and shrugged. I vaguely recognised her from the packing section, but there were hundreds of us working in there every day. I hadn't ever spoken to her before.

I dropped her arm and dashed left then right. I couldn't get inside but I had to know the truth. Had my friends been among the victims?

I couldn't get close to the inferno. Tears ran in streams down my face, making grooves through the charcoal smog that settled on my skin. I fell to my knees and wept. I don't know how long I stayed like that but eventually I crouched and got myself to standing, returning home with a heavy heart.

That afternoon, Ron ran out of school, weeping. He ran all the way home and straight into Ma's arms.

'What's the matter, sweet 'eart?' she crooned, rocking him in her arms.

It took a while for Ron's sobs to stop racking his body. He gulped down air and finally juddered to a halt, enough to speak anyway.

'It's me mate. Me mate Frank is dead. 'E got 'it by the bombs last night. They're all dead.' And with that Ron collapsed into crying again.

There was nothing any of us could say. We'd been lucky so far. The war, though it raged around us, had left us and our neighbours intact.

Ma had been friendly with Frank's mother Cybil, and the family had lived only a few doors away from us. The entire family of three boys had perished by all accounts, while sheltering in the town hall during the air raid. The death of our friends hit us hard, especially Ron.

It could have been us. It so nearly was us. If we needed a reminder of the reality of wartime then that was it. Night after night we'd witnessed the bombings, feeling they would never end. Those German buggers rained down their incendiary bombs on us Londoners, and each night we struggled into the relative safety of whichever shelter was closest, whether our dank old shelter in the yard, or the shelter under Bermondsey Baths on Grange Road, and prayed that we'd make it through the night.

Our borough was a stinking mass of rubble and twisted metal. Auxiliary firemen were out on the streets day and night, hosing down the smoking ruins of our beloved city.

Girls weaved through the wreckage on bicycles, dodging the bombsites to get to their work in the factories. All the young men seemed to have disappeared, all conscripted into the Army, and facing Lord knows what horrors fighting in France. Down in our neck of the wood, the docks were ablaze like the depths of Hades, struck into oblivion as prime targets for the Jerries. There was no work down there any more, the warehouses and cold stores were strewn with bomb damage or burnt to cinders, leaving their charred carcasses as the only sign they'd once been a thriving centre of commerce, along with those smells of burning spices that billowed for days after each raid.

Despite all this, I'd never before felt we were in true danger, which I know sounds odd given the Blitz we were living through. But that all changed after the town hall was struck. We realised we had to get out of London. We had to get as far away as we could or we were sitting ducks.

There were too many deaths. Too much misery. How much longer could we go on like this? My best friends might have died. Ron's pal and his family were wiped out. Our borough was being ripped apart brick by brick, limb by limb.

One thing was for sure, it was time to pack our bags and leave our dirty, ragged and beloved city.

CHAPTER 13

Evacuation

Once Ma's mind was made up, that was that. She marched past the smoking wreckage of our borough to the council offices, where she asked to be evacuated.

Ma wanted me to leave work and go with her because of her illness. Despite the fact I loved my job, and my new-found friends, I knew I had to go with my family. I didn't want to stay at home with Pa either.

I bid a tearful farewell to Helen and her family. They were staying put, saying they couldn't imagine living out of our city. Inside, I agreed with them. I was devastated at the thought of leaving but I knew it was too dangerous to stay.

My friends Margaret and Nellie had gone with their families when they were evacuated at the start of the raids and I hadn't had a chance to say goodbye. Our community was splitting apart. Our borough was becoming an unrecognisable hellhole, our friends and neighbours dying or being sent off to disparate places far from the inner city. We were the next to go. I wondered if I'd ever see any of my friends again and felt immeasurable sadness at our departure.

But Ma was determined to leave and so we packed our suitcases, with dread in our hearts. We had a jumper and extra pair of socks each, one pair of pants and our long johns and nighties. It wasn't much.

A week later, we were told to wait outside the ruins of the town hall for a coach to take us to Euston Station. Les had chosen to stay, working at the tanneries as long as he could. He'd hugged us all for a long time when we said our goodbyes. I understood why he didn't come with us. Our lives were in this filthy, chaotic borough. We belonged here, it was home to us. He had friends and his work, and had escaped from under Pa's roof, so I could see why he stayed, though I tried to convince him to come with us. I didn't want our family to disintegrate, like our neighbourhood. He could see as well as I could that his life was in danger every second he was living and working in London, but he was adamant.

'Don't you forget to clean yer teeth each night and say yer prayers. God can 'ear you even above the sound of the bombs,' said Ma, as she held him tight.

'Come wiv us, please, Les,' I begged, as I folded my arms round his skinny body. He was taller than me but seemed more fragile somehow. Ever since the morning when Pa burnt him with his cigarette, he seemed brittle, unreachable. Part of him was locked away from the rest of us, and nothing we could do could ever seem to get close to him again.

'Don't you worry about me,' he said, smiling though his eyes looked wet. 'I'll be right as rain, you'll see. Don't suppose those Jerry bombers are lookin' for me anyway.' He gave Ron a playful clip round the ear, and Joanie a final hug before he sloped off. As he walked away, the sky was billowing with black smoke and the brick dust that filled our nostrils.

I could hardly bear leaving him behind to an uncertain fate, but it was his choice and he was 16 years old, almost a man. Old enough now to make his own decisions.

Ma sighed. 'You won't convince 'im, 'ilda. 'E's stubborn, just like his mother!'

With that, I forced out a small laugh, before picking up my suitcase and closing the front door behind us. I'd tried to find my friends Rita and Lil to say goodbye to them too. The factory had been shut after the shelter was hit, and there was no way of finding them. I knew that Lil lived in Rotherhithe and Rita down the Old Kent Road but we never met at each other's houses. We all wanted to escape the hungry mouths, dirt and clamour of being at home, so we'd only ever seen each other in work or, afterwards, at a dance hall.

I was terribly sad to leave without knowing if they were okay. My world felt like it had exploded, along with the bombs, and was scattering into a million pieces around me.

Pa had opted to stay in London because of his work, and his 'pals' most probably. I admit I was relieved to see the back of him, and his fists, though who knew for how long? I'm not a vengeful person, but my most secret thoughts were that if Pa didn't survive the raids that thumped down on our part of London, then it wouldn't be the worst thing. I'd never have said that out loud, but by God I knew I felt it.

We clambered onto the bus, gripping our cases and barely speaking. There were plenty of young children in the queue to get on board, their mothers standing by the roadside sobbing and clutching hold of handkerchiefs to wave them off. All of us had our gas masks, a label pinned to our jackets – even though it was a warm morning in May – and our few belongings. The departure of the bus was unbearably sad. The children wailed as they waved to their mothers, who ran alongside the bus as it moved out on the first leg of our journey.

The bus took a tortuous route round the city, and it felt like hours before we reached Euston Station. There were sandbags piled against the buildings, people stepping over piles of debris as they continued about their business. Great jagged remains of offices and houses towered precariously over the bus, looking for all the world like they could fall on our heads at any second. Our city looked like the survivor of a disaster that all too often threatened to overwhelm us all.

At Euston we got off the bus and trooped into lines to wait for the train, which would take us to our unknown destination. Auxiliaries with tin hats and clipboards allocated us to trains. I felt a shiver as I boarded. I knew in that moment the feeling of leaving everything I'd ever known and heading towards an unknowable destiny. I felt like the certainties of my life – my family, friends and work – were suddenly lighter than air, drifting away from me as if they had never been real at all. It was disorientating and very, very frightening.

Most of the journey was spent in subdued chatter. Ron and Patsy were still affected by the town hall's dramatic end, and so we spent the train trip looking out of the windows, wondering where in God's name we were going, how long it would take to get there, and how long we'd have to stay away from our city. As the bombsites and the buildings fell away from us, I felt broken hearted at leaving London. Lord knows when I would see my friends again, or whether they'd survive this terrible war. All the familiar sights and sounds vanished as the grey skies opened up and miles of blank, flat green landscape rolled out around us. Every now and then I caught a glance of myself reflected in the train window. My face was set into a sombre expression, my mouth a thin line.

It was almost summer but the season seemed nameless, the countryside outside unbearably sullen and bleak. I had never seen such big skies, so devoid of buildings and cranes, ships masts and soaring warehouses. The small towns we rumbled through disappeared as quickly as they arrived, a few people ploughing fields, tractors moving through the landscape, scarecrows waving a little in the breeze.

It looked like an alien world. I wanted to go home, and we hadn't even arrived.

The train moved swiftly onwards. The rocking motion

had soon lulled Joanie and Ma into sleep, but I sat there the whole time, dry-eyed but devastated at leaving my life behind. Apart from hopping, we'd never been anywhere further than a tram ride away, and those were pretty rare trips where we dodged on and off without paying.

It was evening before we arrived at a dark station that felt like the middle of nowhere. That night we were too tired to take in our surroundings. We stepped off the train and were directed to a large hall and told we were in Northampton, wherever that was! Ma held Patsy while I distributed the milk and biscuits offered to us by the council officers. There were about 30 of us, mostly children on their own, rubbing their eyes and crying with exhaustion and homesickness.

Then the door opened and a man came in, saying he was the local doctor. He checked us all for lice, before muttering to the three officers who had greeted us on our arrival. A woman in her fifties clapped her hands and asked us to pay attention. She told us that families from the area were coming to select us, and if there were any families among us it was best to split into smaller groups; mothers with babies, older siblings splitting apart, as that would make the process 'easier'.

Easier for who? I thought, feeling suddenly cross at this manner of our greeting. We weren't farm animals to be prodded and poked, and taken home if we passed muster. We were real people, flesh and blood, and there was no damn way they were going to separate us. Ma and I looked at each other, both having the same feeling. We edged closer to each other, and I said, above the noise of the crying children, that we would all stay together.

The woman, who wore her hair in a severe-looking bun, arched her eyebrows at me. 'It would really be best, dear, if you took our advice and separated. Surely you understand that?' she said, her voice high-pitched and bossy.

I stood up a little straighter.

'It would not be best for us, and please don't call me dear. I'm not your dear, not at all,' I said, my voice wavering a little but resolute. There was no way I would leave my sick Ma to cope on her own, and no way I would let them split the children up.

If it was possible, the local councillor raised her eyebrows even higher at that, but she said nothing, except to turn to the lady next to her and add, 'Well I never!'

At that, I grinned. There was no way a stuck-up old woman from goodness knows where was going to have the final say when it came to my family.

We huddled a little closer, and Ma squeezed my hand for support.

Minutes later, people from the village started arriving. They picked out children and young mothers to take back to their homes. Some children were separated from their brothers or sisters and their cries filled the hall. My heart burnt for those poor little mites. So far from home, and so alone. I could not have spent a night away from my Ma in this strange place and I was 20 years old!

Ron grabbed hold of my arm, while Patsy clung to Ma. Joanie sat on her suitcase, curling her hair around one finger, looking bored. One by one the mothers with babies, and the children all alone, were picked off. The night was wearing on. We were yawning, desperate to find a bed and sleep, but we still had nowhere to go.

Eventually there was only our small cluster left in the hall. Several people walked out, shaking their heads. The bossy woman walked over.

'You'll have to separate, that's final. If you don't, there's nothing we can do for you,' she said in clipped tones.

'Then there's nuffink you can do for us,' said Ma quietly, and with that she grabbed Patsy by the hand and started walking towards the door.

'We ain't stayin' 'ere to be looked down on by the likes of you,' she added.

With as much dignity as we could manage, we picked up our belongings and headed out of the door, stumbling into the dark streets. It was a May evening but there was still a chill in the air, a leftover from spring. We pulled our coats round us, looking this way and that at a world which was a million miles away from what we were used to. The road seemed empty – so different from the chaos of sights and smells at home.

The blackout was in force. A few cars went by, with their taped up headlights showing small slits of light. We had no idea where we were going and what we would do, but we had to get away from those self-important officers.

Ma looked up and down the road, then made a decision and turned left. She started walking up to front doors and knocking. I had never been more proud of my mother. She showed steely determination to find us somewhere, anywhere to stay and keep us from being apart. I could see that she would knock on every door in this odd town until she found us a bed or shelter. She was exhausted, but never defeated. She was never going to let her children sleep on the streets.

The houses were terraces, like in Spa Road, but they seemed unfriendly and silent. One by one doors were opened, revealing toothless old men, bedraggled young mothers, smoking men in vests, and face after face looked us up and down, then slammed the door shut before we'd had a chance to open our mouths. Time and time again, we found ourselves staring at the front door, feeling the reverberations of its swift closure.

We knew we looked sad and tired, but we realised we also looked 'different'. Somehow, they could tell we didn't belong there. We were just a family of destitute slum dwellers from London. No one wanted us. We were poor, flea-ridden and common. We were the lowest of the low to these people, and by God they showed us that. I could sense Ma's shame at being considered poor by these unfriendly people, but I knew she would never admit it to us in a million years. I couldn't help but love her with fierce pride as she brazenly walked up to each door.

Eventually, Ma put down her suitcase and strode up to the last house on the long row of terraces. She knocked and waited. We hung back, trying not to look as tired and as defeated as we felt. I shushed Patsy who had started to cry softly.

Ma knocked again. Finally the door opened.

A woman with greasy brown hair and a pinafore stood looking at us.

'What d'you want?' she asked with a Midlands burr to her voice. It sounded strange to us after the East End sounds we were used to.

'We need an 'ome. We've been evacuated 'ere an' we've nowhere to stay. Will you take us?' Ma said.

The woman looked us up and down, openly appraising us.

'We're clean and we ain't got no lice,' added Ma, her voice sounded desperate now. It was late and it really did look like we might have to find a bench somewhere and huddle together overnight.

'Can you pay?' the woman asked and sniffed, folding her hands on top of her large belly. She was a small but stocky woman with wide hips and pendulous breasts.

'Of course we can,' answered Ma.

'Well then, I'll take you all except the boy. That's my final word.' The woman looked like she would brook no argument.

Ma started to speak and then stopped. She looked around wildly, as if another door would open and we could all stay there instead. Finally she looked back at the woman.

'Please take us all, we don't want to be separated...' Ma looked wretched.

The woman simply shook her head, but at that moment the door of the terraced house opposite opened, and a young woman called out to us.

'Oi, Jean, I'll take the boy.' She'd obviously heard every word.

We all looked round, as one, to see who had spoken.

Her face was dark against the hallway light, she carried a baby on one hip and there was another child hanging onto her leg.

Ma looked at me, briefly, and I nodded. This was the only solution, for tonight at least.

Ma turned to Ron and held both his shoulders.

Ron immediately burst into tears.

'I won't go, Ma, I don't want to go there, I want to be wiv you,' he sobbed.

Ma took a deep breath and hugged him tight.

'It's only for tonight, Ronald. We'll work it all out in the mornin'. Be a brave boy for yer Ma.'

At that, Ron cried even harder. There were rivulets of snot running from his nose. He grabbed Ma's arm.

'I won't go. I don't want to go there, Ma. Please let me stay wiv you, please.'

Ma peeled Ron off her. Her face was a picture of maternal anguish.

'Darlin' it's only for tonight. Now, come on, take that lady's 'and. She ain't goin' to bite you,' said Ma.

The younger woman was hovering nearby. Close up she looked okay. She had blonde wavy hair tied up in a turban and a pinafore.

'Take care of 'im, won't you?' begged Ma to the woman, who shrugged her response, and rather roughly grabbed Ron's hand and marched him back to her house. Ma and I watched him go. He struggled with her tight grip, turning round to look at us, his face twisting with misery as he was taken inside and the door shut.

With that, our new landlady gestured to us to follow her inside the dark interior of her hallway.

She showed us into the tiny space which was barely as big as our old flat in Bevington Street. Somehow, it felt poorer still even than there, as the walls were streaked with dirt, the kitchen coated in a layer of grease, and the general smell of the rooms was a combination of urine and fat frying. I watched as a line of cockroaches froze on the walls as we entered the small kitchen, which didn't even have a separate scullery.

'You can stay in here,' the woman said sharply, and pointed towards a tiny room at the back of the kitchen. We trooped inside, almost fainting with tiredness.

Once alone, Ma shut the door, and leant against it for a moment, her eyes shut. I took in the contents of the room. There was a single iron bedstead with a stained mattress. Underneath it was a potty. There was a small sink in the corner, a fireplace that looked like it hadn't been lit in a long while, a long-handled broom and a chair. That was it. The sum total of the next phase of our lives. How were we going to manage? We stood there, gazing at the miserable space that was our new home, no one saying a word.

Patsy started wailing. Ma desperately tried to shush her so we didn't get thrown out of this house, however mean it was. Ma and Patsy got onto the bed and Joanie and me curled up on the floor. We had no blankets, and I had a hunch that the landlady Jean would refuse us any further help – she was already reluctant having us there. I whispered to Joanie to keep her coat on – thank goodness we'd worn them up here – saying they'd be as good as blankets and anyway we were used to sleeping with our coats for extra warmth.

Just as we were settling down to sleep there was a great hammering on the front door. We all bolted upright and Patsy started crying again. There was the sound of the door opening then an exclamation, the noise of hobnail boots running across the floorboards and the door flew open, revealing our brother Ron.

He was in floods of tears, saying over and over again, 'I want me Ma!'

I leapt up off the floor and pulled Ron into the room, checking him over in case he'd been hurt.

'What is it, Ron, lovely boy, what's wrong?' I asked, pulling him into my arms.

'I'm not goin' back there. The lady was mean to me. She said I was a nasty littl' boy from a slum an' told me to look after the babies, then she said she was goin' out an' that's when I ran.' Ron was panting with fright.

'It's alright now. You're safe wiv yer family,' I murmured, stroking his thick hair. He was 12 years old but in some ways seemed younger.

'I ain't goin' back there, I ain't,' he cried, his skinny body racked with sobs.

'Come on, you're goin' nowhere. Settl' down 'ere wiv me an' if that ol' landlady causes a fuss we'll tell 'er wot for,' I reassured him. We lay back down on the floor. There was barely enough room to move but we finally managed to get a few hours' rest.

I slept fitfully though, my dreams interspersed with the sound of air-raid sirens and trains that I tried to board but could never seem to manage to get onto. I stood on ghostly platforms watching the trains snake away from me, leaving me with a longing to be on them, heading for home, perhaps.

I woke up in a daze the next morning. I was woozy with lack of real sleep, and for a minute I thought I was back in our bedroom in Spa Road. I smiled and stretched then opened my eyes. The reality of our situation came crashing down on me once again.

I surveyed the room, sighing. There was a lot of work needed to make this halfway habitable. As the others got themselves up and went for a wash out by the tap in the yard, I got down on my knees and scrubbed that bloody floor. When I'd finished that, I swept out the fireplace as best I could, and looked around for newspaper to start laying it.

With a determined whistle I carried on with my chores. It was up to me to keep everyone as cheery as possible. I finished the jobs with renewed vigour, unpacking the rest of the belongings into neat piles. My head felt thick with exhaustion, but it was another day, and things always looked better in the daytime.

Ma swept her eyes round the room, and I could see the distaste on her face. Jean, our host, was as singularly unwelcoming as the night before. She insisted that Ron sleep alongside her son on the floor of the only other room apart from the kitchen. Ma reluctantly agreed.

*

It took only two days before Ma took action. With determined grace, she fitted her hat on her hair, covered her worn clothes with her coat and picked up her basket and purse, before leaving the house. She looked like a woman on a mission. Later that day she returned with writing paper and a pen. This must be serious. I'd never seen Ma spend our precious pennies on luxuries such as these.

She handed them to me, and she dictated a letter to Pa over my shoulder, telling him in no uncertain terms that we were living 'badly', and either we came home or he'd better find us somewhere else to live. Well, I couldn't believe her nerve. I bit my lip, hoping that Pa would do what was best for his family.

I don't think any of us could believe it when a letter arrived from him a couple of weeks later saying he was coming up to Birmingham with his mate Charlie, and would pop in to see us on his way back to London.

It was late afternoon when the truck containing Pa and his friend pulled up in our street. We heard a loud beep from the road, and at once Ron and Joanie ran out to see what the commotion was.

'Oi, kids, your old pa's 'ere, can you believe it?' came a shout from the front.

Ma and I wiped our hands on our aprons, and she paused to fix her hair before we both went outside. Pa was there but he'd lost weight and looked ill. He saw the shock register on our faces.

'Don't you worry about me, Em, old girl, I'm on the sick an' getting' paid for bein' 'ere, can you believe it?' he said triumphantly. 'Too much of the good times, that bloody doctor told me. I need to stop the drink though. I know I've been 'ittin' it 'ard lately, it's cos me 'eart was broken wiv you all bein' up 'ere without me.'

He jumped down from the cab and stumbled. So they'd dropped by the pub on their way here, I noted, not that I was surprised. So much for listening to the doctor. And all that rubbish about his heart being broken, well I knew just what to think of that. I sniffed as if there was a bad smell in the air, but there was more news to come.

'I've got you all a place in the country,' he beamed, clearly delighted with himself.

'What d'you mean, Ted?' said Ma, frowning. Was this another of his tricks?

'Well now, you won't believe this, but Charlie 'ere an' I drove into Birmingham. We were goin' through this small village an' low an' be'old a man jumped out in front of the lorry!' At this point Pa paused for dramatic effect. ' 'E said, "You've got to 'elp me, I've run out of fuel." Well, you can't be too careful these days an' so we said, "'Ow do we know that you're not an inspector of fuel?" an' 'e replied. "Course I'm not! I live 'ere. Give me a lift up to Braunston an' I'll show you." '

Pa shifted on his seat. He loved telling a tale, and they almost always revolved around him and his antics. 'So we drove up the 'ill an' there was a pub in the village called The Plough an' the geezer says to the publican, "Who am I?" An' the landlord replies, "You're Ted Slater," an' so Ted Slater called for three pints an' we 'ad a lovely evenin'. 'E got 'is petrol an' we got an 'ouse.'

'What do you mean, you got an 'ouse?' said Ma, frowning. She didn't know if this was one of his fanciful stories after one too many.

'No, really, Em, I've got us an 'ouse, a beautiful littl' cottage, I promise you,' Pa laughed, shaking his head at our

disbelieving faces. 'I told Ted Slater about the air raids an'
'avin' to hide in the shelter in the yard, or runnin' from the
pub to the Underground an' sleepin' on the platform till 6
a.m. when it's the all-clear, an' I says to 'im, "It's lovely 'ere.
'Ow nice it must be to live 'ere." At which point 'e says, "Why
don't you then?" It was then the publican says, "Mrs Evans
'as two empty cottages in Cross Lane. Why not take Ted
down to see 'er?" So that's what we did. We went an' saw
'er. I says, "How much is the rent?" an' she says, "Three 'an
six," an' I says, "Are you kiddin'? We'll take it!" an' I paid 'er
a month upfront there an' then.' Pa finished with a flourish,
and sat back, satisfied, waiting for our reaction.

If Ma balked at the thought that Pa had enough money
swilling about to pay for a month's rent on top of his beer,
then she didn't say a word. He'd sent little of it up to us to
feed his children.

Ron was the first to react. His excitement spilled out. 'A
cottage, wiv trees an' country an' that?' he said eagerly, his
face shining as he turned to our old man for an answer. The
house in Nottingham was hardest for Ron out of all of us.
Night after night Ron was subjected to the landlady's boy
wetting himself on the floor next to him. Every day, Ron
was forced to go into his new school in urine-smelling short
trousers, on top of itching with the fleas that inhabited every
crevice of the piss-stained house.

'Yep,' said Pa. 'Trees an' birds an' there's a canal be'ind the
cottage, plenty for kids to do.'

Well, we were speechless. Pa had come up with the answer.

And so it was arranged. He'd go back to London, pack
up the furniture and bring it back to our new home with
his mate Charlie. We would have to wait just a few short
weeks before we would have our own cottage to live in. It

sounded like heaven. Joanie and Ron were beside themselves with happiness.

Before he left, Pa gave us the news that Les had become an auxiliary fireman, fighting the Blitz infernos. Ma's face fell. Her firstborn son had joined the war, albeit on home soil. She clutched her hands to her heart.

'Now don't go worryin' yerself, Em. 'E'll be alright. Les always knows 'ow to keep out of trouble,' said Pa, lighting himself a rolled up cigarette.

Ma looked at him in disbelief before shaking her head. She'd taken the news hard, as any mother would.

''E 'as to find 'is own way, Ma,' I said, hoping to soothe her.

She touched my arm, and swallowed down whatever she had wanted to say. Finally she nodded, and I gave her a hug.

'Les'll be alright, you'll see. I'm proud of 'im doin' 'is bit for the war,' I finished, hoping a bit of patriotism might lift her mood.

It worked. At that, she smiled. 'Yes, 'e's a good boy and 'e'll do us all proud.'

Even so, I felt worried for him. There were often stories of firemen being trapped by flames down at the docks or falling beneath collapsing buildings. He was a brave lad, braver than his father, and I was proud of his spirit. But he was just a boy, really, and the thought of him struggling with great burning buildings filled me with horror. The last time we'd seen him was on the eve of our departure from London. He must have known then that he would join the firefighters but hadn't said a word. That was like Les, these days. He kept his thoughts and feelings close to his chest, and we had to get used to our wilful, cheeky brother going his own way and making his own decisions, like a man.

I held Pa accountable for Les's decision. Les was always

disgusted with Pa's avoidance of his national duty. To me, it seemed that Les was trying to personally make up for Pa's inadequacies by throwing himself, literally, into the flames of warfare. I vowed to myself that if anything happened to Les, Pa would feel the full force of my wrath, and I shuddered to think of my 16-year-old brother battling the fires that lit the horizon night after night.

Pa's visit was a short one. He stayed for a couple of hours, then left with his pal, saying he'd be back to collect us. I watched him go with mixed feelings. I wanted to believe he'd be as good as his word but time after time he'd let us all down. Would this time be different?

CHAPTER 14

Bombshells

Miraculously, it was. A few weeks later, Pa turned up. He'd been up to the cottage in Braunston, which we learnt was near Coventry, and given it a fresh coat of paint and even put up some wallpaper. He'd never done anything like that for us before and I was immediately suspicious. I even wondered if he'd met a lady friend in the village, as there was no other reason I could think of for him doing all that decorating. Unless, of course, he was trying to look like the family man to the people he'd met. I supposed that might be behind it. He'd brought the beds, piano, table and chairs from Spa Road all the way up to the village. We scrambled into Charlie's lorry and off we went.

When we arrived we couldn't believe our luck. The village was just as Pa described: small and quaint, with a church in the middle. Our house was down a lane that bristled with plant life, trees and late flowers. There was even a canal, just as he'd said. At the end of the lane was a small cottage with pretty net curtains and swallows flitting out of their nest under the eaves.

For a moment we fell silent, spellbound by the heavenly vision. Was this really our new home, or was it a cruel trick of Pa's and we'd have to go back to that horrible, infested room in Northampton?

Pa pushed open the front door.

'We're 'ome,' was all he said. In that briefest of moments, I could have kissed him!

Ma and I struggled in with our belongings while Pa sauntered off to the local pub. We unpacked, all the while exclaiming delightedly at the view from the cottage kitchen and at the pantry.

From that day onwards Ron and Joanie were free as birds, playing outside, running through those fields and up and down the lanes as if they'd spent their lives cooped up in cages.

In contrast, my life got harder. Ma's health was getting worse by the day, and I was constantly worried about her. Pa even brought the big bed downstairs and into the kitchen, so she could sleep there rather than attempt to climb the stairs. I could see what ordinary things like washing or cooking took out of her, so I took over her chores. I became even more of a mother to my siblings, in effect. I'd always looked after them, but somehow it was different now. Ma couldn't do it anymore, so I stepped in for her. My days were filled with washing the bed linen, scrubbing and drying clothes, peeling potatoes, queuing up at the local stores for our rations and scolding the younger ones for running wild. Joanie was a young woman of 14 but she hated doing the chores, and would use any ruse to get out of them. I scolded her, but didn't blame her for it. What young girl would want to spend her days scrubbing shirts?

I was determined to get a job, though. I missed Peek Frean's – the independence it brought, my friends Rita and Lil, and the money it brought in. Seeing the German aircraft only increased my desire to do something practical towards the war effort. I'd seen the posters urging us women into the factories and I wanted to join the fight in whatever way I could.

Even tucked away in this tiny village, we weren't immune

to the conflict. At night we heard the heavy throbbing of the German bombers overhead, making their way to Coventry to create bloody mayhem there as well.

On nights like those, the droning of the engines filled the sky. I looked, fearfully, out of the cottage windows and saw the black shapes make their steady way across our patch of sky. My heart sank into my boots thinking of our friends in London. So many people were dying every day, and I could only stop and wonder what had become of our neighbours and friends.

It wasn't long before I found work in a munitions factory. Rootes had been a car factory but was now making armaments. I caught the bus into Coventry and arrived expecting an interview like at Peek Frean's, but instead they were desperate for able-bodied workers. After a short medical examination during which my teeth were scrutinised and my blood pressure was taken, I was declared fit for war work and was taken to the factory floor.

Well, the noise was unbelievable. There were great machines making shuddering noises, a dense acid smell of the chemicals being used in the production of the bombshells, and the heat of intense, hard labour. From the minute I got in there, I loved it.

I was taken to a large space that looked like an aircraft hangar, and I gasped when I saw the rows and rows of thousands of upright shell cases. *There are enough down there to win the war*, I thought.

'Welcome to Rootes,' said a friendly looking girl, about my age. She wore red lipstick and had blonde hair, which was tied up in rollers underneath the factory-issue turban, and to me looked very glamorous despite the fact she was wearing her uniform.

'My name's Betty. I'm goin' to look after you,' and she held her hand out for me to shake. I was amazed at her accent.

'You're from London,' was all I managed to say, amid the noise and heat of the factory floor.

'Born an' bred in Putney, an' proud of it,' she said, with a wink. 'I was evacuated wiv me family at the start of the war. I want you to tell me everyfink you know about London. Gawd I miss it, and me friends there.'

At that, I nodded my head. There was little I could say. I missed my home city and pals too.

'Now come on, let's get you changed into your overalls an' we'll get ta work. The war won't win itself, you know!' she laughed. I liked her immediately, and knew from that minute we'd be firm friends.

Betty took me to a small room in the bowels of the building. There was little there apart from a mess of pipes and wires, and rows of grey lockers against yellowing walls. It was even hotter down here, and I pulled a face.

'You'll get used to it,' she smiled. ' 'Ere's your locka an' your key. Keep 'em safe cos there ain't no replacement,' she said, looking away as I changed out of my skirt and blouse and into my uniform.

I felt like a proper worker, part of the war effort, and I grinned at the sight of myself in the small cracked mirror on the wall.

'We like to keep ourselves neat an' lookin' smart. Can't let those Jerry bastards rob us of our looks, eh?' Betty joked.

'Right, up we go an' I'll show you the ropes.'

Back up on the factory floor, Betty took me to a line of bombshells, standing upright in rows like sentinels.

'This is where you'll work. It's 'ard work, this ain't for

cissies. 'Ow d'you feel about some 'ard graft?' she asked, suddenly serious.

It was obvious the war took on an immediate meaning here. We were the supply lines for our troops and this was dangerous work as well.

'I've spent me life graftin' 'ard. Don't you worry about me. I'll do what I 'ave to,' I said.

Betty nodded. She pointed to a line of girls all scrubbing the insides of the cases in preparation for the chemicals to be poured in. 'Now you've got to 'ave your eyes an' ears open to do this. Them there chemicals, well, if there's a mistake they could go off at any minute. Girls 'ave bin killed while fillin' shells so you've got to 'ave a steady 'and an' a strong nerve.'

I gulped, but I knew I had both.

'If you spend a few minutes watchin' Evie work the machines, she can show you the ropes. Oh an' watch out for those chemicals – they're 'ot as they're bein' poured so keep your 'ands well clear. I've got another couple of girls to settle in so I'll see you later.

'Oh an' don't worry if your 'ands go yellow, that's them chemicals,' she added. 'They call us the Canary Girls so it ain't all bad!' With that, Betty gave me a cheery wave, as if we weren't all surrounded by potential explosions, and left to find the other new recruits.

' 'Ello,' I said to Evie. She was a tall, mousy looking girl but she said a polite 'hello', and I was soon learning the ropes.

I started cleaning the insides of the cases and I soon learnt why it was dangerous work. Within minutes I'd cut my arm badly on the jagged metal edges. Evie sent me off to the factory nurse who gave me a stern look before cleaning the wound and tying bandage around it.

'You've got to be extremely careful, Hilda,' she said, her cut-glass accent sounding strange in the hubbub of the factory. 'Those cases are razor sharp. Didn't the girls warn you?' She finished my bandage with a safety pin.

'They did, but it's my first day,' I said.

The nurse gave me a look, and said, 'Well, be careful, Hilda, we don't want worse accidents than that.'

I walked back to my area feeling a fool, but determined to do my best next time round.

The rest of the day went past in a flash because I had to concentrate so hard. When the five o'clock hooter went, and we all went down to the changing room, Betty came up to me and said, ' 'ilda, we're all goin' for a quick one in town before goin' 'ome. You comin?'

'I'd love to,' I replied, grabbing my coat and hat.

I felt guilty for leaving Ma with all the chores, but the chance of a bit of freedom and company with girls my own age was too tempting to pass up. So me, Betty, Evie and a few other girls whose names I hadn't yet learnt, went into a pub in Coventry.

Where I came from it wasn't the done thing for women to go to pubs, but now there was a war on, all the rules seemed to have changed. We were free in a way we'd never been before, despite the restrictions of wartime.

'What you 'avin'?' said Betty at the bar.

'Oh, I don't know, I ain't never been to a pub before,' I blushed, feeling very naïve all of a sudden.

'Don't worry, 'ilda, 'ave a port 'n' lemon like me. You'll like that. You're one of us now, a Canary Girl. We've got a reputation in these parts!' she joked, squeezing my arm for reassurance.

We took our drinks to a table. Well, I felt so grown up! The taste of the port took some getting used to, but I sipped it and joined in with the jokes and banter around the table.

I hadn't laughed so much in ages. It felt good to have friends and be out of the house.

'So then, 'ilda, 'ave you got yourself a fella?' said one of the girls. Her name was Phyllis and she was sporting a new engagement ring on her finger, which we'd all duly admired. Her accent was a strong Cockney one as well. She was from Stepney, and had been evacuated to a nearby village with her mother and three siblings.

'A bloke, that'd be a fine thing!' I chortled. 'I ain't got time for a man. I got enough on me plate wiv the kids an' me Ma bein' ill,' I said, with a shrug.

'I'm sure you'd like a gentleman caller tho', wouldn't you, 'ilda?' said Betty with a nudge.

'Oh blimey, you're makin' me blush,' I said, enjoying the attention.

'Alright, 'ilda, it's a mission. We're goin' to find you a fella, you see if we don't,' said Betty and raised her glass. 'To us girls – and the lads we're all goin' to marry!'

'To us girls,' we all said, in unison.

Back at the cottage, I walked back in to find Ma lying on her bed, white as a sheet.

'Where are the others?' I said. 'What's been goin' on?' I knew that something was wrong. The warm, happy feeling disappeared in an instant, replaced by a sense of dread rising from the pit of my stomach. I looked at the chair that had been broken into pieces, lying on the floor of the kitchen.

'Now, don't react, 'ilda, but me and your Pa 'ave 'ad a fallin' out,' she said weakly. Her eyes wouldn't meet mine. They were bruised and sore looking, like she'd been crying.

'What 'appened, Ma? You've got to tell me,' I said in a panicked voice, rushing to her bedside. My eyes searched Ma's face as she spoke.

'Nuffink unusual, 'ilda. Your Pa 'ad spent the money to pay the grocer down the pub so I gave 'im wot for,' she answered, her chin wobbling just a little.

'So what did 'e giv you in return?' I demanded, feeling the anger in me rising.

She sighed. 'I'll 'ave to tell you, I suppose, cos Ron saw it 'appen. 'E 'eard a racket an' looked through the letterbox an' saw your pa go for me wiv one of the chairs...' her voice trailed off.

I looked at her, horrified. ''E beat you with a chair?'

She nodded. 'Then Ron, bless 'im, charged in wiv a spade an' told your Pa that 'e wasn't to beat me no more, an' 'e was goin' to giv Pa one wiv the spade. Of course, Pa just laughed, an' turned on him, so littl' Ron turned on 'is toes an' ran off, his Pa chasin' 'im. I haven't seen 'ide nor 'air of either of 'em since.'

All the goodwill he'd created finding us a home went as if it had never come. He couldn't change, he was a black-hearted villain, and he beat the mother I adored and the siblings I mothered as if they were my own. I got up from the table. Dinner could wait.

'I'd better go an' find Ron. Pa'll be in The Plough by now, 'e always is at this time of night. Don't you worry, Ma, now I'm workin', we'll have money for the grocer. I'll get Ron an' put the meal on. You rest up. It'll all be okay.'

I said those words as if things would turn out fine, but at that moment I was pretty sure they never would. All thoughts of meeting a fella went out of my head. I couldn't risk finding one like That Man, by God I couldn't do that. I put my coat and hat back on and went out into the evening to find my brother.

CHAPTER 15

Courting

'Go on, 'ilda, let's go out for a drink an' a dance!' said Joanie, who was 15 going on 20, curling her thick black hair with one finger, staring intently at me.

'Oh I ain't in the mood tonight. Go yerself. I'm tired, I've been at it all day at the factory an' me feet are sore.' I rubbed my left foot as I freed it from my boots, wiggling my toes with the satisfaction of being released after a long day standing up, cleaning out the shells. My back hurt and my forehead felt tense after so many hours spent concentrating on not spilling the incendiary filling, which could set the factory ablaze.

I'd been working at the munitions factory for three months. I held my hands up to the dim light of the gas lamp. They were starting to go yellow, like the skin of the rest of the girls at the factory, because of the chemicals we were using. It was almost a badge of honour, to show we were working hard for the soldiers in France and elsewhere. Still, I didn't like the way they looked jaundiced, even in this light.

' 'ildy, come on, I ain't goin' to go by meself, an' there's a good band on at The Horseshoe. You'll miss out. Please,' Joanie pleaded, cocking her head to one side.

She was definitely the beauty of the family. She had big dark eyes and lustrous black hair, Ted's colouring, while the rest of us had inherited Ma's lighter brown hair and brown eyes.

'Oh go on then, I give in. I'll come wiv you, Joanie, but I'll expect you to buy me a drink,' I yawned, thinking how nice it would be to put my feet up and stay by the fireside tonight. Autumn was coming, and even though the days were fair enough, the nights were starting to draw in, and sitting by a cosy fire was a very attractive prospect.

'Thanks, 'ildy, you won't regret it, I promise you,' said Joanie, as she scampered up the stairs to start getting ready.

She always liked to spend hours brushing her hair and dressing in front of the mirror. I didn't know what took her so long, though. We only had one fancy dress each, and that had to be washed and dried each time we wore it so we'd have something to wear on nights like these. I sighed and rested my head back on the chair. I was only 20 years old but sometimes I felt like an old woman. I'd spent my life cooking, cleaning and washing for my family. Maybe it was about time I got out and had some fun.

Later that evening, Joanie and I walked into the village to catch the bus to Weedon, where the dance was being held. The bus was packed with village girls, and we cooed ' 'ellos' to each other and caught up on the gossip.

At the pub we decided to sit towards the back. I went off to buy us a drink while Joanie sat at the table. I wasn't surprised to see a couple of soldiers sitting with her when I got back. Joanie was such an attractive girl, she always got lots of attention from the fellas.

'Oi, 'ildy, meet Sid an' Albert. They're stationed at the barracks 'ere an' are on leave an' want a bit of entertaining,' she said, winking up at me.

Both men stood up as I put the drinks down on the table.

'We'd 'ave bought you girls those. The next ones are on us! By the way, me name's Sid and this is my mate Albert, 'e's the one wiv the carrot-top!' The taller of the two held out his hand to shake mine.

I said ' 'ello', and smiled at Albert, who indeed had a crop of red hair. He smiled back at me. They seemed like polite lads, I thought. No harm in being polite ourselves. So once we'd all sat down again, we talked until the sounds of the band striking up brought Joanie to her feet.

'Come on, everyone, we don't want to miss a minute,' and with that she grabbed Sid and they went arm-in-arm out through to the back to the dance area.

Albert and I smiled shyly at each other, then he offered his arm for the same.

'I'm all right, thanks,' I said, feeling a little shy of this handsome soldier and not wanting to appear too forward. But I let him open the door into the back room for me, and the two of us joined Joanie and Sid as the first notes from the band struck up.

Twice Albert asked me to dance with him, and in the end I agreed, thinking all the while that I'd better not lead him on. With all the trouble at home between Ma and Pa, I knew I could never bring a boy home. Pa would've hit the roof, and me and Ma would've got a new pair of black eyes for it.

But Albert and I chatted throughout the evening, and I swear his eyes twinkled at me as we talked. We discovered we had shared tastes: we both loved the sound of the military bands and big band music, and we both loved walking in the countryside that was so new to the pair of us.

At the end of the night the boys offered to walk us to our bus but I refused, thanking them for a pleasant evening before turning away, with Joanie in tow, chattering about Sid having nice eyes.

'Look, Joanie, I don't want to rock your boat, but those boys are just back on leave. They'll only be 'ere for a couple of weeks at the most an' they'll be out wiv every girl in town, so don't 'old your breath for 'em.' I felt I had to be realistic.

'An' another thing – if Pa found out either of us was courtin', 'e'd come down on us like a ton of bricks, an' you know that's true,' I finished, wishing I didn't have to say it.

Joanie didn't look worried in the slightest. She was the only one of us that Pa had never hit so she had less to fear from his rages. 'There's a dance on tomorrow night as well. I said we'd go.'

I turned to look at Joanie. Her face was alive with mischief. 'Why the 'ell did you do that?' I said. 'We'll get into trouble!'

'No, 'ilda, I've thought it through. We'll sneak out once Pa's in the pub. You know 'e spends all evenin', every evenin' there these days. Anyway, I like Sid an' I'd like to see 'im again. As you say, 'e'll be off fightin' the Jerries, an' who knows what'll 'appen to 'im.'

Well I didn't have an answer to that!

The next night, we left the house only when Pa was safely ensconced in his local. Ma had insisted that I go out with Joanie, saying I would at least keep her on the straight and narrow. I could tell Ma was pleased I was out enjoying myself like the young woman I was, rather than being an extra pair of hands at home.

The boys were there, as they said they'd be, looking nervous. 'We thought you weren't comin',' said Albert. 'Let me get you both a drink. Port 'n' lemon alright for you?'

'Yes, thanks,' I said, flummoxed that they hadn't stood us up, or started chatting to other girls. There were plenty of them in there and we were almost an hour late.

'Sorry, we get a bit o' trouble at 'ome wiv Pa,' I explained to Sid as Albert went to the bar. ' 'E don't like us comin' out, an' Lord knows what 'e'd do if 'e thought we was wiv a coupl' of soldiers.' I shrugged my shoulders.

'That ain't right,' replied Sid. 'But then again, 'e don't know we're not good blokes so maybe 'e's just protectin' you.

If I was your father, I wouldn't want you bein' taken in by wide boys. There are plenty of those about, let me tell you.'

We all grinned at that, and I wondered if that's what Sid and Albert were, a couple of wide boys out to meet girls like us for fun before being shipped off to war. They didn't seem to be ladykillers though. They both seemed sweet and polite, but looks could be deceiving.

I shook my head and told myself to stop getting silly ideas. We barely knew them and they'd be off soon. Both men were posted to Weedon Barracks. Albert, who was from Bow in east London, was on leave from fighting with the REME (Royal Electrical and Mechanical Engineers) in North Africa. Sid was from Shoreditch, and they'd become friends while serving together.

Albert described the scorching heat and the flies that followed him everywhere in Africa. We listened, fascinated, until it was time to go through for the dance. This time I let Albert have three dances with me, and we spent all evening chatting and laughing. We had the same sense of humour, and by the end of the night I felt like I'd known him for ages.

This time we let the boys walk us to the bus station. Sid and Joanie had a small kiss, while Albert and I shook hands more formally. We'd all arranged to meet the next night. I knew I should really be at home looking after Ma in the evenings but for some reason I was enjoying our nights out and I didn't want them to stop.

We did the same again for the next two nights. Then on the next night Albert asked me if I'd go for a walk with him. Normally, I'd never have gone with a man on my own, not in a million years. I'd been brought up to mind my manners, even if I was from a Bermondsey slum! But something about

Albert made me feel safe. I was pretty sure he wouldn't try anything on, even if secretly I was starting to want him to.

We walked along the lanes until we got to a bench by a field. The moon was huge that night, a big autumn moon that made me shiver. Albert, or Bert as I had started to call him, took off his coat and wrapped it round my shoulders. We sat there talking for a while, watching that moon looking down on us, feeling like we were the only people on the planet.

Then Bert turned to me and said, ' 'ilda, what would you say to bein' my girl?'

I could see his face. He was deadly serious and staring at me as if his life depended on my answer. I hesitated for a moment, and then I heard the words coming out of my mouth. 'I'd say, I'd like that, Bert,' I replied, feeling my stomach do cartwheels.

He looked at me for a minute, and then leant in towards me and kissed me ever so softly on the lips. I kissed him back. My first ever kiss. It felt strange and wonderful. I know it sounds like a silly romance novel, perhaps, but I really did feel my heart skip a beat, and thought, *'ilda, you're in trouble 'ere*.

He put his arm around me, I could feel him shiver slightly, either with cold or with the excitement of his declaration. We sat there for ages, and kissed a bit more, until I said, 'Gawd, Bert, what's the time? I'll miss me bus an' then I'll be in trouble!'

'Alright, 'ilda, don't you worry. We'll get you 'ome whatever 'appens,' he said as we hurried back to the pub. Joanie and Sid were waiting for us outside.

'Come on, 'ilda, we're late. What 'ave the pair of you been up to?' she said with a wink and a nudge.

I couldn't reply. My mind and heart were racing in unison.

I'd got myself a fella. A decent, lovely fella. The world had suddenly become an unimaginably exciting and wonderful place.

We ran as fast as we could for the bus, and managed to get it with seconds to spare. We waved off our boys, then sat talking and giggling nineteen to the dozen all the way home. Joanie was delighted I was Bert's girl. She said she'd become Sid's girl as well that night. 'They must've planned it together, bless 'em,' she said with delight.

'Gawd, we'd better calm down before we get in. Can't 'ave the old man gettin' an 'int of what we're up to,' I cautioned.

By the time we crept back into the house, it was pitch black. Ma was fast asleep and Pa was nowhere to be seen.

'Thank the Lord for that!' exclaimed Joanie and we both crept up to bed, trying not to wake Ron and Patsy.

The next day, I tried to contain my feelings, a mixture of excitement and nerves, but Ma spotted it immediately. When I got home from work I told her I was walking out with a young man. She nodded her head and smiled, telling me to take care and to keep him out of Pa's way, if I knew what was good for me. She knew we'd been out, of course she did, but she didn't judge us or condemn us. She realised that as young women, one day we'd fly the nest, and meeting a sweetheart was the start of it.

She kissed my cheek, sighing, 'You're all grown up now, 'ilda. I can't believe it. It's like you were a babe in me arms only yesterday. You were me firstborn, an' you're me best friend, an' I want only good for you. As long as this chap Bert is worthy of you, then it's okay by me.'

I gave her a big hug. She was in good spirits this evening, and the swelling in her legs had subsided enough to allow her to go out for a walk with Ron and Patsy that afternoon, so things seemed to be looking up, for all of us.

That day we also received a letter from Les, telling us he was on shore leave and coming to visit. It was a shock to learn that he'd enlisted with the Merchant Navy, lying about his age. The letter was written in Les's hand but there was no post mark, nothing to say what ship he'd written from or which part of the world's seas.

Ma had read the letter aloud, and we all listened attentively, excited to be seeing our brother again.

Les appeared at the cottage gate just a day later, and we tumbled out and surrounded him, hugging him and touching his arms to make sure he was real. It was a Saturday morning and Pa was out with his mates, probably in the pub, so it was just us siblings and Ma to greet him. He looked older. He carried his kit bag over his shoulder and I could see why the Navy had believed he was a man. The war had drawn lines on his young face, but he was still our Les and we chatted and fussed over him till he was quite fed up with our attentions.

'Enough, Ma,' he said as she brought him yet another cuppa and a slice of her homemade cake.

'Don't go spoilin' me or I might not want to go back,' he added.

I saw Ma wince. Of course she didn't want him to go but she also knew he was dead set on being a hero.

'What's been goin' on then?' Les asked, biting into the sponge.

Joanie and I glanced at each other, then turned our blank faces to him and shook our heads. I hadn't decided yet how to tell my protective brother that I was courting. I didn't know how he'd react.

'Oh nuffink much. 'Ere, 'ave another biscuit,' I said airily, passing the plate to him. Pa was in the pub most nights, and sometimes days as well, so it felt like it was just Ma, Les, Ron, Joanie, Patsy and me, all together enjoying good times again.

Later that evening, I asked Ma if she didn't mind me meeting Bert again. She waved me off with a smile, and so Joanie and me slipped off to smarten ourselves up.

We came back downstairs and found Les with his Navy coat on, standing in the hallway.

'Thought I'd come an' see the local nightlife for meself,' he said with a wink.

Joanie and I looked at each other again. What could we say? How could we dissuade him? I couldn't think of a single reason why he shouldn't come, apart from the obvious. And, kissing Ma on the cheek, he opened the door and we walked through, as quiet as mice, our heads racing with excuses that we weren't quick enough to blurt out.

'Don't you want a rest, Les luvvie?' I said, finally, with a fixed smile on my face. I had to find a way of keeping him at home. 'Ma's been desperate to see you. Don't make 'er miss you even more. You don't want to come wiv us. It's just a borin' old dance, nuffink excitin', we're not in the city now, you know,' I said, my voice slightly higher than usual.

Les looked at me, realising something was afoot, but I smiled back at him, careful to keep my face as bland as possible. He seemed to be fooled, but wouldn't give up on his plan to come with us. 'Now, 'ow often do I get the chance to see me sisters out on the town, eh?' he replied, pulling his coat round him and placing his cap on his head. There was no stopping him.

The three of us walked to the bus stop together, and stood, stamping our feet on the tarmac because of the cold while we waited. All the while I was thinking, *how do I get rid of Les?* It was a terrible thing for a sister to think, but I was desperate not to stand up my Bert. I kept racking my brains but couldn't find an answer.

We boarded the bus and made our way to Weedon. Joanie was not meeting Sid that night for some reason, but I had arranged to meet Albert at our bench, a little way off down a lane. There had to be a way of diverting Les. When we reached Weedon, I made an excuse that I was going to meet a girlfriend, and that I'd meet up with Les and Joanie a bit later. Les and Joanie headed off in the direction of the pub, while I turned to walk to our bench, and there was Albert himself.

He'd wanted to meet me off the bus rather than make me walk on my own. That was just like him, thoughtful and gentlemanly. I walked up to him and said ' 'ello'. He took my arm and bent to kiss me.

At that moment we heard a loud 'Oi! What the 'ell are you doin' wiv me sister?'

We turned in the direction of the noise, and saw Les running towards me, his face a mask of fury.

'Oh Gawd, that wasn't supposed to 'appen!' I cried.

Then Les brought his fist back and slammed it into Albert's nose. A direct hit. One that Pa would've been proud of.

Albert reeled back, and I grabbed Les's arm and screamed, 'Get off, get off 'im. 'E's me fella!'

At that moment everything went quiet. Les swivelled his head round to meet mine and gawped at me. 'Your fella?' he shouted.

'Yes!' I said. ' 'E's my Bert!'

And, with that, Les dropped his arm, looking from me to Albert with a bemused expression. Albert, meanwhile was holding his nose, which was now streaming with blood, while I dug out a hankie from my bag.

'Gawd, 'ilda, why didn't you warn me?' said Les, looking shame-faced.

I was furious at Les for hitting my boyfriend. How dare he come over all Ted Johnson on us and use his fists to settle things! I was also angry at myself for letting this happen. I should have come clean and told Les I was seeing someone. I'd created all this because I'd been a coward, and now my Bert had a sore nose and a bloody uniform to show for it.

I turned to Bert, sure he would take one look at me and walk off. He wouldn't want to carry on with a girl whose brother attacked him for walking out with his sister. My heart slumped down into the pit of my belly. He would leave me for sure, and I'd be left broken hearted, and with an irate brother to boot.

What happened next was a total surprise.

Despite the fact that Albert was crouching on the roadside, holding my hankie up to his sore nose, he held out his right hand. I gazed at it, unthinking for a moment, then before I could speak, Les's arm reached over and he shook his hand.

Now who could believe that!

I blinked, then decided that if we were going to do this, we'd better do it properly, so by way of an introduction, I said, 'Bert this is my brother Les. Les this is my Bert.'

'Pleased to meet you,' came the muffled response from Albert.

'Likewise,' came Les's reply.

They both looked so gormless, I almost burst out laughing.

'I think you owe us all a drink, Les,' Albert quipped, grabbing my arm and easing up onto his haunches.

And, with that, we all walked off towards the pub, arm in arm.

CHAPTER 16

Pa's Comeuppance

'Oh, Bert, I can't believe you've got to go.' I said softly, my head resting on Albert's shoulder. 'We've barely 'ad time to get to know each other.'

As I spoke, Albert nuzzled his lips against my hair, kissing the top of my head and holding me even tighter. We were sat on 'our' bench, looking at 'our' view together, the last rays of the autumn sun setting as our time together drew to a close.

'I've got to go. Them's me orders, 'ilda. I'll think of you every day. I'll write to you, I promise. It'll be like we've never been apart,' he replied, his voice choking with emotion. Albert had received his posting back to Africa for tomorrow. His fortnight's leave had come to an abrupt end, and he was due to be shipped off back to the hot desert to fight for King and country once more.

I'd only known this man for two weeks but it felt like a lifetime already. I could hardly believe it was such a short time since we'd met. Our idyllic evenings spent walking and talking, and more often than not kissing and cuddling, were over and all that remained was the sweetness of those few days.

'I don't want you to go,' I said.

It was a pointless statement. He had to go. He was risking a court martial seeing me this evening. Albert was meant to be on guard duty at his barracks, but a mate had covered for him so he could abscond to come and meet me for our last night together. If he was found out he'd be in serious trouble, but it was testament to his feelings for me that he risked it. It was the most romantic thing anyone had ever done for me.

'I don't want to go, I want to stay 'ere wiv you, 'ilda. I want to take you to the flicks an' show you where I live in Bow, I want you to meet me Ma an' Pop, an' all me mates down in the East End. They'll love you as much as I do,' murmured Albert.

At that, I sat up with a bolt. 'You just said you love me. I 'eard you, Bert. Did you mean it, or is that something all the soldiers say to their girls?' I said, half-joking, half-dreading he hadn't meant it.

'I do, 'ilda. I love you. You're the girl for me. An' if I get out of this bloody war alive, I'll bleedin' marry you to prove it,' he said, firmly, pulling me back into his arms.

I struggled free. This was too important to mishear. 'You mean it then, Bert, you love me?' I asked, searching for the truth in his eyes.

They stared back at me, silent and safe, full of the love that, deep down I knew, was there.

I felt the same way. If I was honest with myself, I'd known since that first evening when he was such a gentleman and made me laugh, with none of the cocksureness some of the wide boys had. In the short time that I'd known him Albert had always been steady and solid: he showed up when he said he would, he barely drank (which was a very appealing quality after growing up with Pa), and he always looked smart. He liked to be tidy, punctual and wear polished boots. He knew the right way of doing things, and my goodness he was handsome. Blow me if he weren't a proper good-looking fella. He could've had his pick of the girls but he had chosen me. I could hardly believe my luck.

'Well, Bert, then I've got something to tell you,' I smiled, snuggling back into the warmth of his arms.

'What's that then, Duchess?' he said with a grin.

'Duchess! What d'you mean by that?' I laughed.

'Only that you're a cut above the other girls. You look like you should've been born a duchess, not a Bermondsey rag-a-muffin!'

With that I hit him playfully. 'I wouldn't mind bein' royalty,' I replied, with fake haughtiness. 'But where was I? Oh you've put me off me stroke, oh yes, I've got something to say to you, Albert. I love you too. I 'ave done since I met you. Now there you go, put that in your pipe an' smoke it!'

'I knew it!' he said with delight. 'I could read you like a book. Well, it was the same for me – love at first sight. I knew you was the one for me, girl. Now let's make a promise, when I get back from the war . . .'

I interrupted him. 'But what if you don't make it back? I can't bear it, I really can't bear the thought of losin' you.'

'Now don't talk silly, girl. WHEN I get back from the war,' he said, putting emphasis on the 'when', 'I'm goin' to marry you, an' you'll become Mrs Kemp, an' we'll live in Bow an' 'ave three kids an' be 'appy.'

He kissed me direct on the mouth, and we stayed liked that for a while before he broke off.

'So we're gettin' wed then,' I said happily.

For a while I'd thought I'd never let a man into my life. Pa had put me off having a family of my own. I always thought, *What if I ended up wiv a bad'un like Ma?*, and that was enough to stop any thoughts of romance stone dead. But Albert had changed all that. With his simple, quiet manner, he'd charmed me in ways that all those cocky boys in the pubs and at the dances could never have done.

'There's one big problem, though,' I said, turning to face Albert, my face serious all of a sudden.

'Your old man,' he replied. My father. The fly in our oint-
ment.

I'd never felt comfortable talking about That Man and
his beatings to anyone outside of my home. But Albert was
different. I felt I could tell him anything, and so I'd confided
in him. I'd told him how we lived in fear of the next attack
and his drunken rages. I shivered at the thought of the beating that would come my way, and possibly Albert's as well,
once he knew.

'I'll 'ave to tell him,' I said, looking at Bert.

He nodded in reply. 'I'll come wiv you,' he offered, and
I knew he would want to protect me, but I also knew there
were ways of telling Pa, and confronting him was never the
way to go.

'I'll see if I can find a moment. It'll be okay,' I said, to
reassure myself as much as anyone else.

Later that evening, after Albert had walked me back to the
bus stop, and we'd said a reluctant goodbye, I stepped into the
cottage. I was meeting Albert first thing tomorrow, getting
the early bus to Weedon before work so we could say a final
farewell. I was dreading it, but tonight I had other things to
dread. I took off my coat and hat and settled down in front
of the remains of the fire, where the embers glowed faintly
in the fireplace. Ma was asleep on her bed in the kitchen. Her
tired face looked at peace, and I tucked her blanket up under
her chin to keep her warm.

I hoped Pa wouldn't throw a fit, but it all depended on
how much he had drunk that night. He'd left just before
6 p.m. and it was nearly midnight now and he still wasn't
home. That was six solid hours of boozing. Things didn't
look good. I wanted to tell him before Albert went away. I
don't know why, I just felt I owed Albert that commitment.

After all, he was my fiancé, or as good as, and it felt important to tell Pa the truth.

I heard his boots on the path outside before I saw his dense shape move into the doorway. Silhouetted against the light of the bright autumn moon, he looked black and fearsome. I took a sharp intake of breath and pulled together all the reserves of courage I had in me. I was going to do this whatever happened.

'Pa, I need a word,' I said quietly, hoping we wouldn't wake Ma who looked deadbeat today.

Pa started for a second. He obviously hadn't seen me. The house was silent except for the faint snores from Ma, and the occasional creaks as the sleeping children moved then settled back into their dreams upstairs.

I gathered myself, cleared my throat and repeated, 'Pa, I need a word, it's important.' I eyed him like a cornered animal eyes its predator.

He stared down at me, adjusting his eyesight in the darkness, swaying slightly. He was drunk, but his mood was still unfathomable.

I slid out of my chair. I stood up and I faced him, square on. 'I've got a fella, Pa. 'E's a good, decent man an' 'e wants to marry me.' I could feel my legs start to shake. I felt like a little girl again.

'You've got a fella,' said Pa, and barked out a short laugh. This wasn't good. He sounded bitter almost. 'You've got yerself a bloke. An' at what point did you think that you should 'ave told your father?'

I opened my mouth to reply and he stopped me with a swift slap.

'Floozy,' he drawled, a thin line of dribble running from his mouth.

My face stung with the impact. I held a hand up to feel

it but I carried on speaking. Lord knows where I found the courage, maybe it was imagining the look on Albert's face when I tell him we're official.

' 'Is name is Albert an' 'e's from Bow. 'E's a Londoner an' from the East End like us.'

'You're a floozy.' Another slap hit me, this one harder, the blow knocking me against the mantelpiece. I gripped it for support. I ground my teeth and turned to face him once more.

' 'E's said e's goin' to marry me when the war's over,' I continued, defiantly. I could feel a trickle of blood from my split lip.

The next blow was more of a practised right hook, almost lazily delivered. It smashed into the side of my face, and I staggered back, hoping Ma would stay asleep in the kitchen at the back of the cottage, praying she wouldn't hear this latest assault.

'Floozy, you fuckin' floozy. 'Ow dare you meet a fella behind my back,' he sneered. 'I didn't bring you up to run around like a vixen on 'eat wiv the first man who sniffs round you, an' more I'll bet. 'As he 'ad you? 'As he? You filthy whore, just like your mother,' he stormed.

'What d'you mean, like my mother?' I hissed, through bared teeth, trying to keep the noise down, but losing myself to this fight. 'After all that woman 'as done for you. She keeps you fed, an' 'as brought up your children. You're right about something: you didn't bring me up, she did. Gawd's teeth, we never saw you except to come 'ome an' take what littl' food we 'ad to feed your sloshed stomach. Bring me up! 'Ow dare you even say it!'

I knew this wasn't the way to deal with Pa, but my fierce loyalty for my Ma burst from me in a torrent of anger. 'Ma 'as always been the kindest, most lovin' wife an' mother anyone ever 'ad, except you 'ad to ruin that as well. You're never 'appy unless you're ruinin' someone's life, ain't that the truth,' I hit back.

I hoped some of my words might actually make it through to Pa's beer-sodden heart, but I doubted it. It felt good to say them though. Twenty odd years of keeping my feelings under wraps, and now everything I thought about my father burst from me.

His reply came instantly. With a lunge, he felled me with a blow to my stomach. I toppled over, the poker and coal shovel clattering on the hearth beside me.

I could hear that Ma had woken up with the noise, and had stumbled into the room as fast as her swollen legs allowed her. She screamed, and tried to pick me up, but I was fighting for breath, with long guttural moans, desperate to drag the air inside me.

I don't know what That Man did next, but by the time I'd managed to sit up and work my lungs, he'd tramped up the stairs, not caring at the noise his boots made on the wooden steps and waking the others, most likely. He had no shame, no understanding that what he did was wrong. All he saw was his injured pride.

Ma helped me into the kitchen and gave me a glass of water. 'What did you say to 'im, 'ilda, to get a beatin' like that?' she asked as she gently wiped the blood from my face.

'You look a state. 'E really went for ya this time. Gawd, 'ilda, 'e'll end up killin' you one day, mark my words,' and she sat next to me, shaking her head.

I recoiled as she dabbed at my face again. Her words did not comfort me, in fact they frightened me, but I knew she was right. We'd gone beyond words to soothe my distress. It was time to do something about my situation. I couldn't carry on like this.

'You've got a cut across your fore'ead as wide as yer 'ead, and another on your lip. Your eyes are black an' blue as well.' She listed my injuries like an inventory.

'What did you say, 'ilda, to get 'im riled up like that?' Ma said, this time more softly.

'I told 'im about my Albert. An' that e's told me 'e's goin' to marry me when 'e's back from the war,' I said plaintively, sipping the cool water and feeling my body recover slowly.

Mum sighed a long sigh. 'Well, that was never goin' to be easy, but what's done is done. You can't take it back.'

'Neither can 'e,' I said, darkly, referring to the black eye already appearing on my face.

The next morning I caught the bus, ignoring the stares of the other passengers. I must have looked a fright. I had a black eye and bruising on my cheek that glowed yellow and purple. I had a torn lip and my mouth had swelled as it healed.

It was the day of my last meeting with Albert before he went back to Africa. I had lain awake most of the night, my body aching with all the new bruises and cuts I'd acquired, and my soul aching at the thought of losing the good man who, I was convinced, truly loved me.

I felt like I'd been hit by a truck. My insides felt parched and dry. Sorrow hollowed me out, made me lose my usual humour and love for life. I couldn't stand to see my Bert go away. Worse still, I couldn't bear to think that he might not survive this terrible war.

I'd boarded the bus with a heavy heart. I didn't care what other people thought of me, I just wanted to see my Bert and hear him say nice things to me, to make it all better.

When Albert saw me his face registered shock. He walked towards me, his eyes tracking my injuries. He saw me hobble off the bus, clutching my hip which was bruised and sore.

He shook his head slowly, like he couldn't believe what he was seeing.

He came to me and I collapsed into his arms, tears flowing. I held him like I was drowning and he was the lifejacket.

' 'E did this to you?' The way he said it was more like a statement.

I nodded in reply. I didn't need to say anything.

He held me to him for a long time.

'An' 'e did this because you told 'im you were seein' me?' he added, in a voice that cracked with emotion.

Again, I nodded.

I could feel Bert shaking. I drew back and looked at him, quizzically.

He was shivering with anger. I could tell he was struggling to keep his feelings in check.

He grasped my shoulder, and drew in breath when I winced.

'That's Pa. We just accept it. There's no point fightin' it. Every time I fight 'im I lose...' My voice trailed off, lost in the moment. There was nothing I could say to make any of this okay.

Without a word, Albert gently frog-marched me to the bus stop, telling me to go to work and he'd meet me later as he wasn't posted till later that night. Our romantic goodbye had evaporated. Albert looked like he meant what he said, and so I went off to work, all the day avoiding conversation with my friends.

It was not an uncommon sight, though. Many women came in to work with their hair covering bruises. We never mentioned it. We didn't want to cause more distress to the wives and mothers who were having a slap for their pains at home. Betty gave my arm an extra big squeeze while Evie and the others talked to me with cheery voices as if I was an invalid. But I was oblivious to it all. All I could think about was Albert, and what he was planning to do. My guts tightened as the day ended. I was worried that he would do something hasty, something he'd regret. I didn't want him getting into trouble with the law, or anyone else for that matter, over my no-good father.

Frantic with worry, I practically ran out of the factory at the end of the day, as fast as my wounded hip would carry me.

Albert was waiting for me.

'I've sorted it,' he said as a simple statement of fact. 'Your Pa won't be bovverin' you any more.'

'What d'you mean, Bert. What 'ave you done?' I asked, fear creeping into my voice. Had he hurt Pa, had he killed him? My mind raced straight to the worst-case scenarios – somehow they didn't seem so outlandish. The only way I could think that Pa's brutality could be stopped would be by the most unthinkable of crimes.

But Bert looked calm, too calm to have done anything so serious. Even so, my heart thumped through my chest, my mouth was dry.

'Tell me. What 'ave you done to 'im?' I said, staring directly into Albert's eyes, wanting to see whether he would tell me the truth, or whether he would lie to cover up something darker.

'I went to your 'ouse an' I called him out on 'is front door step. I told that man if 'e ever touches you or your mother again, 'e'll 'ave me to reckon wiv,' said Albert with a hard smile. 'I told 'im, 'ilda, an' 'e knew I was serious.'

I felt a rush of relief. 'What d'ya mean, Bert? Didn't you fight 'im? Did 'e go for you?' I said with disbelief.

' 'E tried to turn nasty, 'ilda, but I fronted 'im up. 'E's shorter than me, an' so I raised meself up and I stood square in front of 'im. I told 'im I'd beat the livin' daylights out of 'im if 'e ever touched you again. Ever.' Bert added with emphasis.

'An' I did it in front of 'is neighbours, out the front of your 'ouse. 'E won't 'it you again, my luv. 'E knows I'd kill 'im if 'e does. An' I would do it, for you.'

'Oh, Bert, I don't know what to say. That's the most romantic thing that's ever 'appened to me. Thank you, thank you.' Tears streamed down my damaged face.

I tried to kiss him but my lip was agony.

He laughed at that, and so I threw my arms around his lovely neck, not caring that it hurt to hold him. In that moment I knew I'd found my man, the man I wanted to be with, and be protected by. If he could stand in front of Ted Johnson, a prize fighter, and threaten him then he was ten times the man I thought he was. If it was possible, I loved him even more. Eventually he gently prised my arms off him.

'Look, 'ilda, I love you an' I'll be the one who takes care of you from now on, d'you understand? It's me an' you now,' he said with a serious expression.

I nodded. 'It's me and you, an' I'll think of you every day. Every day I'll pray you get 'ome to me, an' we'll get married, an' have lots of children an' be 'appy,' I added, like a mantra.

We hugged for the last time. Albert bent his head and kissed me.

This time I didn't care about the pain in my mouth. I couldn't believe my sweetheart was off to war. I couldn't believe this was the last time I would see Albert for goodness knows how long. I wouldn't admit to myself that he might never come back. I was sure in that moment that fate, or destiny, or whatever it was that brought lovers together, would not take him away now that we'd found each other. The sight of his proud, upright body as he walked off towards the barracks brought a lump to my throat.

He turned round and waved for the final time. I waved back, my handkerchief in my hand until I could see no more of him.

That night, I couldn't sleep for weeping. Already I missed him with a passion. I went over and over his words to me, praying that they'd come true, that he'd survive the bloodshed in Africa and come back to me so we could raise a family together. It seemed such a small, inconsequential dream set against the larger forces that ripped at our world in such unfathomable and treacherous ways.

At least Pa had been out when I'd returned. But I didn't care what Pa did now. My Bert had stood up to him, and I could only hope it was the start of a new life for me, free of my father's dark shadow.

The next day, my eyes were puffy and red, my battered face sore and swollen. I had downturned lips and felt on the brink of shedding yet more tears all day. All the girls at work noticed it.

'What's got into you, 'ilda? You're the life an' soul of the party normally,' bantered Betty, giving me a nudge.

'She's sighin' after 'er sweetheart,' said Evie, who was also from London, cocking her head to one side to take a long look at me. I was busy concentrating, pouring some of the noxious chemical mixture from a jug into one of the open-ended bomb shells. I had to go carefully as one tiny mistake could cost my life and those of the girls around me, so I had a minute to hide the tears brimming behind my lashes.

' 'Ere, 'ilda, come an' 'old this shell for a moment, I've got to pop to the lavvy,' said another, and I was forced to join the others and answer their good-natured teasing.

' 'Ere she is, all shy an' blushin',' said Betty.

'Alright, girls, I ain't shy. It's just my Albert, well 'e's gone back to the war, ain't 'e, an' I don't know if I'll ever see 'im again,' I confessed.

'I know a good cure for fallin' in love,' cried Evie, with a huge grin on her face. 'You should come up the pub wiv us tonight. There's a new lot of boys on leave an' I've 'eard there's a few good-lookin' ones left for us.'

'Yeah, 'ilda, you'll soon forget Bert when you see the new boys,' winked Betty, giving me another shove.

'You're turnin' into a right mope these days, ain't she, girls?'

'But I don't want to forget my Bert. 'E's said e's goin' to marry me when e's out of the Army,' I said, dolefully. 'It wasn't like your love affairs wiv handsome soldiers. This was the real thing. It was love,' I added, a little put out that she had implied Bert could be replaced with a cheap fling.

'Don't take it the wrong way, 'ilda. Betty don't mean nuffink by it. She just meant that a lot of the soldiers say all that luv stuff, dearie,' said Evie, returning to her shell. 'Look busy girls, the foreman's on his rounds.'

We all scattered back to our posts, leaving me holding the upturned shell. When the foreman had passed by and we had made a good show of working, we huddled back to continue our conversation.

'Come on, 'ilda, a night out won't 'urt you, an' if your Bert says e's goin' to marry you then it won't 'urt to cop a look at the competition,' said Betty, putting her arm through mine. 'We miss you. You've spent too much time fallin' in love. We want you back an' out 'avin' fun wiv us.'

I looked at Betty. She was my best friend at the factory, the only one I would share confidences with. 'It just don't feel right. I don't want to see the competition, Bet. I've found me man an' I'm Bert's girl now so you lot go an' 'ave some fun wivout me.'

I felt good saying that. I was 'Bert's girl' and that's how I wanted everyone to know me.

Betty smiled, 'An' 'e's lucky to 'ave you. Don't you ever forget that, 'ilda.'

CHAPTER 17

Goodbye, Ma

1943

My heels echoed as I walked the length of the long, hospital corridor. The smell of carbolic soap and disinfectant permeated the building. The floor was shining and I thought to myself, *My Gawd what 'ard work it must take to get a shine on it like that.*

It was the enormity of the tragedy that faced us that made me notice the tiny details, as if the thought of Ma's illness was too large and present to take in. Instead, all I could concentrate on was the ground beneath my brown shoes as they moved me ever closer to Ma's bedside.

Before I knew it, I was standing in front of the ward doors, clutching the small posy of violets I'd picked that morning for Ma. I was dreading seeing her, if truth be known. She'd looked so old, so ill, so frail the last time I'd seen her, as we bundled her into the ambulance to take her to the big hospital in Coventry.

I knew it was the best place for her. Life had simply become intolerable for her at home, as she was barely able to stand these days, and she hated being a 'burden' on us.

Of course, she was never a burden to me. I would've done anything to help her get better, but despite the care I'd lavished on her, her dropsy meant she was getting worse by the day. We all knew her heart was giving out. We didn't need the cost of a doctor to tell us that anymore.

She'd complained of pains in her chest for years now and I did what I could to help. These last weeks had been spent caring for Ma day and night. Joanie, now a blossoming young woman of 17, was looking after our younger siblings Ron 14, and little Patsy who was 7, as well as doing the housework and cooking, while I dedicated myself to caring for her, when I wasn't at work.

Every morning I'd wake her up with a cup of hot tea and help her up to sitting position, so she could sip it. I held the cup for her as her hands shook something terrible. Then I'd brush her hair with small gentle strokes and feel her relax under my ministrations. She'd want to use the potty then, so I'd help her out of bed, trying not to put too much weight on her poor swollen legs and ankles, and I'd put the potty underneath her bottom, hoping nothing would spill onto the sheets. She would joke that she was my baby now, and not so long ago she'd have done that for me as a babe in arms. I'd smile, trying not to show her how much I loved her for braving the indignities of her illness. When she'd finished, I'd wipe her down with some rags that I'd have to boil up before leaving the house for work. After that, and depending on how she felt, I'd steer her to the kitchen table so she could eat a small bit of breakfast or, if she wasn't up to it, I'd bring her some bread and jam in bed, brushing the crumbs off the sheets afterwards so she didn't feel uncomfortable. All of this was a labour of love, and I wouldn't have swapped places with anyone in the world.

Before I left for the munitions factory, I'd make sure she had a clean nightie on and a book by her elbow so that she could read if her sight was good enough. All day she'd spend in that bed in the kitchen, lamenting the fact she 'should be up and doin' the 'ousework' while her good-for-nothing husband lounged around in the local pubs, or ambled off with his mates to earn day's work painting and decorating somewhere. It was my privilege to care for her, though, just as she'd cared for us.

In the hospital, I could see the ward in a kind of cross-hatched fug through the window of the ward door. Steeling myself, I opened the door and slipped through, careful to close it behind me. The scent of carbolic was even stronger in here. There were lines of beds forming regimented queues down each side of the long ward. At the end there was a green screen blocking sight of one of the beds. In the middle, at the front of the ward, was a small wooden table and a nurse sat scribbling notes.

I walked up to her, cleared my throat and asked where Emily Johnson was. She looked me up and down, before telling me to follow her to the end of the ward where Ma was lying in bed, her head resting on two white pillows. She was tucked into bed with crisp, clean sheets that I noted were whiter than any I'd ever seen before.

'Ma,' I coughed nervously.

Her eyes were shut. She looked asleep. She looked smaller than I'd ever seen her. Her once matronly form, which was fleshed out by repeated childbirth and hard graft, had shrunk to a tiny skeleton.

From her came a great cough, and her eyes fluttered open. Dazed, and seemingly unfocused, she blinked again and looked round at what had woken her.

'Ma, it's me, 'ilda,' I said, touching the sallow skin on her arm.

' 'ilda, is it really you?' she said, and her voice was like a little mouse's. I had to bend over to hear her.

' 'Course it's me, Ma, it's your 'ilda. Now, what's all this I see, takin' a rest, shouldn't you be up an' about, makin' the ward shipshape?' I joked, while stroking her lovely hand, which was callused from years of domestic drudgery.

She lifted up her hand, and found mine, trembling a little as she moved, and smiling weakly. 'Chance'd be a fine thing. 'Ow are the littl'uns?' she asked, trying to turn herself towards me.

'Now don't you go tirin' yerself out. Let me 'elp you,' I bustled, as I punched her pillows to make them plump again, and settled her back down to carry on talking.

'They're right as rain. Don't you worry about them indoors. Joanie's doin' a fine job of sortin' them out,' I laughed. We both knew that Joanie was a reluctant stay-at-home surrogate for Ma, but she did it and you couldn't say fairer than that.

'Oh bless 'er. I miss 'em all. Give Joanie, Patsy an' Ron a kiss an' a big cuddle from me,' she said and her eyes became all watery.

I squeezed her hand gently. 'It's okay, Ma, we're okay an' that's what matters. We've got each other, ain't we?'

Except, of course, it wasn't okay. I could see the greying pallor of her skin, and hear the rasp of her lungs as she breathed. Her face was puffed up and she spoke with a thickness to her voice. She didn't look long for this world, and it was the sight of her like that, that I'd been dreading. I didn't want to see the truth. I didn't want to acknowledge that the rock of my life was about to leave me, but there was no denying it.

I couldn't let her know, though. She had to think there was hope, or what else did she have?

' 'As Pa been in to see you?' I asked, knowing the answer.

A shadow passed her face and, inwardly, I kicked myself for asking a question that was bound to upset her.

'I expect 'e's busy, 'ilda. Don't you think about 'im. 'E'll come when 'e's good an' ready,' she said, looking like she almost believed it.

' 'Course 'e will, Ma,' I murmured, not daring to say what

we both thought. That hell would have to freeze over before That Man gave anyone but himself and the bottle a second thought.

'So, are they bein' kind to you in 'ere, Ma?' I changed the subject, looking round as I spoke. There were several empty beds, the rest were filled with other, older women, in various states. One was coughing loudly and retching into a metal kidney bowl. Another was waving her hand to get the nurse's attention. All in all, though, it looked like Ma would get the best treatment she could hope for, even though there was a war on.

Just at that moment, a nurse wearing a starched uniform came up to me, and asked if I was Hilda Johnson. When I said that was my name, she asked me if she could have a word in private. I nodded, saying to Ma, 'Be back in a minute,' and looking as reassuring as I was able, though my stomach had sunk to my boots.

'I am sorry to inform you, Miss, but we need the hospital beds for the soldiers coming home from the front. I'm afraid your mother Emily will be discharged back to your home in the next couple of days.'

I stared in disbelief. The nurse with the clipped Home Counties voice was telling me Ma had to leave. 'But 'ow am I meant to look after 'er when I'm at work all day?' I said, my heart thumping with a mixture of anger and something else, something that recognised that as working-class people we were the last on the list for help of any kind. I stared back at her, my disbelief showing on my face. I didn't bother to hide it.

'I'm sorry but that's how it is, Miss Johnson. We don't have enough beds to look after our wounded personnel and so all non-urgent patients must be discharged. Now, if you'll excuse me, I have work to do.'

And with that, the starchy nurse walked off, leaving me staring after her, feeling like I'd been punched in the stomach, again.

Two days later, the nurse was as good as her word. Ma was brought back from the hospital, and carried back into her bed downstairs.

'Don't you worry, Ma, we'll look after you better than those bleedin' doctors. Who needs 'em, eh?' I said brightly, pulling a shawl round her bony shoulders.

Inwardly, though, I didn't have a clue how we'd cope. Ma was looking worse by the day, and all my time, when I wasn't working, was spent making sure she was fed and clean. There was nothing I could do to stop the relentless march of her illness.

As the days went on she became weaker and weaker. Albert had been gone two years now, but that special time with him seemed like a fairy tale. I missed him but had so much to do sorting the others, doing the bulk of the house-work and looking after Ma, that I rarely had time to worry about Bert, which was a small blessing.

One evening, just as I was settling the others upstairs, I heard the front door bang open. Pa had kicked it in by the sound of it. Instantly, my nerves sharpened and the hairs on the back of my neck rose. I could sense trouble as if it were something tangible, something real. I kissed Ron on the forehead, and he burrowed down into the blanket. He knew to keep out of the way. I made my way down the stairs, Pa's voice getting louder the closer I came.

'Get off your lazy backside an' get me dinner, for fuck's sake. You're actin' like a spoiled brat in there. I know you ain't well but a man's got to eat,' he bawled.

I stopped at the kitchen door to see him with his face right up to Ma's, shouting at her like she was a wicked child.

'Pa, leave 'er alone. Why don't you pick on someone your own size,' I said, my voice low and steady. I was weary of this game we all played: Pa being the big, bad wolf. He'd taken Bert's threats to heart, and had left off beating me, though he carried on bullying Ma with impunity.

'Oh go fuck yerself, 'ilda! I want me wife to make me dinner, an' I want it NOW!' he said, reaching for his belt as if he would strike her with it.

The fact she was lying there, pale and lifeless, didn't seem to bother him. In Ted Johnson's head, his needs came first. He could see how frail she was, and yet he seemed to enjoy her powerlessness, her vulnerability. He shouted again, the spittle from his mouth flying into her face. He was working his way into a rage, and so I stepped in, hoping he'd divert his foul-mouthed scorn at me instead.

'I'll make your dinner, Pa. Get yerself washed. The jug's full of water an' there's soap by the sink. Dinner won't be a minute. Ma ain't well, but I can do it.'

Surprisingly, Pa seemed mollified by my reasonable tones. He pulled off his coat and cap, swaying as he did so and poured out water, which he proceeded to wash himself with.

It only took me a minute to ladle some stew into the big plate reserved for the man of the house. He sat, glaring at us both, while he chewed his meal, thoughtfully. I waited until he'd finished, forcing myself to smile and look calm so I didn't provoke him. He grunted and pushed the plate towards me. I picked it up and rinsed off the remains. With that he leant back in his chair, and then, without a word, got himself up to standing and slouched up the stairs to sleep.

I let out a long breath, my shoulders slackening with the release of their tension. I didn't trust him not to disturb Ma again. That night, and each night afterwards, I slept in the chair by her bed.

A couple of times in the night she woke coughing and I held water to her lips to taste.

'Thank you, darlin'. Don't know what I'd do without you,' she said, gasping for breath.

'Don't be silly, Ma. I love you. Now get yerself some rest an' I'll do the same.'

Several days later, I saw that Pa was smearing boot polish into his hair to blacken it. Age had finally caught up with him, painting silver streaks into it. I stood there for a minute, wondering if I was witnessing Pa's latest attempts to find himself a new skivvy now his first one was unable to care for him. Dad had always been a vain man, taken with his appearance. It was nothing new. And neither were his affairs, of which he'd had many.

I tried to sneak past him, but as I reached for the door handle, he said, ' 'ilda, I've been meanin' to speak to you.' He spoke slowly, and turned round to face me.

My hackles rose and I looked up at him. Waiting. 'Go on, Pa, spit it out,' I said in as steady a voice as I could manage. However much I tried to be strong, he frightened me and I could never quite get past that.

'I've been thinkin',' he said with a long pause. I kept waiting. The silence between us was heavy, ominous. Then he moved. He undid his belt and pulled it from his waist. I stood and stared. I knew what was coming, and I knew that if I ran I only stalled the inevitable. 'You don't show me the respect I deserve in me own 'ouse.'

I swallowed the bile that rose to my throat. 'An' so, what 'appens to those who don't show their old man proper respect, eh?'

I shook my head. I couldn't speak. I couldn't talk. I stared at him like a dumb animal.

'Cat got your tongue?' He spat his cigarette to the ground. 'Well, if you ain't goin' to say anything, then I'd better show you what 'appens, hadn't I?' Pa moved towards me.

A bolt of panic ran through me and I turned, fumbling for the door handle. He was too quick for me. All those years boxing for money, it had all led to this moment. He took the belt in one hand and whipped it so it sent a sharp sting against my back.

'Turn round an' face me,' he commanded. But nothing would've made me look back at him. I stumbled over as the next lash of his belt struck. He struck again, then again. I was getting the thrashing of my life. I was a young woman of 22 but That Man still had total control over me. His power radiated from him. I'd known all along that I would probably pay for my Bert standing up to him the way he did, and I'd almost thought he'd forgotten about that day. How could I have been so stupid? He'd just been biding his time over the past two years.

And now the full force of his revenge was being thrashed out on me. I could feel the welts form on my back and legs. I covered my face with my arms, crouching on the floor against the wall while he carried on striking me. I think I cried. I may have screamed. The lashes kept coming, time and time again. It must've been several minutes into it and I had a moment when I thought, *This is it, he's finally goin' to kill me*. Then he threw down the belt and hauled me onto my feet.

He dragged me up while I fought him with the little strength I had. Then BAM, another blow landed on me, this time from his fists. I staggered back into the wall again, knocking one of the pots off the mantelpiece. He stopped then and walked round the parlour. He shook his right hand briefly to get the blood moving in it again, then quicker than I've ever seen him move, he slammed me against the table, winding me. Choking, I held onto the edge like it was the raft from a sinking ship. I was going down.

To my mind, Pa had destroyed Ma's health as much as if he'd stuck a knife into her frail back. He did it with words and with punches, grinding her down until, finally, her body and mind were on the verge of giving up completely. Would he do the same to me? At that moment I knew I had to get out of there. I realised with shocking clarity that it was me or him. I couldn't carry on living under the same roof as this monster. It only took one beating, one shove down the stairs, one drunken night reaching for the bread knife and I was a goner. He'd broken his word to Albert. It was time for me to go.

'You fuckin' cunt, I'll show you what it means to disrespect me, I'll fuckin' show you,' and he was showing me all right.

I staggered to my feet, holding my face. Every part of me was in pain. But I said nothing to him. I wouldn't give him the satisfaction, not this time.

At last he stopped. He was out of breath. He clutched his side as he panted, then looked over to me. I didn't hesitate. I turned on my heels and I fled from that cottage. I had nowhere to go but I just had to get out, to put some distance between Pa and me. I was in shock. It was the most brutal attack I'd suffered at his hands yet, and it had frightened me more than I dared admit.

I ran till I too was out of breath, and stood wheezing and retching at the roadside. I slumped down into a field at the side of the road, and examined my torn, bruised skin while weeping fat tears. How could I leave Ma? How could I leave Ron, Joanie and Patsy? They were the reason I went on living every day.

Except, I had a reason of my own now. Albert had taught me that I deserved to be loved in kind, gentle ways. I did not deserve to be brutalised. Yet the thought of saving myself from almost certain destruction at That Man's hands by leaving, was almost too much to bear. I couldn't leave them, could I?

I cried even harder. I felt torn in two by the decision I had to make.

Once the shock of the beating dissipated, I reviewed my options. Albert had said I had a refuge with his parents if I needed it. It wouldn't hurt to write to them and see if he was serious.

Yet, even as I thought it, I felt deep guilt at the idea of leaving Ma at the mercy of her husband. I knew he wouldn't touch Joanie or Patsy. Neither of them had ever felt the power of Pa's fists as they were both his favourite children, and even Ron had been spared the belt, so it wasn't like I was leaving my younger siblings to get 'my' beatings. But it was Ma I was worried about. Who knew how long she had left to live? And wouldn't my leaving, cause her even more suffering?

I walked back to the house slowly. With wary steps, I entered the cottage. Pa was nowhere to be seen, thank goodness.

I crept into the kitchen, hoping Ma would be asleep and I could have a sit down and a think by myself, but she was there, looking for all the world like she was waiting for me.

'Come an' sit next to me,' she said.

I started. 'All right, Ma, everything okay? D'you need anything?' I asked, as I moved towards her. She patted the bed next to her shrunken body.

'You alright, girl?' she murmured, stroking my hair from my face with a gesture that told me she'd heard everything.

I didn't trust myself to speak so I nodded instead.

'It's time for you to leave, 'ilda,' she said, simply, as if she had read my mind. I looked up at her. How could she have guessed my thoughts? Again, she stroked my hair and bent over to kiss my forehead. 'You've got to go. You know that, don't you? There's no tellin' what 'e'll do if you stay.' Her voice trailed off, leaving a silence between us.

'But what about you, Ma? An' what about the others? What'll you do when Pa is on the rampage again?' I replied, a single tear rolling down my cheek.

'Sweetheart, there's nothing you can do about your old man. 'E won't ever change. 'E won't ever stop behavin' the way 'e does. But one thing's for sure, you've got to save yerself. We both know I ain't got long left.'

At this point I tried to interrupt but Ma kept talking.

''ilda, listen to me. You've got to be a grown-up an' listen. I 'aven't got long left an' that's a fact. There's no point beatin' about the bush. What Pa does to me now don't matter, but what 'e does to you does matter. I'm tellin' you, 'ilda, it's time for you to leave. I want you to go. It breaks me 'eart seein' you takin' 'is beatin's. Do it for me, will you? Leave 'ere an' go an' find yerself a better life. Will you do that for me?'

By now I couldn't stop my tears. They flowed down my face, an unstoppable torrent of sadness. I couldn't bear to acknowledge the truth of Ma's words, and yet I knew she was right. It was time to go.

The next day, I sent a letter to Bert's parents, Albert and Dolly Kemp, asking if I could stay with them. I could hardly believe I was taking my future into my own hands. It felt so foreign, so independent and so disloyal of me to consider leaving my beloved family.

A few days later I had their reply. Of course I could come. Their Albert had told them all about me, and how he planned to wed me on his return. I read the letter and I knew my life with my family was over. My survival instincts, honed by life in the slums, had kicked in. It was this alone that drove me to pack my things. I told the others I had a job in London and that was the reason for my move. I didn't want them to know the truth in case it got back to That Man.

The morning of my departure, I sat with Ma quietly. We sipped our tea, and I gazed at her face. I knew this was our last goodbye, and I would most probably never see my mother again. The moment of departure arrived and I found I couldn't tear myself away.

'Go for me, I mean it. I want you to go an' make yerself a life. I love you, 'ilda. I'll always be there wiv you, in your 'eart. Don't ever forget it,' she whispered.

I kissed her hair, breathing in her scent, wanting desperately to commit every trace of her to memory.

I have no words to describe how painful this parting was. I didn't want to make false promises about returning, because I knew once I got away from That Man I had to stay away.

I kissed Ma one last time, told her I loved her, and picked up my small brown suitcase and walked out of the cottage. As I turned up the lane, I looked back for one last look at the house. I whispered, 'Goodbye, Ma,' and turned away, looking up the lane towards the bus stop, and my future.

Jellied Eels

They were as good as Bert's word. Without a murmur, Albert and Dolly Kemp took me in, much as you might give a home to a waif and stray. I arrived on their doorstep at teatime with my suitcase in one hand and the look of someone fleeing a war zone.

It was ironic that for my own safety I had to flee to London, which was still under attack as England was still at war with Germany. The intense bombing of the Blitz had abated, however.

I knew the instant I got off the train at Euston Station that I'd made the right decision to come back, even though my heart was broken, leaving my family behind. I jumped on a bus and watched as unfamiliar streets went by. The ravages of the past few months had left my city a smoking wreck, but as soon as I smelt the sooty air and saw my first glimpse of the Thames, I knew I was back home at last. I could've shed a few tears for the forlorn city I witnessed, but too much water had gone under the bridge to weep fresh tears. My heart warmed at the sight of Londoners stepping over rubble and making their way, with determined faces, to the shops or work. It was business as usual, and I was going to celebrate that rather than mourn the city as it had been before the German planes had redesigned it.

I changed buses, just as Dolly had said to do in her letter, and finally I was standing in Old Ford Road, Bow. I found number 508, and knocked.

*

Dolly opened the door, and I found myself pulled into an embrace by Bert's mother, as if I was her own daughter. 'Come in, luvvie. Don't stand there gettin' cold. We've got the kettl' on so we'll 'ave a nice cuppa an' you can tell me about your journey,' she said before I'd even opened my mouth.

I followed her down the dark hallway, noting the peeling wallpaper and the damp stains on the walls. The floors were plain boards with a wrinkled mat at one end. There was a bucket of water and a bucket of sand by the doorway, which I had to skirt round. There was also a stirrup pump. Most Londoners had them, especially in the East End. They were kept in case of incendiary bombs.

Dolly, who was the image of her son Albert, with her round open face, light auburn hair and kind eyes, opened a door at the end and led me into a small kitchen. There was a tiny yard out the back which was strewn with washing. Long johns and enormous drawers were flapping in the breeze, and the whole house permeated a damp, dank smell. It wasn't a palace, but Dolly's kindness more than made up for any lack of home comforts.

Dolly waddled over to the range, where a kettle was ratting, exhaling its steam with a whistle. She was a large woman, but she had the kindest face I'd ever seen apart from Ma's. She poured steaming tea into two china cups.

'Get this down you. Why don't you warm your plates there, duckie?' she added.

My plates? What could she mean? I hadn't brought any plates with me.

I must've looked puzzled, because Dolly laughed all of a sudden and said, 'Them's the rhymin' slang – "plates of meat" are feet! We don't bovver sayin' the whole thing so we just say "plates" instead. You'll get used to it, dearie.'

With that I laughed. Even though I'd grown up only a few miles from Bow, I'd never actually heard proper Cockney rhyming slang being spoken. I'd heard people talk of it, of course, but never actually heard anyone using it. Our neighbourhoods might have been part of the same city, but they were separate and contained, and so it was like entering a new world, and one I liked instantly.

Bert's younger sister Dorothy was sat at the kitchen table, smiling at me shyly. His brother Frank was also living there, though he intended going off to sea with the Navy. Frank was the same height as my Bert but, I realised later, looked the spit of his father, with a proud, upright air about him.

At this point I hadn't seen or heard from Bert since he'd asked me to marry him. I had no idea whether he was alive or dead, and this was the hardest part to bear. Since Albert left to rejoin the fighting, I'd had many sleepless night, tossing and turning as my mind refused to rest, wondering where he was, and whether he was still alive and in one piece. I didn't make a fuss, of course. It was hard for post to get back to England. Many people hadn't heard from loved ones, and if Bert was in Africa it would be harder still. Most women had a lover, brother, husband or father out there doing their bit and we all had to get on with life, but in the long bleak nights I yearned and prayed for him. It was all I could do.

His parents had had no word from him either, and yet, despite this, they took me in without question. I could hardly believe my luck. All of a sudden, I felt my eyes swim with the tears I'd been holding back on my journey. Dolly's thoughtfulness reminded me of Ma, and suddenly I felt the loss of her and my siblings as a fresh wound.

'Now there, there, 'ilda. Don't you cry. It'll all work out, don't you worry about that. 'Course you'll miss your family. Why don't you go an' 'ave a lie-down an' I'll call you when dinner's ready. And from now on, no more callin' me Mrs Kemp, I want you to call me Mum.'

Well, I couldn't have been more grateful. I needed to be on my own to start the process of coming to terms with leaving Ma when she was so desperately ill. Had I done the right thing? Whatever Ma said, I knew she'd miss me. And there was no one now to stop Pa and his tempers. I was pretty sure that if the others kept out of That Man's way he'd leave them alone. He'd only ever really gone for me, Les and Ma. Even so, I was worried about them, and now there was nothing I could do to help.

With a sigh, I wiped my eyes and started to unpack. I hadn't got much with me. The clothes I stood up in plus a nightie, my best brown skirt, a dress and an extra blouse. I took off my coat and placed it on the chair in the corner of my room. I had my own room! The first time in my life I'd ever had such a thing. There was a single bed with a blanket folded over the bedstead and a mantelpiece on which to put my hairbrush and face powder. A memory came to me of Bert calling the piano at the dance 'the Joanna', and I chuckled to myself. I liked the strange language; it felt like a tangible link to my sweetheart.

I didn't stay up in that room long. I wanted to make myself useful, so I donned my apron and went back to the kitchen. Before I knew it I felt at home. Bert's father, Albert, Sr, came home from work at just past 6 p.m. Albert, Sr, was a quiet man, softly spoken, even though he was from the roughest part of the East End. He seemed gentle and unassuming, and I warmed to him immediately. He was so unlike my Pa. He was a wax bleacher and his factory had survived the Blitz.

He didn't go straight out to the pub after work. He kissed Dolly on the cheek, then gave me a wink and told me I was welcome and to make myself at home. That was that. I became part of the family from that second onwards and I grew to love Pop, as he was known, and Dolly as if they were my own.

The next day I decided to take a walk back to my old street. Across the Tab, and to the rubble piled high on Spa Road. Our home had been hit by a flying bomb. If we'd have stayed we'd all have perished.

I walked past the hole that remained where once our home had been and I felt nothing, no nostalgia for those times, no twinge of sadness except for our neighbours and friends who copped it in the blast. I skirted the remains of the town hall that had suffered a direct hit only two years earlier. I called on neighbours further down the street, there were a few houses still intact, and learnt how many of the people we'd known and grown up close to had died in the bombing raids.

Helen and her family were among the dead, and I bowed my head, letting the tears flow. I was used to witnessing such carnage. The war had realigned my sense of tragedy. There had been so much death and devastation, it was almost commonplace, though I said a whispered prayer for Helen. My borough felt like a ghost town. Even now, the dust from the buildings seemed to block out the light. There were shards of glass still untouched, twisted black metal and bricks lying in heaps.

I walked round to my old workplace, Peek Frean's. The shelter had been hit on that fateful night when the town hall was bombed, and I had always wondered if my best friends Lil and Rita had lost their lives there. I gulped down my sadness. So many lives had been lost, so many good people dead, and yet Pa survived the lot.

Pa often boasted that he'd survived many a direct hit without a scratch. He'd talk about his 'lucky escapes', including one night during a heavy raid, when he and his drinking pal decided not to shelter under one of the railway arches they usually staggered to from the pub, and instead went into London Bridge Station and slept on the platform. That night the arch was hit and hundreds of people were killed or wounded. At times I would say to God: how is it that good people die but scoundrels, thieves and bullies like my old man, survive? It didn't make any sense, not to me anyway. Not that I wished him dead, I just couldn't understand the justice in it.

Peeks Frean's was still going, though, which cheered me up. I decided to go in and see if there was anyone I knew. One of the receptionists spotted me and told me they were desperate for workers now that people had fled the city or been killed. I demurred for a minute then agreed. I needed to work. I wanted to send some money back to Ma, and give some to Albert's parents of course.

'Start tomorrow,' she said.

So the next morning I got up, washed my face and neck, scrubbed myself dry and brushed my hair, thinking how strange life was. It was like time hadn't moved on at all. I was about to start work again in familiar surroundings, and yet everything was different.

Not for the first time, I sent Bert a prayer, asking that he be saved a soldier's death, and begging him to come back to me. I wrote to him every week. It was the highlight of my weekends, putting pen to paper and letting him know my news. I never knew if he'd received anything I'd written, but I'd promised him faithfully I would do it and so, regardless of the fact we hadn't heard hide nor hair from him, I wrote.

I told him I'd left Ma and the youngsters to save myself from Pa's rages. I said how much I missed Ron, Joanie and Patsy, especially Patsy as she was the baby of the family. I told him that his mother and father were well, and had taken me in after I turned up on their doorstep. I thanked him for coming into my life, and taking me away from the violence of my own. I begged him to write back, even just a word, to tell me he was still alive and still my Bert. I signed it 'Love, your Hilda' and kissed the words before I sealed the letter.

I had no trouble conjuring up a picture of his face, or his smile. It was like we'd been destined to meet, and whatever anyone said, I made it known I was 'Bert's girl'.

Unbelievably, Rita was still at the factory, with her bright red lipstick and her turban tied up in a jaunty knot on top of her head.

'Rita!' I exclaimed, falling into a bear hug with my friend. 'You're still 'ere! Those bombs didn't make a dent on you!' I laughed.

' 'Ilda, I can't believe it's you. We 'eard you got 'it down at Spa Road, an' I thought you were a gonner!' she said, hugging me back with fierce happiness. 'Well that's it, you've got to come out wiv us girls. There ain't a soldier in London who 'asn't 'eard of the biscuit girls!'

At first I hesitated, saying I had to write to Bert, but Rita insisted, and before I knew it I'd promised to go out on the town. She told me every Saturday night they'd go to a dance, sometimes even up in the West End, enjoying the freedom the war gave us. Well, I was in a tizzy about what to wear just thinking about it.

'But where's Lil?' I asked, scanning the room for her blonde curls scraped loosely under her hairnet.

'Aw Gawd, 'ilda, didn't you 'ear? She took an 'it, under the arches. She 'ad no chance.'

I looked at Rita. The shock still registered in her eyes. It mirrored my own. I felt a sudden swoop of grief. I suppose

I'd assumed both Lil and Rita had died, but I wasn't prepared for the reality of losing Lil. Not at all. Tears instantly stung my eyes.

'I'm sorry, I didn't know, Rita. I was in the Midlands wiv me family, I didn't 'ave a clue. Poor Lil,' I answered, and flung my arms around my friend. We hugged and wept until there were no salty tears left. So many good people dead.

'Well, one thing's for sure, she wouldn't 'ave wanted us to mope about. She'd 'ave been the first to go out an' 'ave whatever fun she could, so we owe 'er that at least,' said Rita, with forced jollity as she wiped her face with one arm.

'She would. You're right there, Rita. Alright, count me in. We'll go out an' make 'er proud,' I replied, giving Rita a last squeeze before being shuttled off to get changed into my overall and hairnet.

The rest of the day I spent in a daze. I was thinking about poor Lil, and I was missing my Bert, and hoping against hope that he hadn't taken a hit as well.

On Saturday, I was back at Bert's parents' looking through my sparse wardrobe of clothes. It felt strange going out without Lil, but Rita was right. Lil had always been the most social of us and had loved a dance. In a small way we were remembering her spirit by bucking up and carrying on, even though the sadness felt like it was suffocating me.

I ain't got nothing nice, I moaned to myself. *I ain't got no stockin's, nor any lipstick. I'm goin' to look a right frump.*

It took me a moment to give myself a stern talking to. I was 'Bert's girl' and I didn't need to look glamorous. I'd leave that to Rita and the others. I wasn't out to attract a man so it didn't matter what I wore. Even so, I had looked wistfully at Rita's stockings earlier that week and wondered where she'd got them. The war had been going on for more than four long years. Nylons were a distant memory. Imagine my surprise when she whispered to me that they weren't real stockings, but a mixture of gravy browning and water painted onto her legs, with a thin line of brown eyeliner drawn to resemble the seam at the back! You could've knocked me down with a feather!

'Oh, it's easy, 'ilda, just mix the browning up and brush it on with a makeup brush, or failing that an egg brush. You won't be able to do that seam yerself, so just bring along your liner an' I'll do the rest.'

It seemed so simple so I thought, *What the 'ell*, and painted on that browning. At first it was a bit streaky but as I got used to applying it I soon learnt how to brush the mixture on so it looked nice and even. *I just 'ope it don't rain tonight*, I thought to myself, putting a dab of powder on my nose after pulling on my dress, a blue calf-length frock made of cotton. *That'll do, 'ilda. You don't need to do any more than that. Remember what Ma said about powder an' paint makin' a girl what she ain't*, I told myself and grabbed my coat.

I said 'goodbye' to Dolly and Pop, and said I wouldn't be late. I could see Dolly eyeing my legs and I hoped she didn't think I was 'fast' like some of the girls I knew at the factory, like Mary, who, despite her namesake, was no virgin. She seemed to have three or four fellas on the go at once, and she boasted that she'd have had more had she the time! She was a beauty, there was no doubting it. She had thick black hair and the whitest skin I'd seen, with huge green eyes. We all paled into insignificance next to her, but she was the life and soul of the party at work, so we couldn't help but love her.

I arrived at the meeting point, a pub in Tower Bridge Road that a few years earlier we'd never have gone into as a group of girls. Things had changed because of the war. Who cared about convention when the whole world had gone mad, when we were surrounded by the smoking relics of the past? Mary was there, so was Rita, dolled up to the nines with her bright red lipstick and curled hair from the rollers she'd been wearing especially all day.

'Over 'ere, 'ilda,' she gestured, waving at me. I smiled and headed over, feeling very dowdy next to these bright young women.

You're a bright young lady yerself, 'ilda Johnson, I told myself sternly, before giving each of them a hug and a kiss.

'What are you drinkin', 'ilda?' came a voice from the bar.

'My usual, please,' I replied, feeling very worldly.

'Your usual, eh? Get 'er, she knows what she wants!'

The girls all laughed. I chuckled back and mouthed 'port an' lemon' before turning to the others.

'Where are we off to then, girls?' I asked, feeling that familiar excitement at being young and out on the town. 'Anywhere nice?'

'Well, there's a dance on at the Palladium, or there's a new one down near Trafalgar Square, if you've got the legs for it,' answered Rita.

'Oh me legs! I 'aven't put the lines up the back. 'Ere, Rita, give me an' 'and, won't you?' I begged.

' 'Ow far are you goin' to draw it up there, 'ilda? Just in case anyone gets to see it, if you know what I mean,' cackled Mary.

'Just above me skirt line, Rita. Ta, duckie. I'm Bert's girl and I ain't lettin' no one but 'im up there, and then not till me weddin' night!' I hollered back and we all collapsed into giggles again.

Soon we were slightly tipsy and, linking arms, we wove our way into the blackout, on our way to a dance in a local music hall. Despite the war, Londoners were still up for a good time, and none more so than us that night. Laughing and joking, we flirted our way into the hall, depositing our coats and heading straight for the dance floor.

There were small tables and chairs round the edges of the expanse of floor, which was not yet populated enough for us to brave a dance. Instead, we busied ourselves touching up our lipstick. Rita lent me hers, and I felt positively decadent as I applied it. I smeared my lips together and showed her my face.

'You'll do,' she laughed. 'Now which young men are goin' to 'ave the pleasure of buyin' our drinks tonight then?' she said, peering over her shoulder.

It wasn't long before a group of soldiers came over and asked if they could join us.

'Suits me, but you can only sit 'ere if you're willin' to buy the girls a round,' teased Mary. She was so forward, it took my breath away! They didn't seem to mind. There were four of us: me, Rita, Mary and a girl I'd never spoken to before, a redhead called Dorothy, or Dotty as she was nicknamed. She kept fussing about her stocking line getting smudged. And there were four of them, all dark haired with uniforms I didn't recognise.

'What regiment are you then? I 'aven't seen a uniform like that before.' I asked, hoping they wouldn't think I was being forward too.

The way the men crouched their heads together, and looked to one another before speaking in halting English, told me they were foreigners, over here to fight the Jerries, and having a good time while they were at it.

'We are Polish,' said the bravest of the four. He was sat next to me, his knee brushing mine as he spoke. I moved away from him, but couldn't resist finding out more – I'd never met a real foreigner before.

'Gawd, you're all a long way from 'ome,' I said, sipping my drink and leaning in to listen to their response.

At that point the band struck up the first note and all at once the floor seemed full of young couples in pairs, dancing as if they'd been there all night. The man shuffled round slightly, sitting even closer to me. It was lucky it was dark as I was blushing with being so close to them. One had already asked Mary to dance, and she reluctantly agreed. Then, as he turned to get off his seat, she gave me a broad wink. Rita was the next to go – the youngest-looking soldier had grabbed her hand and practically dragged her onto the dance floor. She didn't look upset by it though.

'Come on, 'ilda, you're next!' she shouted, but was whisked into the dance by her partner.

That left Dotty and me fidgeting slightly while the men tried in vain to make conversation. They'd joined the war as a way of getting out of their rural villages, and were here on leave. They were going back to the front line in a few days' time, and were trying to squeeze the last drops of fun out of their stay.

We tried to talk above the music but it was impossible. The man sitting next to me, whose name I didn't catch, shrugged and held out his hand. 'We can't talk, so let's dance,' he said.

I looked at his outstretched hand and hesitated. Was I being unfaithful to Bert by dancing with this handsome officer?

'Go on, 'ilda, there's no 'arm in it, it's just a dance,' said Dotty, and nudged my arm.

Reluctantly, I took his hand, praying that Bert wouldn't mind, and before I knew it I was whisked onto the dance floor and had danced two or three in a row.

Breathless and laughing as we tried to make stilting conversation, I eventually gestured that I needed to sit down for a while. I sat back at the table, the other girls were nowhere to be seen, and the officer sat next to me. This time his knee brushed mine and I knew it was no mistake. Before long, the three others flopped back into their chairs.

'Blimey, I'm starvin' after that dance! Why don't we go an' find some supper?' pouted Mary.

We collected our coats and headed off to Manze's. It was still early, and we were just in time to catch them before they closed. The windows on either side were taped up to prevent shattering. There was a queue snaking round the serving area, which spilled into Tower Bridge Road.

'Just in time!' said Rita.

'Vat do you vont to eat?' said the officer, his name was Alex, or Aleksy in Polish. The girls rattled off their choices, leaving just me, wondering if I should let them buy my dinner.

'And vat do you vont, Hilda?' said my officer.

I couldn't help but notice he had big brown eyes and a mop of unruly dark hair. He was a dish, as Rita would say, but my heart belonged elsewhere. I just didn't want to lead him on.

'She loves jellied eels. Get 'er some of those,' said Rita, who held onto my arm, sensing that I was feeling uncertain.

'I'm not sure I should...' my voice trailed off. I did love jellied eels, and a plate of those didn't mean anything, did it? We sat on the wooden chairs with our elbows leaning on the marble table tops, chattering non-stop. The men were laughing and talking in their strange language, and eyeing us girls with undisguised delight. Alex came over with a pile of plates. He put down my eels, the waxy flesh of the fish and the jelly quivered as the plate touched the table.

'Eat,' he commanded, and so I picked up my fork and started.

I couldn't resist jellied eels. The creamy flesh of the fish slid down my throat. I licked my lips. 'Nectar!' I laughed. Next I swallowed a forkful of the clear gelatinous aspic. Before long I'd finished my plateful.

'That vosn't so hard,' said the officer. His voice was soft. He was definitely flirting with me.

I stood up abruptly, almost knocking my plate and fork off the table. I couldn't sit there and be eyed up like a tasty dinner, I was practically engaged. It wasn't right by Bert.

'I'm sorry, I 'ave to go. Thank you for the eels, but I've got to be back wiv my fella's Ma an' Pa tonight,' I blurted, stressing the word 'fella'.

The handsome officer looked momentarily taken aback, then nodded. 'Ah, so you have a boyfriend. My apologies. May I walk you home though?'

'No thanks, it's too far. I'll be gettin' the bus. Thanks all the same,' I was gabbling. Reaching for my coat, I said a hasty goodbye to the girls, and ran out of that pie 'n' mash shop like there was a hound on my trail.

Gulping in the evening air, I made a dash for the bus stop. It didn't matter how handsome that officer was, I knew in my heart that it was Bert I wanted to be with, even though I might never see him again.

CHAPTER 19

Victory

1943–45

There was a knock on my bedroom door. Dolly opened it, holding a crumpled letter aloft. It was almost six months after my trip to Manze's with the officer, and I'd heard nothing from Bert in all that time.

' 'Ilda, we've 'ad a letter from Albert. 'E's alright, duckie! E's alive and doin' 'is bit for King and country!' Dolly's voice was shrill with relief.

'My Bert, my Albert, oh my Gawd I can 'ardly believe it, e's alive,' I gasped, running over to Dolly and giving her a kiss on her cheek and a big bear hug.

We couldn't contain our excitement at hearing from Albert and practically danced on the spot. I took the letter from Dolly's outstretched hand, and saw that the letter was shaking as I held it.

'Does 'e mention me? Does 'e remember me?' I asked, as I scanned the writing, hungry for every last drop of contact with my sweetheart. It was the first time I'd seen his handwriting. His script was small and neat. There was nothing fussy about it. It was plain and straightforward, just like Bert. I'd stayed faithful to 'Ginger', as his mates in Bow called him, but did he still feel the same way about me? Had he stayed faithful to his Hilda?

Then I saw the words that made me stop still, hardly believing my eyes. He'd written a note to his brother Frank, asking him to take me to a jeweller in Lewisham that a pal had recommended to get me … an engagement ring! He'd even sent back money to pay for it! All my fears dissolved. He had meant it, as, deep down, I knew he had, but, my goodness, the relief at seeing those words was overwhelming. I burst into tears.

Instantly Dolly looked taken aback. 'Now don't you go cryin' like that, 'ilda. You've got to get yerself busy gettin' a ring to make Albert proud.'

'I know, I know,' I sobbed, the feelings I'd been repressing for endless months bursting from me in a torrent of emotion. 'I've been so worried, Mum, I just didn't know if 'e was thinkin' about me, or whether 'e 'ad even survived.'

'Well,' said Dolly, 'the war ain't over yet, but when it is, an' when our Albert is 'ome safe an' sound we'll 'ave a big celebration.' She smiled, pulling me into a hug.

Dolly was a large woman with a big smile. In contrast, her husband, Pop, my Bert's father, was a small man but gentle and sincere. He showed me more kindness in the months I lived with them than my Pa had shown me in my lifetime. I loved him with the fierceness of someone who has never received that fatherly love closer to home.

My real Pa was still up to his usual tricks, I supposed. Ma and I wrote to each other often so I knew that Joanie was courting Sid still, and that Ron was looking more like Les every day. Ma never told me her worries, or ever alluded to Pa and his ways. In a way I was grateful I didn't know the details, as I might have been tempted to jump on the train back to Coventry.

Pop was so different to Pa, but he had his demons. He was a melancholy man. He had been cursed with low moods since returning from fighting for his country in the Great War. He'd been awarded the military medal but had been blinded in his left eye after a gas attack in the trenches, and had never recovered his peace of mind. Dolly, of course, was the matriarch of Bert's family. Family life seemed to revolve around her, and there were constant streams of relatives and friends, children and neighbours, coming in and out of the home. And now they'd be my family for real. I couldn't have been more excited had Dolly said the Queen was coming for tea.

One hot morning in August 1943, just a day or two after receiving Bert's letter, Frank and I got on the bus to take us into town, and then changed for the Lewisham bus. I could hardly breathe I was so excited.

Frank was a nice enough chap, and he assured me he had similar tastes to Ginger, so whatever we chose would be alright with Albert. We stepped through the bomb-damaged city with a spring in our step. There were rumours afoot that the war was going our way and would soon be over. People certainly seemed more chipper, somehow more confident in the future than they'd been for a long time.

The jeweller was in the high street, the windows all taped up. A little bell jangled as we opened the door to enter. Inside, it was gloomy and dark, though it was late morning. There were rows and rows of rings in all shapes and sizes sitting in little boxes on plush velvet cushions.

' 'Ow are we ever goin' to decide?' I asked in wonder, my eyes raking the glittering display with trepidation. It was the first piece of jewellery I'd ever been bought. I had a necklace and a watch, which I'd bought out of my wages, but this was a proper piece of jewellery. Lord knows how Bert had saved the money from his soldier's wages. He must have made real sacrifices to do it.

I was determined I wouldn't let him down, and so we scoured the display cases. Frank picked out a gold ring with an ornate pattern.

'Oh no, Frank, I don't want nothing showy,' I said,

dismissing his choice with a wave of my hand. 'Bert'll want me to pick something elegant.'

Even though I'd only known Bert for a few short days, I knew enough about him to know he'd want to treat me to something that didn't shout too loudly.

'Wot about this one?' I said, pointing to another, but that too was garish with a coiled design around the ring.

'No, not right,' said Frank. 'Keep looking, Hilda.'

Frank was the only one in his family who spoke 'proper'. He pronounced his aitches and hardly ever used rhyming slang.

We moved slowly around the cases, the shop girl watching us out of the corner of her eye. Then, all of a sudden, I saw the one. 'Blow me, but ain't that the prettiest ring you've ever seen?'

I waved Frank over. 'Look at that one,' I said, my heart beating like I'd been running. I was sure I'd found the perfect ring.

'It's lovely, Hilda, but don't you want a bigger diamond?' replied Frank.

'What do I need a bigger diamond for, Frank? Best spend the money on the weddin', or on the food for afterwards.' I was always a practical girl. 'I don't care about the size of the stone, I just want me Bert back from the war an' I'll be 'appy. An' in the meantime, I'd like to try on that ring, please?' I ventured to the shop girl who came over, eyeing us up and down as she approached.

I stood up a little straighter when I saw her doing that. I wasn't going to let anyone look down on me while I was buying my engagement ring.

The assistant took out the ring and placed it in my upturned hand.

Carefully, I placed it onto my wedding finger. It fitted

perfectly. I moved my hand left to right, admiring the way the solitaire winked at me in the dark shop. A single diamond sat within a flower made of white gold. There was a small line of etched marks either side of the flower that ran the whole way round the ring. It was the loveliest thing I'd ever seen.

'That's the one for me,' I turned to Frank. 'But will Bert like it?' With that I handed my precious ring to Bert's younger brother.

My heart skipped a beat. I was so sure it was the one, but Bert had to like it too. I looked up at Frank who was gazing at the ring intently, then he nodded his head. His expression was serious as he looked back at me. 'I think he'll love it, Hilda. It looks just perfect to me.'

I clasped my hands to my heart and grinned. It was like a fairy tale. I really couldn't believe this was happening to me.

Frank took out a wad of notes from his trouser pocket and began counting them out in front of me. I'd never seen so much money!

'Gawd, Frank, it's too expensive. Look, I'm bound to find another ring. Put that one back,' I pleaded, all at once feeling guilty for spending so much of Bert's hard-earned cash.

'Don't you worry about the money. Bert's sent more than enough back for it. You'll both even have a few pounds left over so stop frettin',' he said, firmly.

The shop girl counted up the notes and pressed a key on the till which sprang open. She wrote out Frank's receipt with a sprawling hand and put the ring in its little box. I'd never felt so much like a duchess before in my life!

We went straight from there to a local photographer to take a picture of me wearing it to send to Bert overseas. The photographer had some fancy hats, so I thought I'd look the part, and chose myself one to wear with a black rim and netting. How glamorous I felt, having my picture taken like a film star. Frank said he'd call back to pick up the pictures when they were ready and out we walked, into the fug of the London summer, me wearing my engagement ring and feeling like I was finally a woman in my own right.

A year passed, and we heard nothing more from Bert. Every day I prayed for him to be safe, but men were still dying in their thousands, and so I didn't expect my little voice to be heard. I wore my ring like a talisman, hoping the promise of our future together would somehow protect Bert from the terrors overseas.

Then one day a letter arrived. The envelope was white, so it wasn't a telegram telling me my Bert had perished. Something wasn't right, though. It was addressed to me, and I recognised Pa's handwriting. Suddenly, I knew.

I held the envelope in my hands for a long time, fearing what I'd find when I opened it but knowing its contents, all the same. I knew she was gone. Hands trembling, I tore it open. The words moved on the page as the tears blurred my vision. Ma had left me, as quietly as she'd always lived her life. She'd slipped away one evening this summer. One minute she'd been breathing, asleep in her chair by the fire. The next minute she'd stopped. It was as simple, and as easy as that.

It was Ron who'd realised and raised the alarm. Pa was having a drink in the garden, and he ran in and took control, sending Ron to find Mrs Worrell who washed and laid out bodies in the village. It was all very dignified, and I was grateful for that at least. I dropped the page onto the floor. There was more in there from Pa, but I couldn't read another word. I crawled into bed and pulled the blanket over me and stayed there, letting the darkness and the warmth soothe me.

I had no tears left for Ma. In a strange way I felt relieved that, at last, she was free from pain, and free from her marriage. I wished I'd been able to say goodbye, but I knew she was in the best place, away from the troubles and hardships of her life. My thoughts were for Les, who was away at sea, and for Ron, Joanie and Patsy. I couldn't be there to comfort them, and that hurt the most. I said silent prayers, asking that they might know how much Ma loved them. I asked that their pain be put onto me so I could carry their burden in some way. I felt guilt at not being there, but also free from Pa's inevitable reaction. I was glad I wasn't there to be on the receiving end when the beer went sour inside him.

Much later, I finished the letter. Ma's funeral was in a few days. I was determined to go to comfort the littl'uns, as I still called them, though Ron was nearly a man now, at the tender age of 15.

Two days later I was met at the station in Coventry by Pa. I hadn't seen him for a year and a half and he had changed. His stocky figure had filled out with a paunch, his face looked puffy from the drink. He'd borrowed his pal Charlie's truck, and he drove me back to the cottage, in silence, barely looking at me.

All three of my youngest siblings tumbled out of the house and into my arms when we arrived. Les had also managed to get back from his posting at sea, and we all cried, and hugged each other. I'd missed them so much, it was like part of me had been missing.

Patsy was so grown up: she'd sprung up in height and had her fair hair cut in a fringe. Ron looked dapper in an old suit jacket of his father's which was too big, and had slicked his hair to the side like a young fashionable man. Joanie was the biggest surprise: her dark hair had turned almost fair and she was wearing it in a fashionable style rolled on top of her head. Laughter and tears of happiness flowed freely.

Pa had ordered two cars, one for the coffin and one for the rest of us, to go to the funeral in the village church. It caused quite a stir among the locals seeing us put on a 'show'. That's how it was for us Londoners, it was a status symbol. It was the first time I'd travelled in a proper car. Pa's pride was at stake so he considered it vital to show his 'pals' he could afford a decent send-off. I'd only ever been in the hopping truck or in Pa's mate's lorry before.

All I can remember about the car journey is the windows steaming up as we were driven slowly along the country lane. Ma was buried in the church graveyard in Braunston after a short service. It was a quiet, simple service. Dignified, like Ma. A few villagers were there to pay their last respects, and they nodded to us as we arrived. There were a couple of bunches of wild flowers, picked by one of the villagers, in vases on the altar, just as Ma would've liked. She was never one for show, that was Pa's domain. Instead, she would have wanted us to remember her with a full heart, not an empty wallet.

Ma had told me before I left that when she died she didn't want a headstone. Whether that was to save money, or whether she wanted to be left alone and in peace, I'll never know, but we respected her wishes, and her grave went unmarked.

After the ceremony, I sat by Ma's grave and told her how much I loved her. I'd already cried all the tears I was capable of for Ma over the years. I felt strangely relieved that she was now safe in heaven, free from Pa and the burdens of her hard life. I felt comforted knowing she was finally at peace and so I shed no tears that day. I spoke to her until the sun started to set and I realised I had to make my way back to my new home.

I returned to London with a heavy heart. Leaving them all was unbearable, but I knew for my own sake I had to go back to my new life.

Dolly and Pop were gentle with me. I was excused from the chores for a few days. I spent most of the time when I wasn't at work, lying in bed re-reading Pa's letter. The girls at the factory were sympathetic and sweet. They hugged me and stroked my arm, and wouldn't let me be alone for a moment. They were so protective of me, that again I felt I'd created a new family, one which sustained me through the fog of those days.

Grief is a strange thing. It came and went in great waves of emotion, catching me unawares, and plunging me into the depths of my mourning, then, just as quickly receding like waves from the shore.

Then on the morning of 8 May 1945, my world changed again. Rumours that the Allies were winning the war had been building for weeks. We waited as a nation, with bated breath. Frank was away at sea, but Dolly, Pop, Dorothy and I huddled round the wireless to hear Winston Churchill declare Victory in Europe.

We could hardly believe our ears. We stood in Dolly's parlour, blinking like we'd spent the last few years underground, and were just emerging into the light. Then we cried, and laughed, but with the sadness of knowing that a whole generation of young men were dead, or brutalised by war.

I put on my best dress, the one I'd worn in my photograph for Bert, and headed out to see what was happening. What I saw was the relief of war ending exploding on our streets. There were people hugging and openly kissing, milling around with huge smiles or glasses of beer. I followed the crowds as they surged into town, making their way to Buckingham Palace.

It seemed no one was at work, London had come to a standstill. The bus drivers were beeping their horns, unable to drive onwards because of the crowds, the shopkeepers were standing on the streets, waving and ripping off the tape that had covered their windows for six long years. As the day wore on, the parties started and the pubs were overflowing with celebrations that would go on all night.

I returned home eventually, to hear the next day had been declared a national holiday. Dolly was already mixing up the last of her egg powder and flour rations to bake a cake.

'There'll be street parties, tomorrow. We'll wear our best dresses, won't we 'ilda, an' show the rest of London 'ow to celebrate?' she smiled. 'An' Churchill, Gawd bless 'im, 'e 'ad something to say on the wireless about the people's struggles, oh yes 'e did.'

'What did 'e say, Mum?' I asked.

' 'E said it was our victory, an' 'e's right, it was our victory over them Jerries. They 'ad my Albert an' my Frank fightin' so the enemy didn't stand a chance,' Dolly chuckled.

We hadn't heard from our Bert since August 1943, but it would be too cruel a blow for him to have died when victory was ours, wouldn't it?

' 'E'll be fine,' I said, touching my engagement ring. 'I'm sure 'e's alive, I am.'

The trickle of troops being de-mobbed began, and the first soldiers arrived home at the end of June. Neighbours and friends saw their husbands and fathers return. Yet still there was no sign of Bert. Then, in July 1945, two months after VE Day, the letter came.

There was a loud knocking at the door. I raced to open it. I took the envelope and hurried to give it straight to Pop.

We all looked at it, hardly able to move. The envelope was white and looked official. The feared telegrams which started 'I deeply regret to inform you . . .' were usually light brown in colour, but I still panicked that this was going to tell us our worst fears. What if Albert was dead? Could I bear it if he'd died so near the end of the war, and so close to us becoming husband and wife and starting the next chapter of our lives?

Pop opened the envelope, he read the few lines contained within it, and then he looked up, with tears in his eyes. Clearing his throat, he said that his son had chosen to be de-mobbed last because he wanted his colleagues who were husbands and fathers to come back first. That gesture was so like him.

' 'E's alive, Gawd 'e's alive,' I sobbed. 'Thank you God, thank you so much.'

'But when's my boy comin' 'ome?' asked Mum, her face shining with joy.

'It doesn't say,' said Pop. 'But it won't be long. This letter was sent two weeks ago, judging by the postmark. 'E could be 'ere any day now.'

All three of us looked to the front door, as if Bert would suddenly appear. I shook my head.

'I'd betta wash me 'air then. I don't want 'im turnin' up wiv me lookin' a fright.'

I skipped into the scullery and ran the cold water into the basin. I didn't even boil up some hot water, I was so impatient to look my best.

It was less than a week later, on a Saturday afternoon at the end of July, when there was a knock at the door. I'd spent every day since the letter fretting and restless, unable to tear myself from the window when I was home from work in case Bert returned. Dolly and I froze. We were cutting up vegetables for that evening's hot pot.

Dolly glanced at me. 'Take off your apron an' go an' see who it is, go on,' she smiled, patting my arm.

I fiddled with the apron ties, and by the time I reached the door, Pop was there and had reached for the door handle.

I swear the rest happened like it was in slow motion. Pop opened that door, and there he was, standing on the doorstep with his Army kit bag slung over one shoulder. He was freckled and pink from spending years in the desert sun of Palestine and North Africa, but apart from that he looked the same. He hadn't lost weight, and his eyes sparkled with happiness. He was wearing his Army uniform, and he looked as handsome a soldier as I'd ever seen.

No one said a word. Pop reached out for him, and they shook hands. It was a feeble gesture in light of the years spent worrying about him, and Pop, realising this, pulled him into a bear hug. Bert grabbed his father, and they stayed like that for a long while.

I stepped back to let Dolly through. This was her moment. Her son who had risked his life over and over again for the greater good. She folded him into a hug, surrounding him with her great berth, which now juddered with the tears she was weeping.

At that moment, Bert opened his eyes, which were also wet, and he saw me.

I gasped, a small involuntary breath. Our eyes met and we both smiled. Suddenly I felt so shy. Here was the man I'd known for two weeks before he'd upped and left to go back to war. A fortnight! It went without saying that I had stayed faithful to him for more than three years of separation, but had he? And did he still like the look of me?

I felt suddenly self-conscious. Dolly, sensing the moment of awkwardness, let her son go and led Pop out into the back. Albert and I were finally alone.

'My 'ilda,' he said, and the ice was broken. Without caring what anyone thought of me, I moved swiftly into his arms.

He threw down his bag and enclosed me in his embrace. I lifted my face for him to kiss me. We stayed like that for what seemed like hours. Eventually, Pop cleared his throat from the adjoining parlour, and we giggled, like naughty schoolchildren caught doing something wicked.

Holding my hand, Bert noticed my ring. He held my hand for a long time, and I could see him full of emotion at the sight of it. The solitaire winked in the sunlight that streamed in through the open door way.

Bert turned to shut the front door and walked me into the parlour, where Mum had put out tea and biscuits. As Bert talked, I could only stare at him, unable to believe he was home, with me, where he should be.

'I'm only 'ere for a month, then I'm posted back to Italy to wait for me demob' was the first thing I really heard. That jolted me out of my dream-state.

'A month? What d'you mean you're goin' back out there? You can't go, Bert. We want you back 'ere wiv us, for good,' I said indignantly, at which Albert smiled.

'It's just for a few months while they demob the married men. And anyway I thought we'd 'ave our own littl' weddin' while I'm 'ere. No point waitin', is there?'

I squealed with delight. Then I realised what he'd said. 'A month! 'Ow can I organise me own weddin' in a month? It ain't possible. Oh my Gawd, a month!'

And with that, Dolly, Pop and Bert collapsed into laughter at the sight of my panicked face.

CHAPTER 20

New Beginnings

August 1945

'Stand still, 'ilda, stop your fidgetin'. I can't pin this 'em up if you don't stand still,' admonished Dolly, as she tried to put the finishing touches to my wedding dress.

Made of parachute silk, the dress pooled into wonderful waves of fabric around my feet. I was standing on a couple of books, one of which was a thick old Bible, so that the final changes could be made. The seamstress who'd made it had finished it off beautifully, but Dolly, who was a stickler for doing things 'proper', wanted to make sure it was perfect.

'But I want to look at meself. It ain't every day I get fitted for me weddin' dress,' I said with a pout. It wasn't like me to act like a spoiled brat, but I was impatient to see the dress I'd waited my whole life to wear.

'Go on, then, get yerself down an' 'ave a look. Me plates are killin' me anyway,' said Dolly with a weary smile.

I jumped off and shuffled down the stairs and into the basement, where Dolly and Pop's bedroom was located, to look at myself in the mirror. I had to stand on tiptoes to see the whole of the dress.

'It's lovely,' I said to myself, gazing at the simple bodice with intricate stitching. The fabric whispered as I moved. 'I look like a proper bride.'

'You are a proper bride, silly girl,' said Dolly, as she bustled in. 'Now you've 'ad a chance to admire yerself, I need to finish what I'm doin' an' get the dinner on.'

I blushed. How silly I was, behaving like I was getting

above myself. I vowed to stop acting like a Hollywood film star, and help Mum by making tonight's stew and dumplings.

Suddenly there was a noise from the hallway, then the sound of heavy footsteps coming down the stairs, two at a time.

'Oi, Albert is that you?' Mum shouted, moving faster than I'd ever seen her move to block the doorway.

'It's me, Mum. You alright?' shouted back my Bert.

'Keep outta 'ere! 'Ilda's tryin' on the dress, an' it's bad luck for the groom to see it before the wedding day. Get yerself a slice of bread an' drippin', and get out. Dinner won't be ready for another hour at least.' Dolly had taken charge.

We heard Bert exclaim 'Blimey!' before his footsteps bounced back up the stairs. Dolly and I collapsed into laughter.

'The men, they don't know wot ter do wiv themselves when it's women's business!' she said.

Dolly helped me out of the gown, and I put my summer dress back on. I turned round, expecting Dolly to have left the room, but she was sitting on her bed, looking at me with such tenderness I felt a swooping sensation in my belly.

'Everythin' alright, Mum?' I asked, my head cocked to one side.

At first she didn't reply, instead gesturing for me to sit next to her on the bed. I walked over and sat by her, leaning my head on her lovely broad shoulders, smelling the scent of soap that always hung about her.

'Now, I don't want to speak out of turn, but did your mother ever tell you about the birds an' the bees?' she said.

For a minute I was confused, then my face reddened when I realised what she meant. 'Mum, I grew up sleepin' in the same bed me old man an' me mother shared, in our rooms in Bevington Street. Then when we moved to Spa Road we were in separate rooms but the walls were paper thin. I don't know much about them birds an' bees, but I know what 'appens between a man an' a woman when it comes to makin' babies. They made enough of 'em!' I shrugged my shoulders.

It was a fact of life, but how I wished it was my real mother who was here right now, giving me womanly advice. I loved Dolly for her many kindnesses towards me, but it was at moments like this that I felt the loss of Ma most keenly.

'I'm not worried, if that's what you're thinkin'. I know Bert'll be good to me,' I said, forming the thoughts first before putting them into words. 'An' the girls down the factory told me it only 'urts the first few times, and then after that, I might even like it.'

With that I dipped my head down, so Dolly wouldn't see the embarrassment I felt at being so honest about such an intimate part of life. Bert and I had slept apart in Dolly's house. Bert was insistent that we start married life properly and wouldn't consider sharing a bed until then.

For the past few days, I'd thought of little else. Was I scared of becoming a woman in every sense of the word? How would it feel to become a wife, to love my husband in physical ways, as well as with my heart? It was a whole new world, and I felt a natural trepidation, however delighted I was to be marrying my true love.

As the day came closer, I had started to feel a tangible sense of loss at being a bride, without my Ma there to guide me. I talked to her in heaven every night, and I asked her to watch over Bert and me while we were getting wed. I desperately wanted to feel that she was there in spirit. It had only been a year since she died, but so much had changed that I worried she wouldn't know where to look for me, if her spirit did ever come back for my special day.

They were silly thoughts. I was lucky to have Dolly and Pop, and my own Bert as well. I had a new family now. Still, I missed my brothers and sisters, despite the fact Ron and Patsy lived in south-east London now. Pa had moved them back before the end of the war. Joanie had stayed up in Braunston with her Sid, as they had decided to settle there, but there was nothing more I could do for the youngest two while they were under Pa's roof.

I'd deliberately stayed away, not wanting to see Pa or antagonise him again. Pa had written to me once or twice since I'd left. He never once mentioned the beating that caused me to flee, though he must've known my reasons for leaving. He never acknowledged the violence in all the years I lived with it, never mind ever apologising for it. And now he had a new fancy woman, a lady called Phoebe who he'd met in Braunston, and had brought back with him to London with my siblings.

Pa, Phoebe, Ron and Patsy now lived in Chapter Road, off Manor Place in Walworth, south-east London. Pa had bumped into a pal whose wife was a cleaner for a landlord and, hey presto, they had a three-bedroom flat up five flights of stairs in another tenement block. Another of Pa's drinking mates had brought the furniture back to London, and they were finally settled. Phoebe was from Hoxton, east London, and had been evacuated to Braunston with her mother. It didn't come as a surprise, not really. Knowing Pa, he'd probably been having an affair with her while Ma lay dying.

But I had my wedding to think about. Joanie and Patsy were going to be bridesmaids, and Ron would be there too. Les was away serving in Italy, as his demob hadn't come through yet, which made me sad. There was only one person who I wished to God Almighty I had the courage to bar from being there, and that was Pa. He'd assumed he would take his rightful place, walking me down the aisle, and I wanted to say 'no bloody way', but Dolly and Pop talked me out of it. They knew, from what I'd told them about Ted Johnson, that if I refused him he'd find some twisted way of turning up and causing a drunken scene. The only way to know for sure that he wouldn't bear a grudge was to have him there.

I didn't want to see him. From what I'd heard, his ways hadn't changed, not that I'd expected them to. He was getting a reputation in Walworth for drunken swagger and beating up Phoebe. 'Leopards never change their spots,' Ma used to say, and in his case she was right. I knew it would stick in my throat having That Man walk me down the aisle to wed my Bert, but I also knew it wouldn't be me who would pay for my refusal, so I vowed to grin and bear it, and just be grateful I was marrying a decent, honest man.

Bert wasn't bothered about seeing Pa. He said he'd face him up a million times if he had to to keep me safe.

Joanie, Patsy and Bert's sister Dorothy were beside themselves with excitement, and all of them looked as pretty as a picture in their matching pink bridesmaids' dresses. Everything was made by hand to save money.

Dolly and Pop had used their life savings to pay for our wedding, along with the money Bert had saved while overseas, and I barely knew how to thank them all. Tradition dictated that the father of the bride paid for the wedding, but as all Pa's money went down his throat, we all knew that he would never put his hand in his pocket for our special day. I was even more grateful to my new-found family, and when I said that to Mum, she replied that our happiness was reward enough.

I vowed then and there to be happy with Bert for the rest of my life. I knew that life was hard, and I didn't expect fairy tales, not after the upbringing I'd had. I knew that things as fleeting as happiness had to be worked at, built up like a muscle. It helped that he was a kind and honourable man, but even so, it would still take hard work to keep a relationship steady, and by God I knew how to work hard.

The morning of our wedding day finally arrived on Saturday, 4 August 1945. I could hardly believe it. I woke up before dawn, with the strangest feeling of excitement and nerves all mixed in together. I felt fluttery and unsettled but also deeply calm and certain. It seemed like a funny mixture of feelings.

I got up and lit the range as although the weather had been fair there was the definite feel of autumn approaching, especially in the early mornings. I made a cup of tea, and sat there watching the day get lighter in the tiny patch of grubby land out the back.

Bert had spent the night at a pal's house so as not to see his bride on her wedding day, not until I approached the altar at any rate. It had felt odd seeing him go, with his Army uniform slung over one arm, ready to wear the next day.

Dolly was soon up and getting breakfast ready. 'You'll need a good breakfast today, dearie,' she said, and put a plate of sausages down in front of me.

Well, I'd never had sausages for breakfast in my life – they were always too expensive to serve for any meal other than dinner! I looked dumbstruck, and Dolly laughed, pushing a knife and fork towards me. She sang as she started her chores, and I ate my breakfast with a churning tummy, gulping down hot tea with plenty of sugar to calm my nerves, chewing on the salty meat that made such an unusual start to the day. I was used to a bit of bread and marg, but I couldn't tell Dolly I didn't want them so I kept chewing, and washing them down with mouthfuls of my tea.

There was a knock at the door, and a man came in bearing

a bouquet of pale pink roses – it was quite the loveliest thing I'd ever seen. He tipped his hat to Dolly and we both looked at my bridal bouquet with undisguised delight. I had never seen a bunch of flowers like it – they tumbled down like a floral waterfall. I could hardly believe they would be mine.

Now go an' get your 'air done an' fix your face,' said Dolly once we'd finished gawping, waving me out of the kitchen.

I sat in my room, carefully pulling my hair out of the curlers that had been rolled up under a hairnet all night. Once I was satisfied my curls were looking just right, I started on my face. My ma's ditty about powder and paint suddenly came to mind and my eyes filled with tears.

I can't cry today, Ma, but I miss you, I said to myself, wiping them away.

I had a small photograph taken in Braunston, just me and her in the countryside. It sat by my bed and I looked at it every night. I took it in my hands now and stroked her face, absorbing her smile. It took a while for my eyes to dry, and I put the photograph back in its precious position on my bedside, knowing it was the last time I'd gaze at it as a single woman. Then I patted on a little face powder and applied rose pink lipstick. I was ready.

I called to Mum, who huffed a little as she made her ungainly way down the stairs. She disappeared into her bedroom. Seconds later, I heard the dress arrive before I saw it. The silk made a sound like water as she carried it. The train trailed behind her and I almost laughed with the joy of seeing such a glorious display of material. It was like the dress symbolised all my hopes and dreams for the future. Here it was, pure and white and beautiful, and with it my desires to be the best wife and mother I could be.

I wanted to be happy. I wanted to create my own family where love was at the heart of every decision, every thought

and every action. I knew Bert and I could do that, I was sure
of it. I also knew it wouldn't be easy but then life wasn't,
was it?

The dress shushed round me as Mum pulled it onto me.
I wiggled my arms through the sleeves, and she did up the
fasteners at the back. From the bedroom she reappeared
again with my veil. I dipped my head back as she fastened
it to my hair with several combs. It was so long, it flowed
down the back of my dress and formed its own puddle of netting. I slipped into satin-covered shoes, and carefully tiptoed
downstairs into Dolly's room, holding my train aloft like I
was the Queen of Sheba.

As I looked into the mirror, Dolly whispered, 'Your Ma
would've been so proud of you, 'ilda.'

'I just wish she could've been 'ere,' I answered, with a
lump in my throat.

I hesitated for a moment longer, searching my face for any
regrets or doubts. There were none. My heart swelled at the
thought of what lay ahead, and I felt suddenly impatient.

'Come on, Mum, I've got a weddin' to get to!'

Bert and I had chosen to have our ceremony at St Mark's
Church in Victoria Park, east London. He'd bought my
wedding ring from Spiegelhalter Bros. on Mile End Road.
It cost three pounds seven and sixpence, a fortune to me. I
knew Bert had been saving his wages during the war, but I
was so touched that he'd chosen to spend it on our wedding.

Needless to say, there was nothing by way of a wedding
present from Pa, except a telegram to wish us luck, even
though he would be there in person. Well, I wouldn't need
him or his 'luck' any more. With Bert's help I was finally free
from That Man and his wicked ways. Bert was everything
my Pa wasn't. He was decent, kind and reliable. I thanked
God every day for bringing him into my life. I could close a

chapter in my life by creating a new one, with my husband and my hopes and dreams for our life together, freed from violence and terror.

The service had been arranged by the vicar. We would have 'Lord and Master of Our Love' as our hymn, a selection of Wedding Thoughts, and prayers for the home 'giving to us joy, fidelity and contentment'. It sounded good to us, anyway. The church had survived the war, albeit with a bit of bomb damage, and it was going to be the place where I became Bert's wife.

'Gawd, is that the time? 'Ilda, you're goin' to be late for your own weddin'! Get a move on!' shouted Dolly.

My bridesmaids had arrived, and were giggling and sighing as they all got dressed. They looked like perfect angels, each in their pink hand-sewn satin dress with puffed out sleeves, and each with their own bouquet.

'Ready?' said Pop. He looked more nervous than I was.

I surveyed the scene – old and new family members looked back at me. 'Ready,' I said, firmly.

The church looked bigger, and prettier than I'd remembered it. There were little arrangements of flowers everywhere. I could feel my heart beating steady as anything. I had waited so long for this day. A strange calm came over me that even seeing Pa at the church entrance couldn't dispel. Pa was wearing his old Sunday best suit, a carnation in his lapel, and his hair was slicked down with boot polish. He held out his arm and I took it though every bone in my body objected. I fixed my smile on my face. Nothing was going to spoil this day.

The first note of Mendelssohn's 'Wedding March' sounded on the organ that filled an entire arch of the church. The congregation stood up, and a blur of faces turned to look as I made my first, faltering steps down the aisle. I smiled as I recognised Ron, and Rita and friends from the factory, and then everything else faded away as Bert turned round to look at me.

His face said it all. He looked proud and humble at the same time. He took off his Army cap and held it between his hands, probably to stop them shaking, I imagined. He might have faced the dangers of fighting enemies abroad, braving the desert raids and fighting for his country, but he looked like his wedding day was his greatest challenge yet.

His eyes were watery, as were mine, by the time we joined each other at the altar. We both turned to the vicar, but not before Bert had given me a little wink to show me everything was alright. More than alright, it was wonderful.

The vicar read his bits. I especially liked his reading 'We must live nobly to love nobly' as, for me, that summed up my man completely. He had been awarded five campaign medals during the war. He was known in the area as being decent and upstanding, all the qualities my Ma tried to instil in us children. And now, here I was, about to marry a man with all those qualities, and more. He knew right from wrong, he eschewed the pub, preferring to spend time with his family and me, and he loved me truly.

The moment came to say our vows. I could hear my voice echo in the vaulted ceiling above us, promising to 'love, honour and obey' my Bert. If it was any other man I might have balked at the word 'obey', but I knew if push came to shove, Bert would know what to do in a crisis, so I was happy to say it.

After we had both said our 'I do's', Bert slipped the ring he'd bought me onto my finger, to join my engagement ring. I looked into his blue eyes and smiled. I was his for now and forever. He grasped my hand tightly and then we went to sign our names in the church register. Everything seemed to pass in a blur.

Walking down the aisle, while our friends and family clapped and shouted, was the proudest moment of my life. I couldn't stop smiling for the rest of the day. We posed for photographs, and even standing next to That Man didn't bother me. Sid Midson, Joanie's fella, was Bert's best man as Frank was waiting to be demobbed. I grinned until my face hurt.

It was the first time we'd all been together since Ma's funeral a few months earlier, and I hugged each of them in turn, tears streaming from my face. They'd all grown up, they were no longer my littl'uns. Joanie had become a beauty in her own right and would soon be marrying her sweetheart Sid, while Patsy looked like a lovely young girl at nine years old, not a baby any longer.

Later that day, once the hullabaloo of the wedding was finally over, Bert and I managed to grab a quiet moment. The guests were all making their way back to Old Ford Road for the rest of the celebrations, and we'd arrived early to get changed and freshen up. It felt so strange, going into the same room to change our clothes. I kept forgetting we were now man and wife, and it was all legal and proper! Bert sat by me while I fussed about with my bouquet and veil. I turned to look at him and he had a great beaming smile on his face.

'What, Bert? What's so funny?' I said, smiling back. Had I missed a joke?

'Nothing, 'ilda, except I'm thinking that I'm the luckiest man alive,' he answered, his smile never wavering.

'Well, blow me, ain't you a poet?' I chortled, but my heart was full with love. I don't suppose I'd ever thought I'd hear a man say that about marrying me. 'An', Bert, I'm the 'appiest woman alive an' I always will be.'

I kissed him again, and it was a little while before we joined our guests. I undressed awkwardly. I'd never taken my clothes off in front of anyone except my family, and it felt odd. I blushed as Bert helped me off with my dress, feeling exposed and a little nervous at him seeing my body for the first time, but he said he'd hide his eyes to spare my embarrassment.

I slipped into my best dress, and fixed my hair. Bert was remaining in his uniform for the rest of the day. He held out an arm for me to take, and together we were ready to face everyone. The beers had been going down a treat. As we arrived, there was a great cheer, and a few ribald comments asking where we'd been, and speculating what we'd been up to. I blushed again – all that was still to come on my wedding night.

The local publican had given us a barrel of beer as a wedding gift, as beer was hard to get hold of due to the wartime shortages, and soon Bert was being offered drink after drink by his pals. I hardly touched a drop. I just wanted to remember everything about the day that had been so special.

By the time we decided to retire to bed, Bert was so drunk he fell asleep straightaway! I didn't mind, though. I needed a bit of time to think of myself as a woman, not a surrogate mother to my siblings, or a young girl fleeing her father.

The next day, Bert was dragged to the pub by his jubilant pals, and the next night as well. By now, the jokes were all about how we hadn't managed to consummate our marriage and so, on the third night, Bert left the pub early and came back to me.

He said hardly a word as he came into our bedroom, but his eyes told me he was ready to make me his. He held me in his arms and sang me a song we all used to sing during the war, 'We'll meet again, don't know where, don't know when, but I'm sure we'll meet again some sunny day'. This was our sunny day. This was the night we became lovers as well as friends.

Nine months later, almost to the day, I gave birth to my baby boy, and we called him Albert, in honour of the man who rescued me from my old life and created a new one in the process.

Looking down at the downy red hair of the little boy mewling like a kitten in my arms, I vowed to him that he would never feel the sharp pang of hunger, he would never feel a hot fist slam into his face, and he would always know what it was to feel truly loved.

Soon afterwards, I gave birth to Brenda, and then Christine. Our family was complete, until tragedy struck and we lost our Brenda in a tragic accident. I will always be grateful for my time with my little girl Brenda, and every day I kiss the picture of her I carry in a locket around my neck. Her death sealed within me the need to live and love with passion every minute of every day, for we never know when and how our loved ones may be taken from us. Later, we even had grandchildren to fill our lives with life and love again, but that was many years ahead of us. My Bert was a proud father and a loving grandfather. He was everything I'd dreamt of.

We had so many laughs, and so many tragedies. So many stories yet to come, but that is a tale for another day. We might not have had wealth, but we had love in abundance, and that would be my inheritance to my children and grand-children.

Hilda Kemp

A Fish Supper and a Chippy Smile:

Love, Hardship and Laughter
in a South East London Fish-and-Chip Shop

HILDA KEMP, CATHRYN KEMP

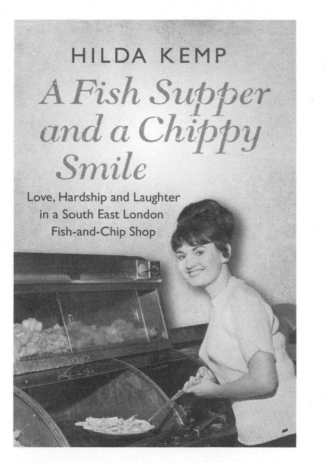

CHAPTER I

Frying Tonight

1951

'Oi, 'ilda, the sign outside says you're frying tonight, but I ain't seeing nothin' done in 'ere!'

The voice, which accompanied a loud cackle, cut through my daydream, startling me into remembering where I was – standing with my back to the door of the fish and chip shop I worked in. The shop had just opened for business at 5 p.m. and already there was a queue of hungry customers on the cobbled street in Bermondsey, south-east London.

'Sorry, Mavis, I was miles away. Don't know what's got into me today,' I replied, before quickly tying my apron round my waist, which was already thickening from the new life growing inside me. 'Bit distracted. Must be this hot weather.'

With that, I smiled to myself. I knew full well it wasn't the weather or the strain of working long hours serving customers and frying fish. I knew it was my third longed-for pregnancy that was making me dreamy: the child who would complete my family, alongside my eldest boy Albert, or Little Albie as I liked to call him, and my darling girl Brenda. This little one, still just a twinkle in the night sky, was making its presence felt already.

At least I wasn't nauseous like I had been with Brenda. Then, the smell of the oily cod and the chips being coated in greasy brown vinegar had turned my stomach. I lost count of the times I had to mumble an excuse to Wally, the owner of the shop and my boss, and stumble out to the outside lavvy in the tiny, dirt-streaked yard, to throw up what remained of my breakfast before I could carry on serving my regulars with a smile and a laugh.

Yes, this time was definitely better, but even so I had a job to do. I would never forgive myself if I wasn't pleasant and charming to the women from the nearby estate. They relied on the shop each Friday evening for a quick, hot supper after a long week working their fingers to the bone with chores and child-rearing. There was little enough round our way in respect of luxuries. Most of us scraped by each week, sometimes having to use Uncle's, the pawn shop, to get by. Life was an endless round of washing, cooking, cleaning and shooing away children as we scrubbed floors and doorsteps. Our husbands went to work wherever they could, returning home at night, expecting to put their feet up and be served their dinner. There was little respite – except for the weekly Friday night treat of a natter in the chip shop queue, and the promise of a steaming hot dinner of crunchy battered fish and golden chips. That was our idea of luxury!

'So, what will it be today, Mavis?' I beamed at my favourite customer. 'Your usual?'

'You know me too well, 'ilda. Always the same for us. My Alfie don't like change, you know that. 'E'll have skate an' chips, the kids'll have rock an' chips, an' I'm watching my figure so that'll do us.'

'Comin' up!' I said, grabbing the metal scoop and burying it deep into the mountain of freshly cooked potatoes, digging out a great pile of glistening yellow chips and flinging them onto the stack of newspaper pages. With one deft action, I grabbed the metal prong from the warming shelf above the fryers, and hooked out a resplendently oily skate which I placed on top. I dropped the tong back into the metal shelf and with a quick series of folds wrapped the meal into submission. Yesterday's rag became today's dinner plate.

I did the same again with the children's order, knowing that tonight the kids would eat, her husband would eat, but Mavis would have to make do with whatever was left from their only hot meal of the day. I glanced around quickly to see that Wally wasn't watching me.

My boss was a short, thin man in his late fifties, with dark hair combed over the bald spot on his head and kind eyes. He was in the back, chatting to his shorter, plumper wife Betty. Seeing he was distracted, I quickly heaped an extra scoop of chips onto Mavis's second bundle, wrapping the whole lot in yet another page from that day's *South London Press*, and gave her a sly wink out of the corner of my eye. Mavis looked back at me and nodded her thanks.

That was all that needed to be done, there was no point saying anything else. I knew how hunger felt. I had gone without my dinner many times so that Albie and Brenda would have enough to eat, and so my Bert would have something in his belly before starting his early morning shift as a delivery driver for Pepsi-Cola. I sighed as I recalled the ache of hunger at bedtime, and how I'd tried suppressing it with hot tea; the lies I told my Bert and the kids, that I was watching my weight, when of course I was not eating so that there would be enough food on the table for them. These were hard times, with harder choices to be made, and it was up to the women of the house to make them. It didn't seem fair, but then life wasn't fair, was it?

For a second I was reminded of another time, much longer ago, when regular meals were like Father Christmas – possible but not probable. Those were the days I felt the soreness of real, aching hunger. I grew up in the slums of Bermondsey, living in two rooms with my Ma, Pa and four siblings. Pa was a casual docker who never knew if he would work from one day to the next. On top of that he was a drunk, and spent the little money he earned in the dingy, dirty drinking holes near the docks. He would drink our food money away, then return home, roaring drunk and filled with bile, and subject Ma and me to violence and beatings. He ate the little food we had, he drank away the little money we had, then he went out and boasted about what a great man he was. Pa had been a prize fighter in the Army, and used the power in his large veiny fists to fight bare-knuckle down by the docks or in The Ring, a notorious hangout for fighters, criminals and illegal bookies in Blackfriars.

No, I admit it, I hated my pa. I still have the broken nose to show how much his love meant to me. He knew how to land a punch on an opponent to cause maximum damage, and by God he gave me some beatings. Many was the time I turned up for school with black eyes or a limp where he'd inflicted hurt on me. Yet, even though everyone in the neighbourhood knew what he was doing to me and Ma, no one ever stepped in to stop him. In our part of the borough it was not the done thing to intervene between a man and his family, however much he hurt and frightened them. There was, and still is, a conspiracy of silence.

He was a mean, sadistic bully, he cheated on my Ma many times, and he walked with a swagger that belied his failures as a man and as a father. Because of him, I knew the sharp pangs of hunger. I knew what it was to feel the cold, and not know when the next meal would be. So, when I saw Mavis sacrifice her food so her children could eat, I couldn't help myself. It was wrong of me to give extra chips. I knew that Wally's business wasn't a charity. He had to make a living like the rest of us, but my nature was always too soft hearted. I couldn't bear seeing Mavis and her kids suffer, and a handful of chips would hardly break the bank, so I risked it for her, and for others when I could. It was all I could really do to help.

My Bert tells me I'm a soft touch several times a day. He always says I'll let anybody tell me a sob story, but it's who I've always been. I brought up my siblings as my mother's helper. I washed their faces, tucked them up in bed, read them bedtime stories and soothed away their nightmares. I've spent my life looking after others, and I couldn't have stopped myself if I'd tried.

But all that happened in another time and place. I shook my head to try and release the thoughts from my mind, hoping they'd fly out and settle somewhere else instead. I always did that to try and clear my head, but it rarely worked. I so desperately wished I could forget the things about my past I wanted to forget.

I leant over the counter and placed the two warm parcels, one distinctly fatter than the other, into my friend's string bag. 'So, how are things, Mavis?' I asked tentatively, hoping she'd hear the gentleness in my voice and guess at the compassion I felt for her, for all us mothers dealing with hard choices and difficult lives.

Mavis's face was lined with worry. Her wispy brown hair was tied back in the turban all us housewives wore, and she was dressed in a faded flowery pinafore and a pink cardigan, despite the heat of the day. In the three years I'd known Mavis, she had always been thin, but today as the sunlight filtered in through the large front window of the shop, she looked gaunt. Her cheekbones stuck out, and I wondered how long it had been since her last proper meal.

'Oh well, you know, things are the same. Alfie's waitin' to start 'is new job. Just a week or so to wait now . . .' Mavis's voice trailed off, and for a brief moment I could see how much it had cost her to tell me even this brief snippet of their lives.

For a moment neither of us spoke. There was no need to. I knew that a week waiting for a job was an indescribably long time when you had mouths to feed. She and Alfie had three children under the age of five, yet Mavis looked older than her 29 years due to the strain of surviving, and the worry of living hand to mouth. I noticed Mavis's worn shoes and her darned stockings, her unwillingness to give up in the face of destitution.

'What's his new job?' I asked, hoping it was true and Alfie really did have something lined up to earn a decent living. His last job driving for a tallow works hadn't worked out, again. Alfie was known for being a drinker. He had a reputation for not turning up to work some mornings, and it cost him and his family dear. As a result, he was turned away from jobs so frequently I was surprised he'd been offered a new position.

'Oh it's a good one, this one,' Mavis replied, her eyes looking brighter with the hopefulness of the poor. ' 'E's got a gig drivin' the meat van which goes round all the butchers in the East End, collecting the fat and offal. We shan't 'ave a worry in our 'eads once 'e's workin' there.' She smiled, avoiding my eyes, and I wanted to believe her so much it hurt.

'Of course fings will get better, dear. They 'ave to, don't they?' I murmured, my hand veering to Mavis's woollen sleeve with the slightest of touches. It was all I could do to give her comfort, to let her know she wasn't the only one who experienced the helplessness of seeing a man drink away the family money. Even so, a feeling of powerlessness swept over me. I couldn't help her. All I could do was give what little I could by understanding her plight, a plight that was so ordinary around here, it hardly counted.

'You ladies goin' to natter all day? I'm runnin' late enough as it is, an' my old man will skin me alive if I don't get back in time wiv 'is dinner!'

The moment disappeared as if it had never been, cut away by the cross words of my next customer, Violet.

'Alright, Vi, I'm comin'. No need to get shirty,' I said, crossly, knowing the small moment of intimacy with my friend was lost. 'Mavis, that'll be four shillings, please.'

I wished then I didn't have to charge her. I felt awkward as I watched her open her purse and carefully count out the money. As she put the coins into my hand I arranged my face into a falsely jaunty smile. Mavis looked away. I knew that sometimes being jolly was too much to bear.

Feeling helpless, I turned to the till, pressing on the buttons that released the drawer for the money with a sharp jolt. The coins clattered into the metal trays and I shut it with force. The damn thing always stuck.

I looked up to say, 'Goodbye, dear. Give those babies of yours a kiss from me' to Mavis, but she'd left the shop, hurrying home with her precious cargo, back to hungry mouths and the leftovers, if she was lucky.

Sighing, I turned to Violet who was listing her order. She was a boisterous woman who lived a few doors down from me. She was plump and loud, and had a skinny hen-pecked husband and five snotty-nosed children who ran wild on the estate. 'Sorry, dear, you're going to have start over. Don't know what's wrong with me today. My head's all over the shop.'

And with that I smiled to myself again. I was back to thinking about my baby, the one who would bring the good times back, who would bring sunshine into our lives. I was absolutely sure of that.

Acknowledgements

I am indebted to my father, Albert Kemp, for his encouragement, anecdotes, and for driving me to and from Bermondsey to relive his past and research our family's background.

My gratitude also goes to Val Johnson, Hilda's sister from Ted's second marriage, as a source of family stories and legend, and for her unswerving support.

Ron Johnson, Hilda's youngest brother, added his memories and stories, many of which were painful, but told with his persistent good humour. Dad, Val and Ron, you are all so like Hilda! Thank you all so much for your many kindnesses.

Lee Ricketts lent me a precious photograph of Hilda with her mother Emily in Spa Road, and Val shared her photographs as well.

I want to thank the Imperial War Museum and the London Docklands Museum for invaluable background information.

I wish to thank my agent Jane Graham Maw at Graham Maw Christie Literary Agency and Publishing Director Anna Valentine at Orion.

I reserve the final thank you for Hilda herself. She was a great lady, and it has been a strange pleasure inhabiting her world and her heart for this, the first book of her memoirs. I love you, Nan.

About the Author

Cathryn Kemp is an award-winning writer and former journalist on national newspapers who wrote her own memoir in 2012. *Painkiller Addict: From Wreckage to Redemption*, published by Piatkus, reveals how she fell ill with a life-threatening illness and became hooked on her painkilling medication. The book is a gripping true story that offers a deeply personal window into one of the biggest medical scandals of this century - drug addiction aided by hospitals and doctors. It is a horror story as well as a love story, a survival story and a battle for dignity and freedom.

Unlike the vast majority of addicts, Cathryn chose not to remain anonymous and has talked publicly about her addiction. Now living and working in Sussex, she is currently setting up the first UK charity to raise awareness of addiction to medicines, called the Painkiller Addiction Information Network (PAIN). Find out more at www.painkiller-addict.com

For competitions, author interviews,
pre-publication extracts, news and events,
sign up to the monthly

Orion Books Newsletter

at

www.orionbooks.co.uk

Prefer your updates daily?
Follow us 🐦 @orionbooks